ENHANCING DIGITAL LITERACY AND CREATIVITY

Enhancing Digital Literacy and Creativity is an exploration of how young children gain digital literacies in 'makerspaces'. The international authors investigate how hands-on experimentation with a variety of materials – from traditional arts and crafts to contemporary digital tools like 3D printers and laser cutters – can aid children in their development of play, creativity and storytelling. From museums to libraries, nursery schools to community centres, this research shows how 'making' supports the development of creative skills and introduces concepts to be explored in a variety of environments and contexts.

Drawing on examples from around the globe, described by a range of international academics, *Enhancing Digital Literacy and Creativity* includes chapters on:

- Virtual reality
- Museum and library makerspaces
- Intergenerational making in families
- Making in schools and nursery settings
- Assessing learning in makerspaces
- Links to previous theories
- Social imagination

This book will be a valuable resource for students and researchers in the fields of education and digital literacies; early childhood teacher educators and practitioners; librarians; museum educators; and makerspace staff.

Alicia Blum-Ross is Public Policy Lead for Kids and Families at Google.

Kristiina Kumpulainen is Professor of Education at the Faculty of Educational Sciences, University of Helsinki.

Jackie Marsh is Professor of Education at the University of Sheffield.

ENHANCING DIGITAL LITERACY AND CREATIVITY

Makerspaces in the Early Years

Edited by Alicia Blum-Ross,
Kristiina Kumpulainen
and Jackie Marsh

Routledge
Taylor & Francis Group

LONDON AND NEW YORK

First published 2020
by Routledge
2 Park Square, Milton Park, Abingdon, Oxon OX14 4RN

and by Routledge
52 Vanderbilt Avenue, New York, NY 10017

Routledge is an imprint of the Taylor & Francis Group, an informa business

British Library Cataloguing-in-Publication Data
A catalogue record for this book is available from the British Library

Library of Congress Cataloging-in-Publication Data
Names: Blum-Ross, Alicia, 1979- editor. | Kumpulainen, Kristiina, 1966- editor. | Marsh, Jackie, editor.
Title: Enhancing digital literacy and creativity : makerspaces in the early years / Edited by Alicia Blum-Ross, Kristiina Kumpulainen and Jackie Marsh.
Description: First edition. | Abingdon, Oxon ; New York, NY : Routledge, 2020. | Includes bibliographical references and index.
Identifiers: LCCN 2019035246 (print) | LCCN 2019035247 (ebook) | ISBN 9780367197865 (hardback) | ISBN 9780367197889 (paperback) | ISBN 9780429243264 (ebook)
Subjects: LCSH: Maker movement in education. | Early childhood education. | Computer-assisted instruction. | Creative thinking in children.
Classification: LCC LB1029.M35 E54 2020 (print) | LCC LB1029.M35 (ebook) | DDC 371.9--dc23
LC record available at https://lccn.loc.gov/2019035246
LC ebook record available at https://lccn.loc.gov/2019035247

ISBN: 978-0-367-19786-5 (hbk)
ISBN: 978-0-367-19788-9 (pbk)
ISBN: 978-0-429-24326-4 (ebk)

Typeset in Bembo
by Taylor & Francis Books

This book is dedicated to our dear colleague,
Dr Kjetil Sandvik.

CONTENTS

FIGURES

TABLES

ACKNOWLEDGEMENTS

This book reports on the project 'Makerspaces in the Early Years: Enhancing Digital Literacy and Creativity' (MakEY), which received funding from the European Union's Horizon 2020 research and innovation programme under the Marie Skłodowska-Curie grant agreement No. 734720. We would like to thank Patricia Baldi, the Project Administrator, for her outstanding support of the project, and our Project Officer, Dr Gianluca Coluccio, for his guidance throughout.

We also warmly acknowledge the support of our International Advisory Board, who have contributed so much to the project: Assistant Professor Cassie Brownell, USA; Professor Anne Burke, Canada; Professor Kylie Peppler, USA; Emeritus Professor Mastin Pinsloo, South Africa; Professor Jennifer Rowsell, Canada; Mark Shillitoe, the Netherlands; Associate Professor Raúl Alberto Mora Vélez, Colombia; Assistant Professor Jon Wargo, USA and Professor Nicola Yelland, Australia.

Finally, we thank all of the children, parents, teachers, library and museum staff, artists and makers who collaborated with us on the MakEY projects. We have, together, created a global community of tinkerers, makers and hackers who will continue to contribute to early childhood theory, policy and practice in the years ahead.

CONTRIBUTORS

Hans Christian Arnseth is Professor of Education at the University of Oslo, Norway. He has published widely on the topic of learning, literacy and digital technologies. Over the last decade he has participated in and led projects that have examined digital convergence and gaming cultures, the use of dynamic representations in science education and young people's learning lives across formal and non-formal settings. He was leader of the National Graduate School in Educational Research (NATED), and Research Director at the Network for IT-research and Competence in Education. He participates in the 'Makerspaces in the Early Years: Enhancing Digital Literacy and Creativity (MakEY) EU project.

Alicia Blum-Ross is a researcher and advocate who works to create spaces for children and families to safely learn, connect and create through digital media, making and technology. She has a doctorate in Social Anthropology from the University of Oxford, and completed a post-doc funded by the ESRC at the LSE, focusing on 'at-risk' teen filmmakers. From 2014–2018 she worked with Sonia Livingstone on the 'Parenting for a Digital Future' research project and blog, and on MakEY. In 2018 she joined Google as the Global Public Policy Lead for Children and Families.

Anne Burke is a Professor in Literacy Education and Early Learning at Memorial University of Newfoundland. She is the Project Lead for the new Discovery Play Centre at Memorial's Faculty of Education. Anne is funded through Social Sciences Humanities Canada on a number of research projects alongside Memorial's Public Engagement office for her research in cultural institutions and digital media. She researches and writes about children's literacy engagements through the evolving role of technology, digital and immersive worlds, multiliteracies, materiality, and critical teacher pedagogies for social justice. Her current research investigates the role of makerspaces in early learning and the possibilities they offer for civic engagement and environmental social entrepreneurship, as well as forms and cultural representations of how making may be conceptualised through STEAM and artistic approaches.

Liz Chesworth is a lecturer at the University of Sheffield where she directs the full-time MA in Early Childhood Education. She has worked in the field of early childhood education throughout her career and has taught in nurseries, children's centres, primary schools and universities. Her recent research has focused upon play cultures, creative pedagogies and young children's embodied funds of knowledge associated with participation in diverse family practices. Liz was a member of the Sheffield MakEY research team and was the Principal Investigator for the MakEY in Libraries project.

Abigail Crocker is a research associate at Memorial University researching folklore with a focus on making in educational and cultural institutions. She is an experienced teacher, with a number of years in the classroom where she has used maker concepts / STEM teaching in her classroom. Abigail considers herself to be a 'maker', as she tinkers with new designs for traditional fibre-craft and jewellery.

Kristín Dýrfjörð is an associate professor at the University of Akureyri, School of Humanities and Social Sciences, Faculty of Education. She has long-term experience as a preschool principal in Reykjavík, has worked for the teachers' union and taken part in the development of the national curriculum at the Ministry of Education both before and after taking up a position as a scholar in academia. Her research interests are: early childhood studies, democracy, policy studies and the connection between science and creativity in early childhood.

Torfi Hjartarson is an assistant professor at the School of Education, University of Iceland. He was an instructional writer and designer, director of a media centre at the Iceland University of Education, and editor of *Netla – Online Journal on Pedagogy and Education*. He leads courses in teacher education at the University of Iceland, and in small measure at the Iceland University of the Arts. He supervises many graduate projects involving digital technologies and instructional design. Research interests include the development of physical learning environments, instructional design, and creative uses of digital technologies in education, in particular at the preschool and compulsory level.

Anna Elísa Hreiðarsdótti is an assistant professor at the University of Akureyri, and head of course of the postgraduate programme in the Faculty of Education. Anna Elísa has 20 years' experience as a preschool teacher and principal and is the author of several developmental projects funded by the Ministry of Education. She has worked as a Consultant at the Centre of School Development at the University of Akureyri. Her research focus is in early childhood education; play, creativity and ICT and technology but also gender and equality in preschool settings. Her project 'They Play to Learn' was placed third in the eSchola eLearning Award 2003.

David Hyatt is a Senior Fellow of the Higher Education Academy, Senate Award Fellow for Excellence in Learning and Teaching and was a Marie Curie Fellow in 2017 and 2018, with secondments via the MakEY project to Australia. There his research interests in learning, teaching and assessment informed his presentations on the project in seminars, conferences and an international expert panel event. He works at the School of Education, University of Sheffield, where he is also the Faculty of Social Science Deputy Director of Teaching Excellence. David is also the Deputy Editor of the *Journal of Education for Teaching*.

Sólveig Jakobsdóttir is a professor at the School of Education, University of Iceland. She heads RANNUM – Centre for Educational Research on ICT and Media. Sólveig's research and development work has been on teacher professional development and ICT; distance education, online and blended learning; ICT and school development, learners' computer and Internet use, literacies and skills, and digital citizenship. Recent projects include evaluation of tablet computers in schools; supporting educators' communities of practice with digital habitats and educamps; and MOOCs for professional development in the area of digital citizenship. She is involved in the Nordic Digichild research network supported by NOS-HS.

Svanborg R Jónsdóttir is an associate professor at the School of Education, University of Iceland and chairs the Research Centre for Creativity in Education. She was an elementary school teacher for almost 30 years. She completed a PhD in Pedagogy from the School of Education, University of Iceland in 2011. Her thesis is titled *The Location of Innovation Education in Icelandic Compulsory Schools*. She has been leading groups of teacher researchers doing action research focusing on creativity in teaching and learning. Her research fields are innovation and entrepreneurial education, curriculum development, creativity in education, school change and self-study in teacher education.

Alfredo Jornet is an associate professor at the Department of Teacher Education and School Research, University of Oslo. Alfredo investigates learning and creativity in and across school, out-of-school and professional settings, with a focus on transformative, participatory design-based approaches aimed at social and pedagogical innovation. Alfredo has been awarded a Marie Curie Fellowship to investigate the role of the arts in education, participates in the EU MakEY project, and leads two work packages of the EU Coordination and Support Action SEAS (Science Education for Action and Engagement towards Sustainability). He is editor of the *Mind, Culture, and Activity* journal.

Louise Kay taught across the primary sector for 11 years and is now employed as a Lecturer in Education at the University of Sheffield. Her current work, in collaboration with Monash University and the Australian Catholic University, explores learning-rich leadership in the early years workforce. She has also been involved in the MakEY project, which aimed to engage young children and marginalised groups in science, engineering, technology and mathematics. Her research interests include pedagogy in the early years, curricular and assessment frameworks, and the impact policy has on children and teachers. She is also interested in the utilisation of Cultural-Historical Activity Theory as a methodological framework.

Skúlína Hlíf Kjartansdóttir is an adjunct at the School of Education, University of Iceland. Her professional experience includes teaching at all school levels, curriculum design in vocational education and educational management, as well as several years of computer games design, software and web management. She is a board member of RANNUM – Centre for Educational Research on ICT and Media and Research Centre for Creativity in Education. Skúlína's research concentrates on mobile learning, game-based learning, digital literacies and creativity, with an emphasis on the pedagogical value of makerspaces. She is involved in the Nordic Digichild research network supported by NOS-HS.

Michalis Kontopodis is a Chair in Global Childhood and Youth Studies at the School of Education, University of Leeds. In collaboration with a wide network of academics, practitioners, NGOs, community organisations and policy makers, Michalis conducts research on inclusive and equitable quality education and children's well-being in a global perspective. His research explores (a) global debt and marginalisation; (b) innovative pedagogies with new media and digital technologies; and (c) the multiple links between child health, ecology and body pedagogies. His books, edited volumes and journal articles have been published in six languages; for further details please visit https://mkontopodis.wordpress.com/.

Kristiina Kumpulainen is Professor of Education and Scientific Director of the Playful Learning Center at the Faculty of Educational Sciences, University of Helsinki, Finland. She also co-chairs the Learning, Culture and Interventions (LECI) research community at her faculty. Kristiina has led numerous research projects and published widely on socioculturally informed studies on children's agency and learning across early years and primary education, cultural institutions and homes. Her research has addressed pedagogies and learning environments that create opportunities for creative, playful and participatory learning. Her ongoing research projects include the 'Joy of Learning Multiliteracies' funded by the Finnish Ministry of Education and 'Culture and Learning by Making: The Educational Potential of School-based Makerspaces for Young Learners' Digital Competencies' funded by the Academy of Finland. She also chairs the Nordic Research Network on Researching Digitalising Childhoods funded by the NOS-HS programme of the Joint Committee for Nordic Research Councils in the Humanities and Social Sciences.

Sonia Livingstone DPhil (Oxon), FBA, FBPS, FAcSS, FRSA, OBE is a professor in the Department of Media and Communications at the London School of Economics and Political Science. She has published 20 books including *The Class: Living and Learning in the Digital Age* (2016, New York University Press). She directs the projects 'Children's Data and Privacy Online', 'Global Kids Online' (with UNICEF) and 'Parenting for a Digital Future', and she is Deputy Director of the UKRI-funded 'Nurture Network'. Since founding the 33-country EU Kids Online network, Sonia has advised the UK government, European Commission, European Parliament, Council of Europe, OECD and UNICEF. See www.sonia livingstone.net

Jackie Marsh is Professor of Education at the University of Sheffield. She is a Fellow of the Royal Academy of Social Sciences, and a Fellow of the Royal Society of Arts. Over the past two decades she has led numerous research projects that have examined young children's literacy practices in the digital age in homes, communities and early years settings. From 2015–2019, Jackie was Chair of the COST Action IS1410, 'The Digital Literacy and Multimodal Practices of Young Children' (www.digilitey.eu), a network of researchers in 35 EU countries who collaborated to further knowledge in this area. She was the co-ordinator of the EU H2020 programme, MakEY, from 2017–2019. She is an editor of the *Journal of Early Childhood Literacy* (Sage).

Monica Mitarcă graduated in Journalism and Communication Studies at the University of Bucharest and has a PhD in Communication Studies. With an interest in the way new media is changing the way identities are conceived, she researched the various facets of digital identities. She teaches journalism and communication studies and participated in research studies such as 'Young Children and Digital Technologies' and MakEY. Other interests are visual studies and film, and especially Romanian film during communism.

Bobby Nisha is University Teacher and the Programme Director for the MA in Urban Design and Planning at the University of Sheffield. With a background in architecture, her research focuses on impacts of spatial perception, with a focus on bridging the gap between physical space and its perceived counterpart, and she uses immersive virtual reality to understand how people experience and navigate through spaces. Bobbi also studies the pedagogic impact of learning with immersive realities such as virtual and augmented realities in makerspace settings.

Beth Nutbrown is a PhD student at the University of Sheffield. Beth's research concerns video game communities and how these communities go beyond game play and in-game communities, and extend into other online and offline community spaces. She is particularly interested in how gaming impacts and informs identity, and the ways in which players express belonging. Beth is also interested in esports and cosplay, amongst other aspects of fan culture. Beth was a research assistant on the MakEY project from 2017–2019.

Margrét Elísabet Ólafsdóttir is an Assistant Professor in Art Education at the University of Akureyri. Previously she taught media art history and theory at the

Iceland University of the Arts, where she continues to supervise students and give lectures. As a founding member of Lorna, an association for electronic arts, and of Lorna Lab, she has been active in the digital art scene in Iceland. Her research subject is focused on media art practices in modern and contemporary art. She is a curator, editor and project manager, and has published extensively on art and culture as an art critic and scholar.

Bryony Olney is a Higher Education Training Consultant for Pearson Higher Education Services. Prior to taking up that post, she was a Learning Technologist at the University of Sheffield, where she co-led, with Dr Bobby Nisha, the HEFCE-funded project: 'Developing Design Consultants of the Future: Embedding Augmented Reality in Learning & Teaching'.

Louisa Haugaard Pedersen is a master's student in Education at the Department of Media, Cognition and Communication at the University of Copenhagen in Denmark. She conducts ethnographic studies of digital and non-digital play and child cultures in both kindergartens and schools. She co-worked with Klaus Thestrup in the Danish-led project 'Next Practice Labs – Taking Makerspaces to the Next Level' in which she had a special focus on 'The Global Makerspace' project that was a part of the EU MakEY project. She also participates in the research groups 'Children, Culture and Media' and 'Ethnographic Studies in Innovative Learning Contexts' based at the University of Copenhagen.

Kylie Peppler is an Associate Professor of Education and Informatics at the University of California, Irvine and engages in research that focuses on the intersection of arts, making and computational technologies. She serves as the Director of the Creativity Labs at UCI and was the former lead of the MacArthur Foundation's Make-to-Learn initiative. She has authored over 100 peer-reviewed publications including publications in the *Teachers College Record*, the *British Journal of Educational Technology, Mind, Culture and Activity, Review of Research in Education* as well as having authored or edited more than 11 book publications, including the *Makeology* volumes.

Svava Pétursdóttir is an assistant professor at the School of Education, University of Iceland. She was a compulsory school teacher for 15 years, teaching first primary classes and then science and mathematics. She completed an Ed.D. from the University of Leeds in 2012. The title of her thesis is *Using Information and Communication Technology in Lower Secondary Science Teaching in Iceland*. She has led a community of practice of Icelandic science teachers and heads the research group on science education. Her research interests are in the field of ICT in education, primary teaching, teacher professional development and science education.

Deborah Rodrigues (aka Tartaruga Feliz) works with art and technology, exploring the intersection of learning, interaction and play as a path to strengthen creativity. With her project Glück Workshops, she works with children in very different parts of the planet, passing on her values and helping them to connect with their creative power. She recently finished a research programme on virtual reality and childhood with the University of Sheffield in England. Before creating Glück, she worked as an illustrator developing characters for Disney Club Penguin, a free-to-play virtual world for children.

Ole Smørdal is a researcher with a PhD in Informatics and is head of EngageLab, an ICT design and development team at the University of Oslo that works closely with educational researchers. Ole has long-term experience in the intersection between design, education and computer science. His interests are related to learning ecologies, infrastructuring, social innovation, empowerment and sustainability. Ole specialises in research that is based on practice partnerships, and adopts design-based and participatory methods in such collaborations.

Klaus Thestrup is an associate professor at the Centre for Teaching Development and Digital Media at Aarhus University in Denmark. He is also a trained social educator from University College South, a dramaturg from Aarhus University and holds a professional master's in children's and youth culture and digital media from the University of Southern Denmark. For more than 25 years he has been conducting developmental work and practical research in media play and digital communication from kindergarten to university level in both formal and informal settings. He was the project leader of "Next Practice Labs – Taking Makerspaces to the Next Level" in the EU MakEY project. Within the MakEY project he also led the subproject 'The Global Makerspace'. Moreover, he led the Danish research project 'Children as Digital World Citizens' (2015) and the Danish research project 'ASSiST – Experiment with Teaching over Distance in the Primary School' (2017–2018). He is currently participating in the EU project 'SEEDS – Social Entrepreneurship Empowering Development in Preschools' (2019–2020). Furthermore, he participates in the 'Children, Culture and Media' research group based at the University of Copenhagen.

Gísli Thorsteinsson is a professor in the Department of Design and Craft Education at the School of Education, University of Iceland. He finished a doctoral degree at Loughborough University, exploring the pedagogical value of using a virtual reality learning environment for improving ideation in the context of innovation education in Iceland. In 1999 he was involved in the development of the national curriculum for ICT and technology education and wrote the curriculum for design and craft education. Gisli has written numerous articles on design and craft education, innovation education, the use of ICT and Open and Distance Learning (ODL) in education and several textbooks about innovation education.

Jenni Vartiainen is a researcher at the Faculty of Educational Sciences, University of Helsinki. She has over ten years of experience in the field of science and mathematics education. Her main research interests are young children's playful science education, scientific literacy, and young children's digital cultures in formal and informal learning environments. Her current research project is 'Joy of Learning Multiliteracies' (www.monilukutaito.com). She has co-created several research-based innovations for STEAM education from kindergarten to high school levels, e.g. Kide Science. Jenni is also active in popularising science. She has manuscripted for a Finnish national broadcasting company a children's science TV show and acted in it (Tiedonjyvä). She has written science-related fiction books for children and pedagogical books for teachers.

Anca Velicu is a researcher at the Institute of Sociology (Romanian Academy). Her main research interests include youth's use of digital technology, parental mediation, media education and the opportunities to use new media for education. Two of the most important projects in which she has participated are MakEY (dir. J. Marsh) and 'Friends 2.0: "Friendship" Quality in the Age of Online Social Networks'. She acted as a co-manager for the relationship with stakeholders in COST Action, "The Digital Literacy and Multimodal Practices of Young Children" (dir. J. Marsh), and is currently the national Romanian contact for the *EU Kids Online* Network.

Dylan Yamada-Rice is a Senior Tutor in Information Experience Design at the Royal College of Art. She is also a Senior Research Manager for Dubit, a company that specialises in strategy, research and digital for kids entertainment brands. Her research is at the intersection of experimental design and social sciences, focusing on the design of digital storytelling, games and play on a range of platforms such as apps, augmented and virtual reality, as well as new content for television. She specialises in experimental visual and multimodal methods.

Justyna Zubrycka is a UX/play designer, creative director and toy maker. She co-founded *Vai-Kai*, a Berlin-based EdTech company that created a wooden interactive doll. She is also a co-founder of, and advisor to the *Toy Pioneers Club*, which enables start-ups to launch pioneering toys.

1

THE MAKEY PROJECT

An introduction

Alicia Blum-Ross, Kristiina Kumpulainen and Jackie Marsh

The main aim of this book is to provide an overview of the key findings of the project 'Makerspaces in the Early Years: Enhancing Digital Literacy and Creativity' (MakEY). This project, funded by the EU Commission's Horizon 2020 Programme, was a collaboration between researchers, educators, library staff, museum educators, artists and makerspace staff in Denmark, Finland, Germany, Iceland, Norway, Romania, the UK and the USA. The project also actively involved an international advisory board consisting of scholars from Australia, Canada, Colombia, South Africa and the USA. Over a period of 30 months, the team explored the role and value of makerspaces in both formal and non-formal educational settings. In this introductory chapter, we explore the concept of makerspaces and offer a rationale for undertaking research on their use in early childhood practice. Early childhood is defined as the period from birth to eight years of age.

There is little doubt that the digital age is impacting on the lives of society's youngest children. Across Europe, many children have access to digital technologies in homes and communities from birth (Chaudron et al., 2015). Whilst a range of work has focused on the development and assessment of digital skills, such as the DIG-COMP study in Europe (Ferrari, 2013), limited attention has to date been paid to the development of the digital literacy skills of young children. Further, it is clear that there needs to be a multi-stakeholder approach to the task of ensuring that young children develop the skills and knowledge required for the digital age. Researchers, early-years practitioners and industry partners need to collaborate in knowledge exchange and the co-creation of new pedagogies and learning environments, including the development of digital tools and solutions that offer children avenues for digital learning, if some of the 'wicked problems' that face society are to be effectively addressed. It is also important that young children have opportunities to foster their creativity and develop the kinds of creative skills that are important for future employment and learning, such as creative design. This can take place through a process of 'making', which has increasingly become the focus of a range of activities related to the 'Maker Movement', which celebrates making across all areas of everyday life.

A maker culture is one in which the process of creativity, design and innovation is key, and some have linked its genealogy to that of craftsmanship (Schrock, 2014), although contemporary maker culture is less focused on the acquisition of a set of specific craft skills over a long period of apprenticeship, and more concerned with a general approach in which anyone with access to the right tools and resources can create (Hatch, 2013). Makerspaces are part of the move to a 'DIY' culture in which citizens take the initiative and become more self-sufficient, made possible through the development of new digital tools and practices (Knobel and Lankshear, 2010). Rather than this being experienced as an individual process, however, makerspaces emphasise collaboration and sharing.

This project arose because of the limited research that has been undertaken with respect to the use of makerspaces in early-years education. This lack of attention to the matter is somewhat surprising, when it is clear that the approaches to practice in makerspaces align with well-established principles underpinning early childhood education, such as child-centred pedagogies, play and interest-driven learning (Marsh, Wood and Chesworth, in press). The MakEY project adopted the definition of makerspaces outlined by Sheridan, Halverson, Litts, Brahms, Jacobs-Priebe and Owens (2014:507), who suggest that:

> Makerspaces are comprised of participants of different ages and levels of experience who work with varied media, but a commonality is that these spaces all involve making: developing an idea and constructing it into some physical or digital form.

Some might argue that the concept of makerspaces is redundant to early years settings, given that making has always been a central practice of educational environments for young children. Indeed, Resnick (2017), in his book *Lifelong Kindergarten*, suggests that other phases of education should look to and adopt the playful approaches to learning that are central to early-years practice. Whilst we agree with much of this argument, a key point to make in this debate is that approaches to making in the early years have to date primarily focused on the use of non-digital tools and resources – junk modelling, painting, construction bricks and so on. When making using digital technologies has been an element of early-years practice, the activities normally involve tablets and cameras (Scott and Marsh, 2018), and there is little integration of disciplines in the approaches employed. The opportunities afforded by makerspaces as they are being developed in many countries enable children to move beyond these more traditional tools and practices to embrace the use of, for example, digital fabrication tools (e.g. 3D printers and laser-cutters) and electronics equipment. This can, in turn, enhance children's learning across science, technology, engineering and mathematics subjects (STEM). For the early years, an approach that integrates STEM disciplines with arts and humanities, known as STEAM, is appropriate, as it enables early-years practitioners to build on their well-established practice of integrating learning across subjects through a topic-focused approach, at the same time as extending the range of tools and resources on offer to children. A further rationale for the focus of the MakEY project was the need to understand the ways in which makerspaces can foster young children's digital literacy skills and knowledge.

Makerspaces and children's development of digital literacies

The importance of digital literacies for social inclusion, quality of life, success in the labour market and economic growth is widely recognised. There is an urgent need for every citizen to develop the knowledge, skills and attitudes required to participate in a complex and increasingly digitised society for personal and societal prosperity. According to the Digital Competence framework proposed by the European Commission,[1] the key areas of digital competence are *Information and data literacy, Communication and collaboration, Digital content creation, Safety*, and *Problem-solving*. In these policy documents, the definition of digital competence underscores confident, productive, creative and critical usage of digital technologies for diverse purposes in various social contexts and with various tools (Ala-Mutka, 2011). Moreover, these areas of digital competence are often viewed as part of the so-called transversal 21st-century skill sets that every citizen should be entitled to develop. Digital competencies are thus seen as intertwined with other transversal skill sets, including critical thinking skills and learning-to-learn, interaction and expression, multiliteracy, working life skills and entrepreneurship, as well as social participation and influence. In the MakEY project, we referred to these competencies as digital literacy to underscore their social and cultural nature, entailing the literacy practices, such as communication, expression, collaboration and advocacy, required for full participation in today's knowledge society (Sefton-Green et al., 2016).

Research shows that many children and young people in Europe have access to various media, digital tools, online sites and apps in their homes and communities (Livingstone and Haddon, 2009). The integration of digital tools into early years and primary classrooms has also increased due to the availability and affordability of computers, mobile phones, tablets and other similar technologies (Yelland and Gilbert, 2013). However, the nature of digital literacy practices among many young people throughout Europe has been found to be uneven (Livingstone and Haddon, 2009). Young people are reported to be adept at using technologies for operational purposes, but they generally lack more advanced literacies, such as critical literacy (Ala-Mutka, 2011). Overall, these findings indicate that mere exposure to technology does not equate with the development of more advanced digital literacies (Li et al., 2016). Moreover, not all young people have equal opportunities to use digital technologies fully due to various social and cultural factors, lack of interest and confidence or social support (Ala-Mutka, 2011). Research also shows an uneven provision of digitally enhanced learning opportunities for children in formal educational settings (Palaiologou, 2016).

Whilst there has been a range of European work that has focused on the development of digital literacies of all citizens (e.g. Ferrari, 2013), scant attention has been paid to educational activities that position children as active, creative and critical investigators, of and with digital technologies. At present, there is a dearth of knowledge on creating learning opportunities for digital literacies that are inclusive for diverse learners with different capabilities and interests, and that are able to accommodate their different personal situations and objectives and combine, for example, formal and everyday learning practices (Kumpulainen and Erstad, 2016; Kumpulainen, Mikkola, Rajala and Kaartinen, 2017). In sum, these realities point to the urgent need for the development and research of novel pedagogies and learning environments for enhancing every young person's digital literacies in meaningful, authentic and consequential ways.

One of the novel ways in which this may be approached is through the provision of makerspaces. Makerspaces prescribe a model of learning-by-doing in which individuals can work on creative design projects that are personally and/or collectively meaningful. The possibility to play with material objects is considered to act as a 'social glue' for people to come together and to engage in collaborative and creative endeavours (e.g. Gauntlett, 2011; Honey and Kanter, 2013; Ingold, 2013). It follows that social interactions and learning practices in makerspaces often cross divisions, such as age, gender or level of formal education and/or expertise (e.g. Halverson and Sheridan, 2014). In sum, making activities account for a complex set of socially and materially mediated practices that encompass not only the process of creating specific artefacts supported by a wide range of technologies and media, but also emotional, relational and cultural processes surrounding their use and construction.

A variety of benefits have been proposed as being accrued from participating in making activities based on intellectual traditions of cognitive psychology, constructivism, experiential learning and design theory (Dewey, 1902; Freire, 1970; Papert, 1980). Research suggests that hands–on experimentation and production across multiple media and digital content supports students' creative and critical engagement in disciplinary and transversal learning with various digital technologies and media (Hughes, 2017; Ratto, 2011). Existing research has proposed that making activities have the potential to support young people's creative and improvisational problem-solving, encourage students' agency, persistence and self-efficacy, and enrich young people's ideas and understanding of STEM and beyond (Bevan et al., 2016). Research has also suggested how making activities can enhance peer collaboration and transform the traditional roles of the teacher/other adult experts and students, enabling participants to develop and draw on each other's relative expertise (Vossoughi and Bevan, 2014). In addition to these academic goals, research on makerspaces in a children's hospital has pointed out their emancipatory and healing value in supporting young patients to feel more agentive in taking charge of their environment, as well as of their learning and wellbeing (Krishnan, 2015; Marsh, Arnseth and Kumpulainen, 2018).

Kafai, Fields and Searle (2014), for instance, examined students' engagement in one type of making activity, that of creating electronic textiles. In a similar fashion to Peppler and Glosson (2013), they concluded that by *making* wearable textiles, students gain a better understanding of the functions of computers and other tools involved in the process. Similarly, by means of designing games, making stories and animations and sharing them with others, children not only learned computational thinking but also came to understand the cultural and social nature of digital literacy practices (Kafai and Burke, 2014; Portelance, Strawhacker and Bers, 2015). In relation to critical literacies, Santo (2011, 2013) has pointed out that when children take part in 'hacker literacies', they both learn to approach technologies not merely as tools for self-expression and production but also learn to reflect on and critically evaluate the societal impacts of technology use. Therefore, as children engage in making activities, they appear to learn to draw on various knowledge(s) and skills (operational) to inform their creative production (cultural) and thus come to understand the ways in which these knowledges are embedded in larger sociocultural contexts (critical).

At the same time, available educational research on makerspaces has pointed out critical features that need to be addressed when considering their educational value (Peppler and Bender, 2013). For instance, makerspaces have been criticised for their narrowly defined goals and, thus, failing to attract and engage the broader population of young people (Blikstein and Worsley, 2016). Research has also warned of the erroneous dichotomisation between abstract thinking and play, a general ethos of more 'doing' and less 'thinking and reflection', and about a dismissive stance towards the documentation and assessment of learners' engagement and learning in makerspaces (Kumpulainen et al., 2017). Also, as Blikstein (2013) points out, educators need to move away from simple demonstration projects typically associated with makerspaces and move towards learning that is more meaningful and contextualised. In all, existing research calls for quality and inclusivity in makerspaces and making activities, and urges further investigation into makerspaces as they relate to creating equitable and deep learning experiences for all children and young people.

One of the contributions that the MakEY project makes to the field is to bring together the fields of maker education and New Literacies in relation to early-years practice. These fields of study have distinct traditions, but each is concerned with how children make meaning using a range of resources. Whilst maker research has largely focused on examining spaces for making, the characteristics and practices of makers and the nature of making itself (Peppler, Halverson and Kafai, 2016), New Literacies has been concerned with examining digital literacies in detail through an analysis of the processes of design, production, dissemination and interpretation of multimodal and multimedia texts and artefacts (Colvert, 2015). Bringing these two traditions together means that the place of texts and artefacts themselves in making becomes significant, whilst still recognising that in many makerspace practices, the focus is on the process of making and not the product.

The research foci

The research projects that were undertaken in MakEY examined a range of issues at three levels of analysis: personal, relational and institutional. First, at the personal level, is the child him- or herself. Factors such as identity and interests impact on the choices children make with regard to engagement in digital production and subsequent learning gains. For example, at the personal level, how do young children's vectors of identity, such as gender and ethnicity, impact on their digital making? The students carry with them the history of their participation in social practices in and outside school. Their *histories in person* (Holland and Lave, 2001; Wortham, 2004) – that is, their unique trajectories of past participation in and across social contexts, sedimented in their identities – are powerful mediators of their present activity. However, students' identities are not determined by their past and present conditions; people and the social practices in which they participate co-develop over developmental time. Moreover, through their imagination, students can project themselves onto alternative futures by enacting *projective identities* (Gee, 2003). Taking part in makerspaces might bring forth a space of authoring new actual and projected identities, which could be important in orientating children towards future participation in activities related to STEM learning. At a personal level, therefore, the project examined the meanings and motivations children attach to their engagement in making activities, and explored how these motivations interact with the demands of the makerspace. The project also studied how children's experiences in makerspaces reshaped their interests in and identifications with digital literacy learning and creativity, examining the kinds of digital literacy skills and creative competences children developed through their participation in makerspaces.

Second, at the relational level, the project team was interested in exploring the nature of social interactions and learning practices, including collective creativity, that arise in makerspaces. Heterogeneity, complexity and conflict are central features of any social practice (Kumpulainen and Renshaw, 2007; Lave, 2008; Rajala and Sannino, 2015), and thus it was felt important to trace the continuous negotiation and conflict between the various agendas, identities and interests of the children, cultural industry professionals, teachers and other stakeholders taking part in the activities. The team was also interested in understanding the ways in which the social and material resources of the makerspaces supported diverse children's joint engagement, digital learning and creativity. At a relational level, therefore, MakEY throws light onto what characterises the social interactions and learning practices that arise in the digital makerspace, and illuminates how diverse children engage in the social interactions of the makerspace. The project also explored how the social and material resources of the makerspace support diverse children's engagement, digital literacy and creative design skills.

Third, at the institutional level, the project investigated the differences that apply when considering makerspaces situated in different contexts, such as Fab Labs, museums and kindergarten classrooms. The team identified the perceived institutional/organisational barriers to the use of makerspaces for children aged 3–8 years in community makerspaces, early-years settings and schools, libraries and museums. The project examined how makerspaces are integrated into these institutions, including considerations of social organisation, space and time arrangements. The project also considered how far the makerspaces studied and their practices create equitable opportunities for children's learning and identity development and how this process operates at an institutional level. The research team questioned what kinds of practices – pedagogical, assessment, material provision – best support young children's engagement in makerspaces in order to identify how this knowledge might be used to inform future provision for makerspaces in both formal and non-formal learning spaces. Finally, the project examined the value of the partnership between academic and non-academic participants in creating makerspaces for young children. In the concluding chapter, we return to these three levels of analysis and identify the project's key findings in relation to each.

An overview of the book

The book provides an overview of case studies conducted in all of the MakEY project countries. In addition, we invited a team in one of our international partner countries, Canada, to outline a study that was relevant to the MakEY project. Collectively, these case studies offer a range of rich insights into the provision of makerspaces for young children in early-years settings, schools, libraries and museums.

We begin with a chapter that offers a theoretical framework for the project as a whole. For many of the Nordic researchers in particular involved in the study, theorists central to Cultural Historical Activity Theory (CHAT) were key to their work. For others in the consortium, new materialist and post-human philosophies underpinned their studies. The chapter by Kontopodis and Kumpulainen, therefore, brings these two separate theoretical traditions into dialogue with each other in an analysis of data from the German project, in which children used Virtual Reality technology in their making. Whilst this chapter is significant for the project in creating a space for such dialogue, it is important to note that the other chapters do not limit themselves to these two theoretical traditions. Rather, each country team draws on specific theoretical frameworks that are relevant for their specific foci for discussion. This means that the book is truly interdisciplinary in nature, as it brings together theories from Childhood Studies, Education, New Literacies, Philosophy and Sociology, among other fields/disciplines.

The book then moves on to outline the empirical studies conducted in each of the countries involved in the MakEY study: Denmark, Finland, Germany, Iceland, Norway, Romania, the UK and the USA. Each of these chapters draws on a rich range of data collected in the case-study sites to examine a range of themes, including how making is framed within both formal and non-formal learning contexts, the kinds of pedagogical strategies that best support young children's learning, and how this learning might be assessed. The chapters also consider the ways in which children's learning can be supported in makerspaces, and they include an analysis of the relationships with parents and others who do not have a formal learning agenda but do have a vision of what they think making can accomplish for their children. In addition to the chapters outlining the projects conducted as part of MakEY, we include a chapter written by a member of the international advisory board, Anne Burke, and co-author, Abigail Crocker. This case study was conducted in Canada and offers additional insights into some of the themes that emerged in the MakEY study, such as the role making has in developing children's sense of citizenship.

The concluding chapter brings together all of this work by returning to some of the questions posed when considering the three levels of analysis discussed previously – personal, relational and institutional. This chapter also identifies the implications of this study for future research, policy and practice. The book closes with an afterword written by Kylie Peppler. A member of the MakEY international advisory board, Kylie is one of the pioneers of the maker movement in education, and her work has informed the MakEY project from its inception. It is an honour to have her close the book and look forward to what this field might offer in future years.

Note

1 https://ec.europa.eu/jrc/en/digcomp/digital-competence-framework

References

Ala-Mutka, K. (2011). *Mapping Digital Competence: Towards a Conceptual Understanding.* Retrieved from: http://ftp.jrc.es/EURdoc/JRC67075_TN.pdf

Bevan, B., Ryoo, J. J., Shea, M., Kekelis, L., Pooler, P., Green, E., Bulalacao, N., McLeod, E., Sandoval, J. & Hernandez, M. (2016). *Making as a Strategy for Afterschool STEM Learning: Report from the Californian Tinkering Afterschool Network Research-Practice Partnership.* San Francisco, CA: The Exploratorium.

Blikstein, P. (2013). Digital fabrication and 'making' in education: The democratization of invention. In J. Walter-Herrmann & C. Büching (eds), *FabLab: Of Machines, Makers and Inventors* (pp. 203–222). Bielefeld: Transcript Publishers.

Blikstein, P. & Worsley, M. (2016). The maker movement: The last chance of progressive education? In K. Peppler, E. Halverson & Y. Kafai (eds), *Makeology: Makerspaces as Learning Environments* (Volume 1, pp. 64–80). New York: Routledge.

Chaudron, S., Beutel, M. E., Černikova, M., Donoso, V., Dreier, M., Fletcher-Watson, B., Heikkilä, A.-S., Kontríková, V., Korkeamäki, R.-L., Livingstone, S., Marsh, J., Mascheroni, G., Micheli, M., Milesi, D., Müller, K. W., Myllylä-Nygård, T., Niska, M., Olkina, O., Ottovordemgentschenfelde, S., Plowman, L., Ribbens, W., Richardson, J., Schaack, C., Shlyapnikov, V., Šmahel, D., Soldatova, G. & Wölfling, K. (2015). *Young Children (0–8) and Digital Technology: A Qualitative Exploratory Study across Seven Countries.* Joint Research Centre, European Commission. Retrieved from: http://publications.jrc.ec.europa.eu/repository/handle/JRC93239

Colvert, A. (2015). *Ludic Authorship: Reframing Literacies Through Peer-to-Peer Alternate Reality Game Design in the Primary Classroom.* Unpublished PhD dissertation. Institute of Education, University College of London.

Dewey, J. (1902). *The Child and the Curriculum.* Chicago, IL: The University of Chicago Press.

Ferrari, A. (2013). *DIGCOMP: A Framework for Developing and Understanding Digital Competence in Europe.* Retrieved from: http://ipts.jrc.ec.europa.eu/publications/pub.cfm?id=6359

Freire, P. (1970). *Pedagogy of the Oppressed.* New York: Seabury Press.

Gauntlett, D. (2011). *Making is Connecting: The Social Meaning of Creativity, from DIY and Knitting to YouTube and Web 2.0.* Cambridge, UK: Polity Press.

Gee, J. P. (2003). *What Video Games Have to Teach Us about Learning and Literacy.* New York; Basingstoke, UK: Palgrave Macmillan.

Halverson, E. R. & Sheridan, K. (2014). The maker movement in education. *Harvard Educational Review*, 84(4): 495–504.

Hatch, M. (2013). *The Maker Movement Manifesto*. New York: McGraw-Hill.

Holland, D. & Lave, J. (2001). Introduction. In D. Holland & J. Lave (eds), *History in Person: Enduring Struggles and the Practice of Identity* (pp. 3–33). Albuquerque, NM: School of American Research Press.

Honey, M. & Kanter, D. E. (eds). (2013). *Design, Make, Play: Growing the Next Generation of STEM Innovators*. New York: Routledge.

Hughes, J. M. (2017). Digital making with "At-Risk" youth. *International Journal of Information and Learning Technology*, 34(2): 102–113. doi:10.1108/ijilt-08-2016-0037

Ingold, T. (2013). *Making: Anthropology, Archaeology, Art and Architecture*. Abingdon, UK: Routledge.

Kafai, Y. B. & Burke, Q. (2014). *Connected Code: Why Children Need to Learn Programming*. Cambridge, MA: MIT Press.

Kafai, Y. B., Fields, D. A. & Searle, K. A. (2014). Electronic textiles as disruptive designs in schools: Supporting and challenging maker activities for learning. *Harvard Educational Review*, 84(4): 532–556.

Knobel, M. & Lankshear, C. (eds). (2010). *DIY Media: Creating, Sharing and Learning with New Technologies*. New York: Peter Lang.

Krishnan, G. (2015). *Designing a Mobile Makerspace for Children's Hospital Patients: Enhancing Patients' Agency and Identity in Learning*. Dissertation manuscript submitted to the Faculty of the Graduate School of Vanderbilt University in partial fulfilment of the requirements for the degree of Doctor of Philosophy. Retrieved from: http://etd.library.vanderbilt.edu/available/etd-08182015-034719/

Kumpulainen, K. & Erstad, O. (2016). (Re)searching learning in and across contexts: Conceptual, methodological and empirical considerations. *International Journal of Educational Research*. http://dx.doi.org/10.1016/j.ijer.2016.08.004

Kumpulainen, K. & Renshaw, P. (2007). Cultures of learning. *International Journal of Educational Research*, 46(3): 109–115.

Kumpulainen, K., Mikkola, A., Rajala, A. & Kaartinen, S. (2017, May). Students' creative agency in a school-based makerspace: A socio-material investigation. A poster presented at the structured poster session: *From Making to Agentic Participation: Perspectives on and Approaches to Fostering Epistemic Engagement in Making*. AERA conference, San Antonio.

Lave, J. (2008). Situated learning and changing practice. In A. Amin & J. Roberts (eds), *Community, Economic Creativity, and Organization* (pp. 283–296). Oxford: Oxford University Press.

Livingstone, S. & Haddon, L. (2009). *EU Kids Online: Final Report*. London: LSE: EU Kids Online. (EC Safer Internet Plus Programme Deliverable D6.5). Retrieved from: www.lse.ac.uk/media@lse/research/EUKidsOnline/EU%20Kids%20I%20(2006-9)/EU%20Kids%20Online%20I%20Reports/EUKidsOnlineFinalReport.pdf

Marsh, J., Arnseth, H. C. & Kumpulainen, K. (2018). Maker literacies and maker citizenship in the MakEY (Makerspaces in the Early Years) project. *Multimodal Technologies and Interaction*, 2: 50. doi:10.3390/mti2030050

Marsh, J., Wood, E. A. & Chesworth, L. (in press). Makerspaces in early childhood education: Principles of pedagogy and practice. *Mind, Culture and Activity*.

Palaiologou, I. (2016). Children under five and digital technologies: Implications for early years pedagogy. *The European Early Childhood Research Journal*, 24(1): 5–24.

Papert, S. (1980). *Mindstorms: Children, Computers and Powerful Ideas*. New York: Basic Books.

Peppler, K. & Bender, S. (2013). Maker movement spreads innovation one project at a time. *Phi Delta Kappan*, 95(3): 22–27.

Peppler, K. & Glosson, D. (2013). Stitching circuits: Learning about circuitry through e-textile materials. *Journal of Science Education and Technology*, 22(5): 751–763.

Peppler, K., Halverson, E. & Kafai, Y. (eds). (2016). *Makeology: Makerspaces as Learning Environments* (Vols 1 and 2). New York: Routledge.

Portelance, D. J., Strawhacker, A. & Bers, M. U. (2015). Constructing the ScratchJr programming language in the early childhood classroom. *International Journal of Technology and Design Education*, 29(4): 1–16.

Rajala, A. & Sannino, A. (2015). Students' deviations from a learning task: An activity-theoretical analysis. *International Journal of Educational Research*, 70: 31–46.

Ratto, M. (2011). Critical making: Conceptual and material studies. *Technology and Social Life, The Information Society: An International Journal*, 27(4): 252–260.

Resnick, M. (2017). *Lifelong Kindergarten*. Cambridge, MA: MIT Press.

Santo, R. (2011). Hacker literacies: Synthesizing critical and participatory media literacy frameworks. *International Journal of Learning and Media*, 3(3): 1–5.

Santo, R. (2013). Towards hacker literacies: What Facebook's privacy snafus can teach us about empowered technological practices. *Digital Culture & Education*, 5(1): 18–33.

Schrock, A. (2014). "Education in disguise": Culture of a hacker and maker space. *Journal of Education and Information Studies*, 10(1): 1–25. Retrieved from: http://escholarship.org/uc/item/0js1n1qg

Scott, F. & Marsh, J. (2018). Digital literacies in early childhood. In G. W. Noblit (ed.), *The Oxford Research Encyclopedia of Education*. Retrieved from: http://oxfordre.com/education

Sefton-Green, J., Marsh, J., Erstad, O., & Flewitt, R. (2016). *Establishing a Research Agenda for the Digital Literacy Practices of Young Children: A White Paper for COST Action IS1410*. Retrieved from http://digilitey.eu/wp-content/uploads/2015/09/DigiLitEYWP.pdf

Sheridan, K., Halverson, E. R., Litts, B., Brahms, L., Jacobs-Priebe, L. & Owens, T. (2014). Learning in the making: A comparative study of three makerspaces. *Harvard Educational Review*, 84: 505–531.

Vossoughi, S. & Bevan, B. (2014). *Making and Tinkering: A Review of the Literature*. National Research Council Committee on Out of School Time STEM. Retrieved from: http://sites.nationalacademies.org/cs/groups/dbassesite/documents/webpage/dbasse_089888.pdf

Wortham, S. (2004). From good student to outcast: The emergence of a classroom identity. *Ethos*, 32(2): 164–187.

Yelland, N. J. & Gilbert, C. L. (2013). iPossibilities: Tablets in early childhood contexts. *Hong Kong Journal of Early Childhood*, 12(1): 5–14.

2

RESEARCHING YOUNG CHILDREN'S ENGAGEMENT AND LEARNING IN MAKERSPACES

Insights from post-Vygotskian and post-human perspectives

Michalis Kontopodis and Kristiina Kumpulainen

Vignette: Niklas engaging with virtual reality technologies

Niklas (pseudonym), a 5-year-old boy, participates in a virtual reality workshop, one form of makerspace associated with FabLab Berlin. Niklas is interested in video games, computers and painting and there seems to be plenty of these materials and technologies around. Interestingly, there is also a toy, an Avakai wooden doll (made by the digital toy startup company Vaikai), with no gender-specific characteristics, which produces a great variety of sounds every time it is involved in some movement, aiming to communicate emotions (in Vaikai terms). Niklas is asked to create a world for that wooden doll, on or with cardboard and with a variety of other tools such as scissors, paint and pencils that are provided. Then he is also asked to create a similar environment for the doll using virtual reality tools. Other boys are present, including his older brother, who has just managed to paint in fine detail his own version of a virtual environment for the doll.

Niklas can see the doll on the desk alongside the painting materials as well as the doll's virtual replication within the pre-designed virtual environment on a 2D laptop screen. For 3D vision he is required to wear an HTC VIVE headset, which is connected through cables to two controllers, one for each hand, as well as a set of sensors and a data processing unit. When he does that, he can no longer see anything off-screen.

While Niklas tries the HTC VIVE headset, he steps on the (offline/off-screen) cable connecting it to the processing unit and almost falls on the floor. The facilitator – a woman in her 30s – quickly catches him so that he doesn't fall and moves the cable further away so that Niklas can focus on the virtual environment as it appears through the HTC VIVE headset. Then the facilitator invites Niklas to use the mouse, select a virtual brush and move it in a certain direction so as to further paint, modify and develop the doll's virtual environment. The facilitator explains to Niklas that he can move his whole body and even walk around if needed for the painting, but within the provided virtual room space, which is marked by virtual walls. Two minutes later, Niklas is crossing the virtual wall, which means that he also moves out of the offline/off-screen marked workshop area; without realising it he slightly touches a (real) chair with his back, which he couldn't have seen as he was wearing the HTC VIVE headset. This gives him a shock – the facilitator intervenes again, Niklas removes the headset, with everybody – him and the other boys – bursting into laughter.

Even if this ethnographic vignette is brief, it nevertheless raises complex theoretical issues, with no easy answers:

- Who is initiating and leading the activity? How and why is Niklas involved in the activity? What meanings, motives and affects are at stake? Do age, gender and ethnicity mediate Niklas's activity, and if yes, how?
- What are the possibilities and constraints entailed in this particular socio-material arrangement (facilitators + Niklas + other children + doll + software + PC + virtual reality headset + cables + sensors + controllers + chairs)? Do humans or Other-than-humans determine what is going to happen next? Does the design of the offline and online space and the design of the toys and technologies available matter? To what extent? How?
- How are broader contexts (e.g. institutional, cultural, societal) relevant for making sense of this particular scene?

The aim of the present chapter is to take this brief example as a point of departure and explore post-Vygotskian and post-human perspectives to investigate and make sense of young children's play and learning in makerspaces. We will also consider how these two perspectives can come into dialogue and provide both alternative and complementary answers to our enquiries into young children and makerspaces. In particular, we will consider some of the core constructs stemming from (post-)Vygotskian and post-humanist approaches to understanding children's engagement and learning with new technologies in makerspaces.

Post-Vygotskian perspectives

Making as culturally and historically situated activity

One could argue that everything in the vignette described above has *a meaning* situated in a specific cultural-historical context in space and time. Niklas is a German male name. *Dolls* entail meaning and can be attributed *roles* matching their design. *Computers, sensors, headsets* entail meaning as well: for example, Niklas was aware, as he explained in a follow-up interview, that these were expensive technologies that he could not have at home. Therefore, participating in this workshop was supposed to be a unique experience. Indeed, this is a *workshop* that is culturally-historically situated in an educational setting, within which children, adults and other people are undertaking certain roles and expected to engage in certain forms of action with the help of available tools, but not in others (cf. van Oers, Elbers, Wardekker and van der Veer, 2008). The workshop would be defined as successful, from the perspective of the facilitator, if

Niklas was keen to attend future events and, subsequently, learn to participate in maker activity while moving from peripheral participation to more active and even transformative engagement (Lave and Wenger, 1991; Stetsenko, 2016).

Post-Vygotskian approaches provide researchers with one potential tool for researching children's engagement and learning in makerspaces as culturally and historically situated activities. According to Engeström (1987), human activity is always situated within communities that are mediated by culturally and historically derived rules and divisions of labour. Furthermore, the object of an activity, leading to an outcome, is shaped by the goals and intentions of the people taking part in the activity and by their use of culturally and historically derived artefacts or tools, both conceptual and material. The ontological premise of Engeström's theory is that activity is always dynamic and that change within a system is also inevitable as the result of people's actions. Hence, the whole activity system can also change and develop as a result of people's activity. For that reason, the analysis of activity systems in makerspaces needs to take into account various levels of analysis, including individuals' engagements in the activity, relational interactions between and across people and available artefacts or tools, as well as the institutional context nested within a system. It is the tool–mediated interactions, and specifically tensions and contradictions that emerge in and across these different spheres of activity, that can help us investigate and understand what is going on in maker activities as a dynamic and multi-layered whole and how this activity can contribute to the learning and transformation of both individuals and communities (cf. also Kumpulainen and Erstad, 2016).

Making as a tool-mediated activity

Our vignette of Niklas and his activity in the makerspace shows how he is eventually motivated to engage in the activity and make use of available *meanings, signs* and *tools* in order to perform a concrete task with the doll and virtual painting, following his brother's engagement in the same activity. At the same time, Niklas may be entangled within broader cultural-historical contradictions regarding, for example, values on *gender* – as boys are expected to participate more in makerspaces than girls – or values related to social class and ethnicity – as playing with expensive technologies that cannot be available at home had a certain symbolic significance and was referred to by Niklas's mother as a reason for her bringing Niklas to the virtual reality workshop.

According to Vygotskian and post-Vygotskian approaches, when these contradictions cause so-called "developmental crises" or "dramatic events" (Veresov, 2004; Kontopodis, 2012), the child then makes use of psychological and environmental resources in order to overcome the contradictions at stake and engage in new modes of functioning, either by appropriating existing *meanings* or creating new ones – thus development happens. This development is at the same time psychological *and* cultural-historical: Vygotskian and post-Vygotskian approaches to teaching, learning and development (in their various versions cf. Daniels, Cole and Wertsch, 2007; Stetsenko, 2016) have indeed thoroughly studied how signs and mediating tools – in our case the HTC VIVE headset and virtual painting tools –

mediate the communication between adults or experienced peers and less experienced children; at the same time, signs and mediating tools shape one's *inner speech* and so-called higher psychological processes such as thinking and imagination:

> [E]very function in the cultural development of the child appears on the stage twice, that is, on two planes, first, the social, then the psychological, first between people as an intermental category, then within the child as an intramental category. This pertains equally to voluntary attention, to logical memory, to the formation of concepts, and to the development of will. We are justified in considering the thesis presented as a law, but it is understood that the transition from outside inward transforms the process itself, changes its structure and functions. Genetically, social relations, real relations of people, stand behind all the higher functions and their relations. From this, one of the basic principles of our will is the principle of division of functions among people, the division into two of what is now merged into one, the experimental unfolding of a higher mental process into the drama that occurs among people. For this reason, we might term the basic result to which the history of the cultural development of the child leads us as sociogenesis of higher forms of behaviour.
>
> *(Vygotsky, 1931/1997, p.106)*

Vygotsky described three phases in the child's developmental process: (a) the social situation of development, (b) the new formation which is typified by a contradiction between the child's current capabilities and his/her needs and desires as well as the demands and possibilities of the environment, and (c) the outcome in new functions. In order to overcome the contradiction between his/her capabilities and desires, the child needs to mobilise intra-psychological maturing processes in relation to cultural psychological and material tools. A structural change in the organisation of functions is brought about by the process of the child overcoming the existing contradiction within his/her activity (Chaiklin, 2003; Kontopodis and Newnham, 2011).

A much-disputed concept in this framework is the Vygotskian notion of the Zone of Proximal Development (Vygotsky, 1930–34/1998). Chaiklin has reviewed all of Vygotsky's texts in which this term appears and questions the definition of the term, since Vygotsky himself does not provide it and there is no outline of a theory for the Zone of Proximal Development (Chaiklin, 2003). Chaiklin argues against the various "commonsense" interpretations of the Zone of Proximal Development and their implications for educational practice. The main features of the Zone of Proximal Development as summarised by Chaiklin are the following: a) it involves the whole child; b) development is concerned with the relationships between psychological functions and not the psychological functions as such; c) development takes place as a qualitative change in these relationships; d) change is brought about by the child's actions in the social situation of development; and e) each age period is characterised by a leading activity/contradiction that organises the child's actions through which new functions develop (Chaiklin, 2003, p.50). New functions in the aforementioned case would entail the links between on-screen painting and off-screen bodily movements within a given space and frame.

While conceiving of child development as a cultural-historical phenomenon, Vygotsky also posed the question as to how human history can lead to a new type of society and a new type of human being (Vygotsky, 1930–34/1998). Concepts such as *appropriation*, and *active subjectivity*, have been central in this undertaking. The notion of *active subjectivity* implies that children as well as scientists or teachers act according to their own intentions and motivations, actively participating in defining how signs and tools are used and meanings are appropriated. Active subjectivity can thus transform a given social situation so that new meanings and new practices emerge (Kumpulainen, Kajamaa and Rajala, 2018, 2019). Niklas could, in the longer term, create new meanings and new ways of *VR design, making* or *hacking* in this frame or participate in such creative processes in collaboration with others, which also explains how civilisations develop. In Russian, the term "mediating activity" emphasises exactly the generation of novelty in every developmental process (as opposed to the term "mediated activity"). Being in the world is transforming the world, not adapting to it, and human development is the process of purposeful transformation of the world (Stetsenko, 2016). Critical educational and critical psychological research (Holzkamp, 1995; Williams, Billington, Goodley and Corcoran, 2017) has been much inspired by Vygotsky as well as by the entire Soviet school of psychology (Davydov, 2008; Leont'ev, 1978; Lompscher and Galperin, 1972) in this frame.

Making as play and creativity

The makerspace context of Niklas's activity also implies a space for creative and playful activity in which something new and personally meaningful can be created by the participants with the help of available artefacts and tools (Honey and Kanter, 2013; Kumpulainen, Karttunen, Juurola and Mikkola, 2014). Ideally, makerspaces prescribe a model of learning-by-doing in which children and older people too can work on creative design projects that are personally and/or collectively meaningful. The possibility to play with material objects is considered to act as "social glue" for people to come together and engage in collaborative and creative endeavours (e.g. Honey and Kanter, 2013; Ingold, 2013). Making activities hence account for a complex set of socially and materially mediated practices that encompass not only processes of creating specific artefacts supported by a wide range of tools, but also emotional, relational and cultural processes surrounding their use and construction (Kumpulainen, 2017).

Vygotsky paid particular attention in his developmental theory to emotions and saw play as the cornerstone of development:

> "An idea that has become an affect, a concept that has turned into a passion" – this ideal of Spinoza's finds its prototype in play, which is the realm of spontaneity and freedom... In short, play gives the child a new form of desires, i.e. teaches him to desire by relating his desires to a fictitious "I" – to his role in the game and its rules. Therefore, a child's greatest achievements are possible in play – achievements that tomorrow will become his average level of real action and his morality.
>
> *(Vygotsky, 1933/2002, online)*

For Vygotsky (1978), the foundation of play arises from children's desires that cannot be met in the moment. Hence, to fulfil their motives, children invent imaginary situations, i.e. play activity, to meet their needs. Vygotsky also argued that children's play, although imaginary, is mediated by rule-based behaviours embedded in their everyday lives. Play hence requires children to abstract and translate the meaning of their real-life practices to their imagined scenarios in play activity. For Vygotsky, such abstraction from concrete to imaginary requires children's use of a *pivot* – an action or object that carries meaning from real life into imaginary play activity. Through the use of such pivots, children begin to exert self-control by regulating their own activity according to the rules of their imaginary play. Hence, for Vygotsky, play performs two important developmental functions: It contributes to children's development of mental representation and self-regulation (Vygotsky, 1978).

In makerspaces, children are afforded opportunities for play and playful interactions with various new (e.g. digital technologies and media) and more traditional tools and artefacts (e.g. associated with craftsmanship, such as woodwork or textiles). Makerspaces hence provide a fascinating context to research children's play and the genealogy of creative practice in general, and how these mediate the learning and development of children, i.e. what they learn to know (cognition) and how they see themselves (identity), as well as how these playful and creative activities shape their relationships, roles and positions with others, as well as their communities and cultures. Here, acknowledging the situated, embodied and multimodal elements of thinking and learning creates conceptual bases for researching children's maker activities as cultural practice. Overall, a focus on the creative and playful dimensions in maker activities can lead to novel investigations and insights in which cognition, affect and bodily activity and knowing are examined in unison and no longer divorced (Roth and Jornet, 2016).

Next, we turn to discussing the post-humanist perspective and its contribution to researching the materiality of making and makerspaces. In so doing, we want to extend our discussions on the meaning of tool-mediation and materiality in, and for, children's creative and playful activity and potential development in makerspaces. We will also consider how the post-humanist perspective can advance our thinking of children's engagement and learning in makerspaces.

Exploring ongoing action from a post-humanist perspective

One could argue that the term *mediation* offers quite fertile ground to begin analysing Niklas's activity in the scene above. Yet, it might not actually disclose what exactly it is supposed to reveal: the involvement of *mediating tools and devices* in ongoing action (e.g. VR headset, software, cables, doll, sensors, controllers). When Niklas moves his (off-screen) body, moves the controller by moving his (off-screen) hand or presses a certain (off-screen) key, there is action on the computer screen as well as on the screen of the VR headset. The two systems (on-/off-screen) are interlinked through Niklas's actions, which in turn are mediated by the controllers, sensors, processing unit and software. Further mediators may entail cables, the broader spatial arrangement, verbal directions by the facilitator or by other children etc.

How virtual reality technologies work is not of importance to the average modern-day user; they are usually *black-boxed*. Little is known about how the processing unit processes recorded data, the coding behind a rather user-friendly painting interface or the multiple connections between all the different parts (cables, sensors, controllers, PC, headset). When Niklas literally steps *on* the cable and metaphorically *out of* the virtual reality environment, some of this black-boxing is reversed – but not for long. The *composition* of all these mediating means does not only impact on the outcomes produced (let's say a 3D virtual interface design), it also impacts on Niklas, as well, by *radically transforming* not only his actions and responses to the screened and mechanic effects but also his *intentions*.

This is the most crucial aspect: the *actor-network* of Niklas + software + controllers + sensors + computer + doll + headset does not just do *more of* or *better* what Niklas would do anyway, it does *different* things and *translates* the activity at stake in ways that neither Niklas *nor* the software program (and its developers) would have necessarily envisaged in advance. From a post-humanist perspective, the contingency and unpredictability of this dynamic *ordering* of humans and Other-than-humans cannot be reduced to any single part – let alone to the agency or intentions of a single human agent – if such a distinct "human" agent exists at all. A "programme of action" emerges symmetrically in this context: it refers as much to the intentions of human beings as to the functions of artefacts, without invoking an a priori distinction between humans and Other-than-humans. The original programme of action is thus "translated" or "transformed" through *technical mediation* into a new one. Both the machines and the person change in the course of mediated action: neither has an "essence"; they have existence, they exist, and they are transformed in their relation to one another. The dimension of *time* is significant here: the software and the computer have obviously been developed by humans; however, their intentionalities are delegated to other actors and thereby *transformed* over multiple layers of time that cannot easily be traced back or reconstructed.

Latour (1994, pp.32–39) identifies four different yet interrelated modes of technical mediation in this frame:

- "translation" of an intention or a programme of action into another one, as described above
- "composition", i.e. relating things that were previously different or unrelated
- "black-boxing", which renders invisible the intermingling of humans and non-humans but becomes reversed when actor-networks fail to work and the various parts of the actor-network are revealed
- "delegation" of action from an actor-network to another one (e.g. from a developer team to software).

According to Latour, all these modes of mediation work *through* humans and Other-than-humans *symmetrically* without humans having a central role – as other paradigms would presume. As a result, no action can be traced back to distinct individual or collective human intentions – "the universe is agential intra-activity in its becoming" as Karen Barad writes:

...the universe is agential intra-activity in its becoming. The primary ontological units are not "things" but phenomena – dynamic topological reconfigurings/ entanglements/ relationalities/ (re)articulations. And the primary semantic units are not "words" but material-discursive practices through which boundaries are constituted. This dynamism *is* agency. Agency is not an attribute but the ongoing reconfigurings of the world.

(Barad, 2003, p.18)

As Karen Barad (2003) postulates, when thinking in terms of becoming, no subjects and objects are presupposed, agency is distributed, matter matters in its intra-active becoming on the basis of which objectivity and subjectivity emerge (see also Law and Moser, 1999). In this frame, terms such as "becoming", which implies open-ended processes, are preferred over terms such as "development" or "learning", which often imply a final stage of equilibrium (Reinertsen, 2016). While (post-) Vygotskian research emphasises the *purposefulness* of human activity, post-humanist analysis shifts the focus to the rather *unpredictable and messy* process of the translation of multiple intentionalities into action (and vice versa). In both cases action is *mediated* – yet, order*ings* or attempts at order*ing*, as John Law (1992) explains, is a term that emphasises the dynamic, messy and open-ended character of everydayness as well as the co-existence and potential conjunction of heterogeneous orderings. Such an approach is opposed to the proposition that culture, history, learning or development can be understood in terms of one single order. Relationality, in its radical post-humanist version, presumes the reality of infinitude:

Relations are based on an alternative ontology, time and space, and on an inclusive rather than an exclusive or oppositional logic. The key to this different logic is a distinction between finitude and infinitude. Whereas oppositions presume the existence of finite terms, relationality presumes the reality of infinitude. In an experience of relationality, subjecthood is suspended; there are no finite terms, but, rather, the undefinable non-oppositional difference of wholeness.

(Metcalfe and Game, 2008, p.191)

Such a perspective does not of course imply absolute relativism and political neutrality – rather, the opposite: across the various streams of post-humanism (Actor-Network Theory, post-phenomenology, post-ANT, post-feminist scholarship cf. Fox and Alldred, 2016), much attention is paid to the knowledge and values incorporated in technology. Design, technoscience, architecture and socio-material arrangements in general are not considered to be neutral: even if their use entails uncertainty, they enable certain things to happen and prevent other things from happening. Acknowledging this has led to long discussions in the field of *Science & Technology Studies* on the broader politics of technoscience and the implications for children and childhood (Lee, 2013; Snaza and Weaver, 2015).

Yet, instead of discussing politics from "out-there" – i.e. from a distanced and disembodied perspective often implied in post-/Vygotskian scholarship, when taking seriously the notion of "mediation", researchers cannot be seen as neutral entities external to the research procedure looking at the results from the balcony of the world as if their presence had no impact on the data. On the contrary, researchers may be sharing motivations, values and collaborating with a few people and not with others, and situated in socio-material arrangements, enabled as well as bound by semiotic, material, spatial and temporal orderings, that shape their roles and interactions with the research participants and materials. Researchers therefore contribute (not always consciously) to the complex dynamics of continuity and change in the mediated orderings that they explore (Hasse, 2015; Kontopodis and Perret-Clermont, 2015).

Seen from this perspective, the question is not how Niklas develops – as an individual – but how to experiment with one's body, i.e. with the socio-material orderings within which children/researchers/facilitators are embedded so that fundamentally new sets of relations emerge that eventually escape various layers of existing knowledge-power relations – be they racial, gendered, age-related, capitalist, geo-political etc. (cf. Murris, 2016; Taylor and Hughes, 2016).

Conclusions

In our chapter, we have introduced insights into some core notions and conceptual thinking behind post-Vygotskian perspectives and post-humanistic approaches that we believe can help us to research and make sense of children's play and learning in makerspaces situated in and across various sociocultural contexts, such as in cultural and educational institutions. At the same time, we understand that our introduction is in many ways limited and ambitious in scope – not the least since the commonalities and differences between post-Vygotskian and post-humanist approaches have been little explored in existing literature. The few exceptions that have addressed such contrastive and comparative analysis include the article by Bruno Latour on inter-objectivity (1996) and the debate it opened in the journal *Mind, Culture, and Activity* (Miettinen, 1999), the work by Estrid Sørensen on the *Materiality of Learning* (2009), the study by David Middleton and Steve Brown on remembering and forgetting (Middleton and Brown, 2005) and the research on *Fabricating Human Development* by Michalis Kontopodis (2009), as well as recent theoretical work by Alex Levant (2017).

According to our still emerging analytic interpretation of these theoretical perspectives, we would like to emphasise that:

- Both perspectives focus on dynamic processes as opposed to more linear models of nature-driven development (cf. Piaget, 1936/1977).
- Both perspectives draw attention to tool-mediation and action as pivotal elements of creativity, play, development and transformation.
- Both perspectives pay much attention to conflicting or multiple intentionalities and the generation of novelty – yet they do that in different ways.
- While fostering creativity, playfulness and experimentation with regard to technology, both perspectives invite us to be rather sceptical of popular

understandings of commercial entrepreneurship and direct our attention to broader societal and ecological problems of our era, and to the complexity technology-in-the-making may entail in alleviating these.

Taken together, we believe that post-Vygotskian perspectives along with post-humanist approaches can guide our empirical research on makerspaces in several worthwhile ways, helping us understand maker activities and makerspaces as dynamic and complex social, cultural and material practices, situated across space and time. For example, *a personal level of analysis* will help us unpack the varied intentions, interests and identities that children bring into play, learning and maker activities, as well as those which they develop in interaction with Others (including Other-than-humans) during their engagement. This level of analysis will also address the diverse ways in which children respond to the demands and opportunities that maker activities impose on and offer to their learning and development. At the interpersonal level, we can investigate the pedagogical interactions and practices that arise in makerspaces between children, facilitators and the various artefacts as *enabled* and *constrained* by the design of the socio-material environment (on-/off-screen). At the institutional level, we can explore how the cultural-historical context and the rules and values of the institution, in which the makerspace is situated, are *interlinked with* and *materialised in* complex socio-technical arrangements that mediate the nature of maker activities, including children's play and learning.

We want to end our chapter with a quote by M. Fischer (2009) who, for us, powerfully summarises various elements present in maker activities worthy of our research attention in our efforts to understand individual and cultural practices and transformations situated in makerspaces designed for children and their communities.

Culture is…

1. that relational (circa 1848),
2. complex whole (1870s),
3. whose parts cannot be changed without affecting other parts (circa 1914),
4. mediated through powerful and power-laden symbolic forms (1930),
5. whose multiplicities and performatively negotiated character (1960)
6. are transformed by alternative positions, organizational forms and leveraging of symbolic systems (1980s),
7. as well as by emergent new technosciences, media and biotechnical relations (circa 2005).*(Fischer, 2009, p.1)*

Acknowledgements

We are particularly thankful to participating colleagues and artists Deborah Rodrigues, Justyna Zubrycka, Dylan Yamada-Rice and Jackie Marsh, as well as to FabLab Berlin and the anonymous parents and children for their consent and enthusiastic engagement in our research. Special thanks are also due to Liz Chesworth for her feedback to an earlier version of this chapter.

References

Barad, K. (2003). Posthumanist performativity: Toward an understanding of how matter comes to matter. *Signs: Journal of Women in Culture and Society*, 28(3): 801–831.

Chaiklin, S. (2003). The Zone of Proximal Development in Vytgotsky's analysis of learning and instruction. In A. Kozulin, B. Gindis, V. Ageyey & S. Miller (eds), *Vygotsky's educational theory in cultural context* (pp. 39–64). Cambridge: Cambridge University Press.

Daniels, H., Cole, M., & Wertsch, J. V. (eds). (2007). *The Cambridge companion to Vygotsky*. Cambridge; New York: Cambridge University Press.

Davydov, V. (2008). *Problems of developmental instruction: A theoretical and experimental psychological study*. Hauppauge; New York: Nova Science Publishers.

Engeström, Y. (1987). *Learning by expanding: An activity theoretical approach to developmental research*. Helsinki: Orienta-Konsultit Oy.

Fischer, M. M. (2009). *Anthropological futures*. Durham, NC: Duke University Press.

Fox, N. & Alldred, P. (2016). *Sociology and the new materialism: Theory, research, action*. London: Sage.

Hasse, C. (2015) *An anthropology of learning: On nested frictions in cultural ecologies*. Dordrecht: Springer.

Holzkamp, K. (1995). *Lernen: Subjektwissenschaftliche Grundlegung*. Frankfurt am Main: Campus.

Honey, M. & Kanter, D. E. (eds). (2013). *Design, make, play: Growing the next generation of STEM innovators*. London; New York: Routledge.

Ingold, T. (2013). *Making: Anthropology, archaeology, art and architecture*. Abingdon: Routledge.

Kontopodis, M. (2009). *Fabricating human development: The dynamics of 'ordering' and 'othering' in an experimental secondary school* (Hauptschule). PhD Dissertation. Freie Universität Berlin, Berlin, Germany.

Kontopodis, M. (2012). *Neoliberalism, pedagogy and human development: Exploring time, mediation and collectivity in contemporary schools*. London; New York: Routledge.

Kontopodis, M. & Newnham, D. S. (2011). Expanding cultural-historical and critical perspectives on child and youth development. *Ethos*, 39(1): 71–75.

Kontopodis, M. & Perret-Clermont, A.-N. (2015). Educational settings as interwoven sociomaterial orderings: An introduction. *European Journal of Psychology of Education*, 30(4): 1–12.

Kumpulainen, K. (2017). Makerspaces – Why they are important for digital literacy education. In J. Marsh, K. Kumpulainen, B. Nisha, A. Velicu, A. Blum-Ross, D. Hyatt, S. R. Jónsdóttir, R. Levy, S. Little, G. Marusteru, M. E. Ólafsdóttir, K. Sandvik, K. F. Scott, K. Thestrup, H. C. Arnseth, K. Dýrfjörð, A. Jornet, S. H. Kjartansdóttir, K. Pahl, S. Pétursdóttir & G. Thorsteinsson (eds), *Makerspaces in the early years: A literature review* (pp. 12–16). Sheffield: University of Sheffield; MakEY Project.

Kumpulainen, K. & Erstad, O. (2016). (Re)Searching learning across contexts: Conceptual, methodological and empirical explorations. *International Journal of Educational Research*, 84: 55–57.

Kumpulainen, K., Kajamaa, A. & Rajala, A. (2018). Understanding educational change: Agency-structure dynamics in a novel design and making environment. *Digital Education Review*, 33: 26–38.

Kumpulainen, K., Kajamaa, A. & Rajala, A. (2019). Motive-demand dynamics creating a social context for students' learning experiences in a making and design environment. In A. Edwards, M. Fleer & L. Bottcher (eds), *Cultural-historical approaches to studying learning and development: Societal, institutional and personal perspectives*. Amsterdam: Sage.

Kumpulainen, K., Karttunen, M., Juurola, L. & Mikkola, A. (2014). Towards children's creative museum engagement and collaborative sense-making. *Digital Creativity*, 25(2): 233–246.

Latour, B. (1994). On technical mediation: Philosophy, sociology, genealogy. *Common Knowledge*, 3(2): 29–64.

Latour, B. (1996). On interobjectivity. *Mind, Culture & Activity*, 3(4): 228–245.

Lave, J. & Wenger, E. (1991). *Situated learning: Legitimate peripheral participation*. Cambridge; New York: Cambridge University Press.

Law, J. (1992). Notes on the theory of actor-network: Ordering, strategy, and heterogeneity. *Systems Practice*, 5: 379–393.

Law, J. & Moser, I. (1999). Managing, subjectivities and desires. *Concepts and Transformation*, 4(3): 249–279.

Lee, N. (2013). *Childhood and biopolitics: Climate change, life processes and human futures*. New York: Palgrave Macmillan.

Leont'ev, A. (1978). *Activity, consciousness, and personality*. Englewood Cliffs, NJ: Prentice and Hall.

Levant, A. (2017). Smart matter and the thinking body: Activity theory and the turn to matter in contemporary philosophy. *Stasis*, 2(5): 248–264.

Lompscher, J. & Galperin, P. J. (1972). *Probleme der Ausbildung geistiger Handlungen: neuere Untersuchungen zur Anwendung der Lerntheorie Galperins*. Berlin: Volk und Wissen.

Metcalfe, A. & Game, A. (2008). From the de-centered subject to relationality. *Subjectivity*, 23(1): 188–205.

Middleton, D. & Brown, S. D. (2005). *The social psychology of experience: Studies in remembering and forgetting*. London; Thousand Oaks, CA: Sage.

Miettinen, R. (1999). The riddle of things: Activity theory and actor-network theory as approaches to studying innovations. *Mind, Culture & Activity*, 6(3): 170–195.

Murris, K. (2016). *The posthuman child: Educational transformation through philosophy with picturebooks*. London: Routledge.

Piaget, J. (1936/1977). *La naissance de l'intelligence chez l'enfant*. Neuchâtel-Paris: Delachaux & Niestlé.

Reinertsen, A. (ed.). (2016). *Becoming earth: A posthuman turn in educational discourse*. Rotterdam: Sense.

Roth, W.-M. & Jornet, A. (2016). Perezhivanie in the light of the later Vygotsky's Spinozist turn. *Mind, Culture & Activity*, 23(4): 315–324.

Snaza, N. & Weaver, J. (eds). (2015). *Posthumanism and educational research*. London; New York: Routledge.

Sørensen, E. (2009). *The materiality of learning: Technology and knowledge in educational practice*. New York: Cambridge University Press.

Stetsenko, A. (2016). *The transformative mind: Expanding Vygotsky's approach to development and education*. Cambridge, MA: Cambridge University Press.

Taylor, C. & Hughes, C. (2016). *Posthuman research practices in education*. New York: Palgrave Macmillan.

van Oers, B., Elbers, E., Wardekker, W. & van der Veer, R. (eds). (2008). *The transformation of learning: Advances in cultural-historical activity theory*. Cambridge; New York: Cambridge University Press.

Veresov, N. (2004). *Zone of proximal development (ZPD): The hidden dimension?* Retrieved from: https://pdfs.semanticscholar.org/b999/cccd4245f76c4bfb43d03c69c722881f82f2.pdf, 20 August 2019.

Vygotsky, L. S. (1930–34/1998). Child psychology (S. Sochinenij, Trans.). In R. Rieber (ed.), *The Collected Works* (Vol. 5). New York; London: Plenum.

Vygotsky, L. S. (1931/1997). The history of development of higher mental functions (M. Hall, Trans.). In R. Rieber (ed.), *The collected works* (Vol. 4, pp. 1–251). London; New York: Plenum.

Vygotsky, L. S. (1933/2002). *Play and its role in the mental development of the child.* Retrieved from: http://yuoiea.com/uoiea/assets/files/pdfs/vygotsky-play.pdf, 20 August 2019.

Vygotsky, L. S. (1978). *Mind and society: The development of higher mental processes.* Cambridge, MA: Harvard University Press.

Williams, A., Billington, T., Goodley, D. & Corcoran, T. (eds). (2017). *Critical educational psychology.* Chichester: Wiley.

3

MAKEATIVE MAKERSPACES

When the pedagogy is makeative

Klaus Thestrup and Louisa Haugaard Pedersen

An introduction to being makeative

This chapter analyses what it means to be practising makeative pedagogy in makerspaces. Being makeative is an approach to practising makerspaces based on an open pedagogy that emphasizes an ongoing flexibility to investigate and invent with any kind of materials and tools, and in any kind of spaces. It is matter of being open to the unforeseen, no matter what materials, tools or location. This pedagogical approach is based on a series of empirical research projects on makerspaces in Denmark. These projects have been facilitated at a municipal school, Katrinebjergskolen, and a municipal library, DOKK1, in Aarhus. The makeative approach evolved from a pedagogical and research method called *Next Practice Labs*, where children, professionals and researchers act together in experimenting communities facilitated in open laboratories. In this chapter we present how the makeative approach evolved through three steps integral to three Danish makerspace projects, highlighted as: step 1) starting makeative acts, step 2) exploring makeative narratives and step 3) developing makeative playgrounds.

Kindergarten in school

The Danish system of education, and some recent changes to it, requires a few words of introduction. In Denmark the term 'kindergarten' normally covers children 3–6 years old, but sometimes children start when they are just 2 years old. Adults working in kindergartens do not hold the title of pre-school teachers, but pedagogues or social educators. This is due to the fact that kindergartens historically have not been considered part of the educational system, but instead deploy a special kindergarten pedagogy. Children start formally in school when they are 7 years old, but in practice they nearly all start when they are 6 years old in a pre-school, or what is often referred to as "Class 0". Pre-school in Denmark only lasts for one year. Almost all the children involved in the Danish MakEY project are 7 years old and were part of this special class. In Denmark, pedagogues still receive their own education training alongside education training for teachers in school. But the adults in Danish pre-schools are both trained teachers and trained pedagogues. This is a result of political ambitions to strengthen the connections between school and kindergarten.

Class 0 is a specific crossing point between kindergarten and school. When entering the rooms where these children go to school, one sees the heritage of the kindergarten tradition in Denmark. The rooms have many shelves with tools and materials for the children to use when, for instance, drawing or painting. As for kindergartens in Denmark, it is possible to say that they, in a sense, look like makerspaces. The rooms inside a kindergarten have spaces for play and activities at tables, but also on the floor, and the children themselves are to a certain extent given the option to decide what to play with and for how long. The actual spaces are intended for activities using body and hands, alone, in small groups or with everybody together. Scissors, pens and glue-guns are among the tools available to use, together with digital media, which have been introduced and used in different Danish kindergartens over the last few years (Howard and Lauridsen, 2017; Skjærris and Knudsen, 2017; Pröschold, 2018). This is also the case with After School Clubs. Makerspaces as spaces to be creative and to play have been part of the kindergarten tradition in Denmark for a long time.

The connection between the first kindergartens in Europe in the 18th century and children's experiments with technology today has been made by, among others, Mitchel Resnick, who is inspired by Fröbel's ideas from the 19th century about kindergartens where children experiment and play with toys, materials and other objects (Resnick, 2017, p.13). Resnick even emphasizes that education for all age groups should be based on how children play in kindergarten. He calls this the *Lifelong Kindergarten*. The new curriculum for kindergartens in Denmark, from 2018, points at play as a central activity for children and furthermore emphasizes that the child's perspective is important (Børne-og Socialministeriet 2018a, 2018b). When children start pre-school, they bring important experiences and abilities with them, so it seems that pre-school in Denmark represents an interesting place to grasp ideas from kindergartens and use them when opening makerspaces in schools, where children get the possibility to be makeative.

A makeative approach – closed and open pedagogy

We owe the term 'Makeative' to the late Kjetil Sandvik at the University of Copenhagen and James Wallbank at Makers,[1] who in 2017, during the MakEY project, started to discuss this term. They based it, among other things, on their thoughts on some of the first results from the project, thus indicating that makerspaces come in many different types. A makerspace can be temporary or permanent, placed in more formal learning spaces, like schools, or in non-formal spaces, such as a museum, a library or a community centre (Marsh et al. 2017, p.61). To be makeative requires using tools, materials, processes and spaces in certain ways. To be makeative has to do with what you then do and how you then play and experiment in a makerspace, no matter whether you are a participant in some activities, or if you lead them. It has to do with the actual space itself, how materials and tools are used in various processes and what children have to offer in these processes. A makerspace is not a pre-defined set of tools or a copy of other makerspaces. Being makeative is a question of orientating from a principle to re-making locations, materials and directions when needed or wanted by those who run a given makerspace. It is, so to speak, more than tinkering with materials (Resnick and Rosenbaum, 2013); it is tinkering with the makerspace itself.

The openness of one's mindset should also include an openness towards other spaces, no matter whether these spaces are local or global, analogue or digital or a combination of these. The Maker movement has its starting point in physical spaces, but it is already part of the development of makerspaces that spaces use the Internet as part of the storage, communication and production facilities available to makers (Peppler, Halverson and Kafai, 2016a, 2016b). It could be argued that, inside the Maker movement, the idea of global connection is present, as it also is when you talk about the FabLab movement, where several FabLabs from several countries worked together from the very start (Gershenfeld, 2012). Before the MakEY project, the co-author of this chapter, Klaus Thestrup, over the years worked in similar ways, leading projects in which kindergartens developed narratives together over Facebook, or exchanged playing with and using apps in Google+ groups (Thestrup, 2019). All these experiments have been characterized as projects where local activities were the basis of communication with others somewhere else inside the country or abroad.

When two or more makerspaces meet across time and space with all the possible differences and similarities between them, one requires a certain view on pedagogy, which needs to be makeative. It becomes even more necessary if one adds the encounters with other kinds of laboratories or groups of people worldwide. The participants in a single makerspace may encounter different views on what digital media can be used for and how, and what materials and tools to use in what order and for what purpose. One may identify a tension between a closed and an open pedagogy, where a closed pedagogy represents a teaching structure and content based on pre-made templates facilitated by the use of digital and analogue materials and tools with pre-defined questions and answers. In short, the structure and content are planned by a defined and specific goal. What goes on outside the maker-space itself is of no interest or will easily be regarded as unwanted and unnecessary disturbance. An open pedagogy, on the other hand, represents a situated structure and content, without pre-made templates or pre-defined goals, but with an emphasis on an ongoing process of questioning and investigation, of and with digital and analogue materials and tools (Pedersen, 2019).

The openness of the pedagogy depends on the flexibility possible in relation to the activities, materials and tools, where children have time and the opportunity to find their own way to make, select materials, ask questions, investigate and express their own points of view. These contexts are like open formulas because they can constantly evolve in various directions, depending on the experimentation itself. An open pedagogy puts an emphasis on situated questions, experimentation and transformation, because the answer is not given beforehand. The participants in a single makerspace will, through an open pedagogy, include inspiration and challenges from other makerspaces as exactly that: new sources of inspiration, which might be transformed into new local expressions, objects and questions. This is in contrast to a closed pedagogy, because that emphasizes responding to pre-made questions and attempting to guess the answers (Pedersen, 2019).

The notion of the need for an open pedagogy is supported by formulations in projects before the MakEY project. Here 'Open laboratories' were seen as locations offering space with any kinds of materials and tools without a specific purpose in advance, but open to unforeseen discoveries made by 'Experimenting communities'. These experimenting communities were established as play, so that children and adults together, through play, could discover ways to use materials and tools. At the very core of an experimenting community was the experiment itself and the capacity to invent. All parties, including teachers, were asking questions and searching for answers (Caprani and Thestrup, 2010).

To be makeative involves adopting an open pedagogy and it reflects a view of children as human beings, which respects how they explore their own perspectives and negotiate meanings through play to express and create their own child culture (Mouritsen and Qvortrup, 2002; Corsaro, 2005; Kampmann, 2010; Sommer, Pramling Samuelsson and Hundeide, 2010). Inherent in their play, children actively repeat, change and improvise so-called formulas (Willett 2015). Together with participating adults, they can come up with new formulas that can be improvised with. Experimentation can turn existing local, cultural and pedagogical uses of narratives and construction into new forms of expression and uses of tools, materials and spaces.

Step 1: Starting makeative acts

The first project emphasized activities relating to construction using LEGO bricks based on three principles: to do, re-do and share. This involved use of the LEGO system to demonstrate the principles behind exchange and creativity used online (Gauntlett, 2015). The project took place at Katrinebjerg school in Aarhus and involved approximately 40 children from a pre-school class over three days. The activities took place in a large empty space, called The Box, which is not designed to have one particular use or a natural centre. It is rectangular, approximately half the size of a gym hall. Two sides of this space open up into hallways and therefore it is difficult to close it off. Due to its open character, the space has to be re-defined each time it is used, and that pertains to both the part of the space that is to be used, how and for what purposes.

The practitioners and researchers involved made LEGO constructions together with the children without a specific goal being defined in advance. The LEGO bricks were in boxes to begin with but quickly spread all over the floor (see Figure 3.1). Pathways through the LEGO bricks were made simply by using a sweeping brush. Soon, the children established small areas where they were building on tables, behind sofas and on the floor. The construction activities were based on this guideline: if you make a construction, others may add to or change it. It emphasized the possibility that one could join in what others were constructing, either

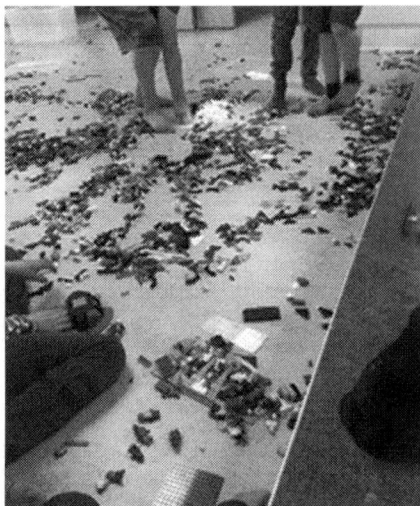

FIGURE 3.1 Children playing with LEGO on the floor in The Box

while it was happening or later. It was an attempt to generate collaborative engagement while making a construction. A few of the children did not see the point at the beginning, but as the days went on, the guideline was largely accepted.

The children were not told in advance to build any specific constructions or to construct a certain number of narratives, but they started to emerge nonetheless. Klaus Thestrup was, for instance, involved with a group of girls in a scenario in which a deadly forest was built on the floor and a heroine had to try to get through this to reach a certain safe point. Klaus was not part of this narrative from the start, but joined in when the forest was in the making. He followed the ideas for the narrative and suggested new elements. This story was finally told and filmed with a smartphone. The story did not exist in this form when the days started but, in the middle of all the LEGO, it came into being for a short period of time. When it was told, it was no longer interesting and other projects began. The example highlights the process that took place in the space. The ongoing construction was the basis and the emerging narratives were possibilities for shorter or longer periods of time.

There is no doubt that the special qualities of LEGO played a significant role in this particular project. There was enough of it so that all the children, most of the time, had access to build what they wanted to. It was easy and fast to start building something, and then take it apart again if needed be and re-do the original construction and narrative if the children so wished. In a space like The Box it is easy to share, as it is easy to see what others have done. The children could spread out in the space and find a specific place to be and build in their own time. The LEGO and the space facilitated basic construction play where other elements like the smartphone mentioned above could be added.

The Box as an empty space pinpoints a space where it is necessary to establish connections and action and it allows a certain culture of doing something together. Makeative acts can unfold in such a space as it all depends on what constructions and narratives are made. Children's play culture seems to fit very well in such a setting, as it is defined by children's ability to improvise over formulas (Mouritsen and Qvortrup, 2002). Of course, children can do this in other spaces and with other materials as well, but the open pedagogy emphasizes the possibility to code and re-code the use of a given space. Doing, redoing and sharing can be under-taken in one physical space, or they can be done in situations where spaces are connected. As a matter of fact, one can argue that each culture has a creative meaning-making centre, which can be activated when meeting other cultures (Gauntlett and Thomsen, 2013). The Box is, in that sense, a playful cultural and creative space in itself, with the potential to reach out to the world.

Step 2: Exploring makeative narratives

This project took place at a school in Katrinebjergskolen, in a library at DOKK1,[2] and at a centre for cultural production called Godsbanen[3] in Aarhus. The last event was part of an international conference on technology, entrepreneurship and educa-tion.[4] These activities stretched over five days during three weeks in Autumn 2017.

At the various locations, different technologies were spread out over the space on the floor or on small tables, and the children were allowed to try out the technolo-gies as they wished. At each technology station, there were grown-ups to help and support if needed. The investigation of the available technologies was the focus of the activity. In the first stage of the Danish MakEY project, as described above, only LEGO bricks were used, but here a number of technologies were presented and utilized. The possibility even existed to combine different technologies, for instance, filming robots being used together with a green-screen effect, which allows two images to be combined, so a robot for instance can be placed at different locations. Due to the fact that the final workshop took place at a conference, some of the technologies were already in place in the room, but one can easily imagine how the children could be involved in placing and combining the different technologies themselves. In an open laboratory it is not identified in advance how something should be done. It is a matter of being open to unexpected possibilities, so that you can discover new ways of telling stories or using technologies.

At DOKK1, a task was given to the children: a spaceship was landing in one corner of a piece of A3-sized paper. Some Ozobots would leave the spaceships and encounter somebody and something, and then return. One central activity at DOKK1 was the use of Ozobots,[5] which are small objects, the size of a thumb, that have a likeness to robots. The Ozobots themselves were also decorated, as one could place a small transparent plastic cup upside-down on them, and then glue different material to them. In groups the children had to build spaceships, draw characters and objects on the planet and then draw a line that the Ozobot had to follow, which programmed the movements of the Ozobot (see Figure 3.2).

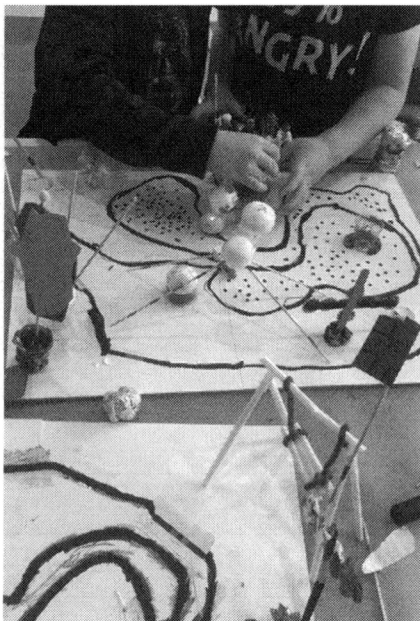

FIGURE 3.2 An Ozobot in a narrative constructed by the children

These Ozobots have a sensor in the bottom of each device so that one can draw a line on a piece of paper and, through the colour of the pen used, the Ozobot is coded to follow instructions, such as go forwards, turn right or left, and so on. The children experimented in a makerspace. The room had one long table and a few smaller tables with materials and tools, such as glue-guns, A3-sized white plates, pens, scissors, wires, feathers and white glue. They started to construct small worlds to extend their Ozobots' narratives. Later on, tablets were added. The actions on the planet would be photographed with a tablet and imported into an app, which enabled cartoons to be made (see Figure 3.3).

Even with this starting point, there were many different planets being created and actions taking place. There was an intention from the leader of this specific narrative to enable the children to create a fairy tale based on a closed dramaturgical structure known from most narratives, i.e. they include a start, some narrative tension and a turning point. But that is not what happened.

The activities with the Ozobots were more of a case of a feast of material and tools than the construction of a single linear story. On the other hand, there were many elements of meaning-making when the children were asked what was happening on the planets. They had stories to narrate and had constructed objects and lines, but the structure was more of a pattern of elements and formulas that one could improvise on, as the lines often had the character of a circle on a rectangular piece of cardboard than a straight line with an endpoint. The narratives presented on cardboard could continue as long as the children

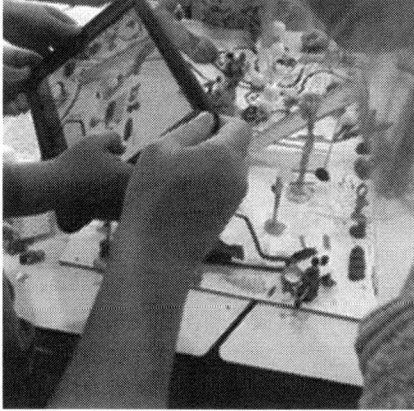

FIGURE 3.3 Developing the narratives with tablets

wanted them to. A circular dramaturgy was also a way to tell a story. The children were occupied with trying out different materials and tools. Whenever a new tool or material was introduced, it had to be examined for what it might be able to do. They looked at what the others were doing and tried to do something similar. Each new material changed what was going on. The lines on white cardboard were made in a different way than just drawing a single straight black line and then observing an Ozobot follow it. Instead, the children were drawing, sketching and making zigzag lines in different sizes and areas, so it was more difficult for the Ozobots to follow the lines. Nevertheless, they were used and placed on the lines and areas and were still running while the children continued drawing in front of them and around them. A road came into being while being drawn and embodied, in that regard, the central element of play. One could say that the children asked themselves at least two questions about drawing and building: *What does this technology do?* and *What can I do with this technology?* (Bird and Edwards, 2015). The second question opens up new and unexpected ways of using any given materials, tools and technologies, but both questions require a pedagogical approach that allows space for this to happen. The children's experiments were, in this regard, an obvious possibility.

The activities at DOKK1 were also the beginning of an open laboratory, where analogue and digital, narrative and construction could meet and influence each other. Later on, this open laboratory unfolded further at Godsbanen, at an international conference, where the children were part of a workshop. In a central space in the middle of the building, a number of familiar and unfamiliar technologies were presented to the children. Ozobots and A3-plates were available, LEGO Mindstorm robots[6] were at hand (Caprani, 2015), small metal robots to be filmed were shared on Instagram and a green-screen effect was introduced.

The investigation of the available technologies was the focus of the activity. In the first stage of the Danish MakEY project, as described above, only LEGO bricks were used, but here a number of technologies were presented and utilized. The possibility even existed to combine different technologies, for instance filming robots using a green screen. Due to the fact that the workshop took place at a conference, some technologies were already in place in the room, but one could easily imagine the children being involved in placing and combining different technologies themselves.

The Ozobots at DOKK1 showed that an examination of the possibilities of a technology and the ongoing construction and changing of narratives can happen simultaneously, even in a space designed for one kind of activity with a few materials and technologies available. It was still possible to be makeative and flexible in the use of Ozobots and the adding on of other technologies. A linear story was not insisted upon, but an open examination of materials and technologies was allowed. The Ozobots could, literally, go in various directions and meet many different objects and characters along the drawn lines. The building of these objects and characters was just as important as drawing the lines. The final workshop differed from the LEGO project in The Box in that it used many different technologies, but it was based on the same starting point. At the start of the makerspace sessions, spread out in the room at various stations were different possibilities and possible connections between them.

In children's play culture, the relation between formula and improvisation is very delicate. It is possible to establish new formulae that are open enough to improvise upon, but the pedagogy has to be open to this and even support an imbalance between the two. The workshop with the Ozobots and lines was quite an open formula, and the narrative could have moved in many directions. The spreading out of technologies can point in the same direction if the connections between technologies are advanced, which is something the children can investigate. Using a Mindstorm robot taken from one station at a green-screen station is one significant example.

Step 3: Developing makeative playgrounds

In October 2018, approximately 135 children aged 6–8 years from the United Kingdom, Australia and Denmark participated in collaborative making activities through the use of a Google+ group called *Global Makerspace* (GM). This digital platform combined these three schools' local communities into one global community, where the children could share and transform each other's ideas into constructions in physical and virtual spaces. This project took place over four days. The central part of the activities in Denmark took place in an open room called The Box. In Denmark, approximately 40 children participated. Again, due to the nature of The Box, some older children participated while passing by, but they did not add anything significantly new to the project and were not instrumental in the actions that took place with the young children involved in the research project.

On the first day, all the children were introduced to the GM platform in small groups in a classroom by the co-author of this chapter, Louisa Haugaard Pedersen. The GM was described as a network, where other children from the United Kingdom and Australia were posting pictures of what they were doing. The

Danish children were told that children in the other countries were hoping to see more of what we were doing in Denmark. The next day, Louisa presented the GM platform to a smaller group of children in 40 minutes. It was important to find out whether the children actually wanted to get a closer look at the pictures on GM. Therefore, she decided to take the computer and place it on the floor so that the children could get a closer look at GM while making a post, and so that it was more collaborative. She told them to select pictures of what they found interesting in their peers' maker activities and think about what might be interesting for other children in the UK and Australia to see.

From day one, the children transformed The Box into one big analogue platform. They made this platform by putting pieces of paper on the floor, walls and windows before they began to draw on it as a 2D canvas. This made actual space for the children to reveal their ideas and create narratives together, before they transformed their drawings into physical constructions made out of recycled materials. The children formed their own maker communities on the floor, instead of sitting at tables working on their constructions with adults. It turned out that, every day, the children would join the same peers at the same spot on the floor with paper on it. The tables inside the room had recycled materials on them. The children would go to these tables to find new parts for their constructions, and then go back to their maker-peer group on the floor. Meanwhile, some of the children took pictures of the maker activities with two digital cameras. This also created child-initiated experimenting communities, which investigated other children's activities.

The children developed a playful approach to research with the digital cameras. This activity consisted of one child holding a camera while peers followed her and investigated the room by taking pictures of selected objects and locations inside it. At the same time, the children experimented with their own collaboration around the camera. It was reminiscent of a research team seeing possibilities and challenges and asking questions about the activities around them and their own activity with the camera. This camera activity established an experimenting community that examined the child-initiated spaces inside The Box. These improvised children-as-researchers teams usually first ran around, but later carefully walked around the different child-initiated maker communities. These camera-related activities indicated that the children played with both physical and digital spaces. They constantly zoomed in and out of the different and changing activities before, during and after they took pictures of the maker activities. This mirrored the process of reflecting collaboratively, because the children around and through the camera constantly asked questions about what other children were doing. At the same time, the children with the camera investigated the camera itself, and visualized the process of their examination.

Louisa also combined the activities with the cameras and making posts on the GM. She positioned herself with a computer at one of the tables inside The Box. Two children were each given a digital camera and then went out into the room to take pictures. Then, they came back to Louisa and the computer to select some pictures and describe them, so they were transformed into posts. The process of presenting the GM and how to use the camera were similar, in that these digital tools were slowly but surely integrated into the activities and play areas on the floor in The Box. The computer was used for analysis and the production of texts and the digital cameras likewise became a tool for reflection and the production of expression and meaning-making. The digital cameras and the computer became tools for communication and transformation based on what was going on inside The Box.

One result was an increasing level of transformation of what the others around the world were doing. One example is a simple black–and–white line drawing of a robot on an A5 sheet of paper, which suddenly turned up on the GM page, originally submitted by students at Aarhus University. It was turned into two big paper drawings coloured with pens, by children at The Box in Denmark and later a painted version known as 'the robot panda' was done and uploaded by children at the school in Melbourne (see Figure 3.4). The communication between countries became a more and more important part of what was being produced and taking place in The Box

It also turned out that The Box was constantly transformed by the children's maker activities. The children spontaneously constructed meanings with regard to how The Box could be used, which transformed spaces inside The Box in parallel with the children's own maker processes. In the final workshop at Godsbanen, the children did not have the opportunity to alter the space they

FIGURE 3.4 The Robot Panda, originally made by a student from Aarhus University and remixed by Australian children

were in, but in this project they did. In that sense, the children had the possibility to transform The Box into a makeative playground with both analogue and digital elements. The global makerspace was in a process of being both three different locally and physically based makerspaces and at the same time part of one common makerspace, placed on a digital platform.

Conclusion

Constructing a trans-glocal play culture

The pedagogy that unfolded during the three steps in the project was open and makeative in several ways. The settings offered an open laboratory where both analogue and digital had a place, and it was open to the world. The space became flexible and was used in flexible ways. The global makerspace in itself pinpointed the need to emphasize an open pedagogy, which could be flexible and adaptive towards new inspirations and challenges from participants outside the single makerspace. The ability to be makeative is needed when encountering somebody on the Internet, whom one does not already know, and the activities served a useful purpose in that respect.

During the project, Louisa developed a term based on what she observed and framed pedagogically in the project, which demonstrates some future possibilities: trans–glocal play culture. This concept concerns how children's play culture works and forms global, local and transformative contexts in-between physical and virtual makerspaces. A characteristic of a trans-glocal play culture is that it grasps how children create transformative contexts when connecting local and global makerspaces through play. This is expressed in the ways children incorporate, and create with, analogue and digital materials and tools in their play. A trans-glocal play culture reflects how play can go beyond time and space, but it also demonstrates how this openness depends on the flexibility of physical and virtual spaces in local and global contexts, as well as the openness of the pedagogy.

Throughout constructing, sharing and transforming different physical and virtual materials, and uploading these processes onto a digital platform, a cyclic web of similarities and differences of makerspaces and pedagogies can form. To be makeative is the capacity to play in every single makerspace, to tinker with the makerspace itself and start playing with and transforming each other's ideas, expressions and objects, both locally and globally. Establishing a trans-glocal play culture offers the possibility to be makeative.

Notes

1 http://makersontheedge.com/
2 https://dokk1.dk/english
3 http://godsbanen.dk/english/
4 www.elig.org/we-share/aarhus17/
5 https://ozobot.com/
6 www.lego.com/da-dk/mindstorms

References

Bird, J., & Edwards, S. (2015). Children learning to use technologies through play: A Digital Play Framework. *British Journal of Educational Technology*, 46(6), 1149–1160. doi:10.1111/bjet.12191

Børne- og Socialministeriet (2018a). *Lov om ændring af dagtilbudsloven og lov om folkeskolen* [Law on change on pre-school and law on public school]. (Dagtilbudsloven). Lov nr. 160 af 24/05/2018. Kbh.

Børne- og Socialministeriet (2018b). *Bekendtgørelse om pædagogiske mål og indhold i seks læreplanstemaer.* [Announcement on pedagogical purpose and content in six curricular themes]. (Dagtilbudsloven). BEK nr. 968 af 28/06/2018. Kbh.

Caprani, O. (2015). Mangfoldige læringsaktiviteter - ét robotbyggesæt [Multiple learning activities – one robot construction kit]. *Læring Og Medier Online.* Retrieved from http://ojs.statsbiblioteket.dk/index.php/lom/article/view/22074/20129

Caprani, O., & Thestrup, K. (2010). Det eksperimenterende fællesskab - Børn og voksnes leg med medier og teknologi [The experimenting communities – When children and adults play with media and technology together]. *Læring og Medier*, 3(5), 1–39. Retrieved from https://doaj.org/article/aba105d1075948f895b345a91f1f92d3

Corsaro, W. A. (2005). *The sociology of childhood* (2nd ed.). Thousand Oaks, CA: Pine Forge Press.

Gauntlett, D. (2015). *Making media studies: The creativity turn in media and communications studies.* New York: Peter Lang.

Gauntlett, D., & Thomsen, B. S. (2013). *Cultures of creativity: Nurturing creative mindsets across cultures* [Main report]. Retrieved from The LEGO Foundation website: www.hacerlobien.net/lego/Cre-003-Cultures-Creativity.pdf

Gershenfeld, N. (2012). How to make almost anything: The digital fabrication revolution. *Foreign Affairs*, 91(6), 43–57.

Howard, P., & Lauridsen, P. (2017). *Kulturudveksling i børnehøjde* [Culture exchange between children]. BUPL – Børne- og Ungdoms Pædagogernes Landsforbund. Unpublished project report.

Kampmann, J. (2010). Børnekultur i et institutionsperspektiv: Spændingsfeltet mellem leg og læring [Children culture in the perspective of institutions: Tension between play and learning]. Tidsskrift for Børne- & Ungdomskultur, 9–20.

Marsh, J., Nisha, B., Velicu, A., Blum-Roos, A., Hyatt, D., Jónsdóttir, S. R., … Thorsteinsson, G. (2017). *Makerspaces in the early years: A literature review.* Retrieved from University of Sheffield, MakEY Project website: http://makeyproject.eu/wp-content/uploads/2017/02/Makey_Literature_Review.pdf

Mouritsen, F., & Qvortrup, J. (Eds.). (2002). *Childhood and Children's Culture.* Odense: University of Southern Denmark Press.

Pedersen, L. H. (2019). *Constructing open and closed pedagogy: A case study of the Global Makerspace-project inside the Danish field* (Assignment). University of Copenhagen, Faculty of Humanities, Department of Media, Cognition and Communication, Section of Education. Unpublished.

Peppler, K. A., Halverson, E., & Kafai, Y. B. (Eds.). (2016a). *Makeology: Makers as learners* (Volume 2). New York: Routledge.

Peppler, K. A., Halverson, E., & Kafai, Y. B. (Eds.). (2016b). *Makeology: Makerspaces as learning environments* (Volume 1). New York: Routledge.

Pröschold, J. (2018, October 29). Digitale børn: Børnehave viser, at iPads og Instagram giver en sjovere barndom [Digital children: A kindergarten shows that iPads and Instagram give a more fun childhood]. *Politiken.* Retrieved from https://politiken.dk/viden/art6794041/B%C3%B8rnehave-viser-at-iPads-og-Instagram-giver-en-sjovere-barndom

Resnick, M. (2017). *Lifelong kindergarten: Cultivating creativity through projects, passion, peers, and play*. Cambridge, MA: MIT Press.

Resnick, M., & Rosenbaum, E. (2013). Designing for tinkerability. In M. Honey & D. E. Kanter (Eds.), *Design, make, play: Growing the next generation of STEM innovators* (pp. 163–181). New York: Routledge.

Sandvik, K., & Thestrup, K. (2017). *Challenging makerspaces*. Presented at the NordMedia conference, Finland, 17/08/2017 – 19/08/2017.

Skjærris, M., & Knudsen, J. (2017). *Den store opdagelsesrejse for de helt små* [The great expedition for the smallest ones]. BUPL – Børne- og Ungdoms Pædagogernes Landsforbund. Unpublished project report.

Sommer, D., Pramling Samuelsson, I., & Hundeide, K. (2010). *Child perspectives and children's perspectives in theory and practice*. Dordrecht; London: Springer.

Thestrup, K. (2019). How preschool teachers and children communicate in a digital and global world. In C. Gray & I. Palaiologou (Eds.), *Early learning in the digital age* (pp. 136–148). London: SAGE Publications Ltd.

Thestrup, K., & Sandvik, K. (2018). Skolen som Makerspace – Leg og læring i kreative rum [The school as a Makerspace – Play and learning in creative spaces]. In I. H. Andersen, H. H. Møller, K. B. Kristensen, & C. S. Rasmussen (Eds.), *Leg i skolen, en antologi* [Play in school: An anthology] (1st ed., pp. 212–234). Copenhagen: UP – Unge Pædagoger.

Willett, R. (2015). Everyday game design on a school playground: children as bricoleurs. *International Journal of Play*, 4(1), 1–13.

4

MAKERSPACES, MULTILITERACIES AND EARLY SCIENCE EDUCATION

The Finnish approach

Jenni Vartiainen and Kristiina Kumpulainen

Introduction

Young children are known to have a strong inner curiosity to explore the world around them (Eshach and Fried, 2005) and they regularly display an interest in science-related phenomena (Baram-Tsabari, Sethi, Bry and Yarden, 2006). The most commonly identified challenge of formal science education is, however, its inability to create a connection with young people's natural curiosity in science as it is experienced in their everyday lives. Therefore, children and youth often find formal science education disconnected from their experiences, literacies and life-worlds (Krapp and Prenzel, 2011; Osborne, Simon and Collins, 2003; Potvin and Hasni, 2014). As a result, researchers in Finland and around the world have emphasised the importance of creating science education that draws on children's everyday lives, literacies and cultures. This includes cultivating approaches to science education that are playful and hands-on and in which the context arises from children's everyday experiences and life in general (Bulunuz, 2013; Kumpulainen et al., 2018a). Also, integrating play into enquiry-based science activities has been reported to enhance children's meaning-making capabilities in science (Akman and Özgül, 2015).

Recently, makerspaces have aroused some interest in Finnish science education, and internationally, as a potential means of creating meaningful and transformative connections between children's everyday and scientific literacies (Kajamaa and Kumpulainen, 2018; Kumpulainen, 2017). Maker activities have also been reported to enhance peer collaboration while diminishing more traditional teacher–child relationships and roles (Kumpulainen, Kajamaa and Rajala, 2018; Vossoughi and Bevan, 2014). In educational makerspaces, scientific literacies are typically embedded in an integrated science, technology, engineering, arts and mathematics (STEAM) curriculum with hands-on creative activities, offering children different opportunities to engage in the learning of science and other important 21st-century skills, such as problem-solving, critical and creative thinking, collaboration and communication (e.g. Halverson and Sheridan, 2014; Litts, 2015; Marsh et al., 2017; Stornaiuolo and Nichols, 2018). Furthermore, makerspaces can, reportedly, have a positive effect on youth's interest in science, enhancing feelings of competence and a willingness to engage in science (Krishnamurthi, Bevan, Rinehart and Coulon, 2013).

While less is known about the educational potential of makerspaces in early childhood education (ECE) (Marsh et al., 2017), emerging research suggests that makerspaces can contribute to children's creative and innovative practice (Wohlwend, Scott, Yi, Deliman and Kargin, 2018). Maker activities are characterised by opening up a creative space conducive to STEAM learning in which children can collaboratively design, plan, reuse, test and refine artefacts for their own and/or collective purposes (Halverson and Sheridan, 2014). Maker activities call for alternative skillsets, knowledge and literacies compared to more traditionally controlled science experiments (Vanderhoof, in press). Yet, very little is currently known about the ways in which children relate to and make sense of scientific literacies during their maker activities in ECE, and how these interact with their earlier experiences and everyday literacies. Furthermore, there is a lack of research and overall understanding of the significance of playfulness in young children's maker activities for the enhancement of their scientific literacies and science learning.

Motivated by these gaps in current research knowledge, this chapter discusses a maker project in Finnish ECE in connection with a national curriculum reform emphasising integrated multimodal and playful STEAM learning activities in early years and primary education (Kumpulainen et al., 2018b). The maker project entailed children making parachutes and skydivers with various tools and materials, and then experimenting with and learning about air resistance with the artefacts they had created.

The maker project discussed in this chapter draws on work undertaken in an international, EU Commission-funded project: 'Makerspaces in the early years: Enhancing digital literacy and creativity' (MakEY). In Finland, the MakEY project interacts with an ongoing national research and development programme, *The Joy of Learning Multiliteracies (MOI)*, launched by the Finnish Ministry of Education and Culture, which develops new pedagogies, learning environments and materials in accordance with the new core curriculum for early childhood, pre-primary and early primary education (Kumpulainen, 2019; Kumpulainen et al., 2018b). In response to the aims of MakEY, the maker project discussed in this chapter responds to the need to explore the potential role and value that makerspaces can have in the early childhood curriculum, with a specific focus on early science education.

Drawing on sociocultural theorising and Green's (1988) 3D model of literacy, our chapter demonstrates how children spontaneously connect their earlier experiences and playful orientations to their maker activities, while engaging in and making sense of their maker activity, including scientific literacies. In this chapter, we draw specific attention to the nature of children's meaning-making during their maker activity at the intersection of the operational, cultural and critical dimensions of literacy. Our work points out how children 'playing with science' creates a pivotal intersecting space for their engagement in scientific literacy practices in the context of making. Our work also underscores the importance of multimodal analysis in tracing the nuanced ways in which children make meaning and learn within maker activities.

Unpacking children's meaning-making through sociocultural lenses

Acknowledging the socioculturally situated, playful and imaginative elements of children's meaning-making creates the conceptual basis for our investigation of children's maker activities. We hold that focusing on the creative and playful dimensions of children's maker activities can lead to novel investigations and insights where cognition, affect and bodily activity can be examined in unison (Roth and Jornet, 2016). We also hold that meaning-making, thought, emotion, play and creativity, as well as the creation of relationships, are an integrated whole. When any of these aspects are left out or broken apart, children's learning and development are hindered (Connery, John-Steiner, and Marjanovic-Shane, 2010; Vygotsky, 1978).

In his genetic law of development, Vygotsky (1978) emphasised the primary role of social interaction for human learning and development and proposed that the process of a child's cultural development occurs in two phases: first on the social plane and then on the intra-psychological plane. For sociocultural theorising, an essential feature of learning is that it creates a zone of proximal development; learning awakens a variety of internal developmental processes that can only operate when a child is interacting with other people in their environment. Once these interactional processes are internalised, they become part of the child's independent developmental achievement (Vygotsky, 1978).

Sociocultural theorising also maintains that play is one expression of meaning-making that occurs across one's lifespan. Meaning-making, on the other hand, is the construction of knowledge to reach an understanding with other people within and across a variety of situations and modes (Vygotsky, 1986). For Vygotsky, play represents a social form of embodied imagination, leading to complex symbolic constructions, behavioural mastery, collaborative protocols, emotional arousal and control, and the production of group cultural lore (Vygotsky, 1976). In early childhood, play emerges as the growing child's motives shift towards the realisation of personal desires. Because these desires are not available in reality, the child seeks to realise them through imagination. Play, therefore, represents the seeds of imagination in development, or imagination in action (Connery, John-Steiner and Marjanovic-Shane, 2010).

Vygotsky underscored two characteristics in play: the creation of imaginary situations and rules. He discovered that children are able to follow rules in play before they can adhere to those in other real-life situations. Play for Vygotsky represents one form of the zone of proximal development (ZPD); action in the imaginative sphere, the creation of voluntary intentions and the formation of real-life plans and volitional motives all appear in play and thus make it the highest level of early years development (Vygotsky, 1976). Taking all this together, a sociocultural viewpoint provides a fruitful lens for understanding children's maker activities with worthwhile insights into understanding play, imagination and meaning-making.

Scientific literacy from the perspective of a 3D model of literacy

Drawing on Green's (1988) 3D model, our work holds that there are at least three dimensions involved in children's scientific literacy practices: i) operational, ii) cultural and iii) critical (see also Marsh, 2016; Marsh, Arnseth and Kumpulainen, 2018). In our work, we are interested in applying and further developing the 3D model of literacy to help understand scientific literacy as it evolves in a child's maker activities.

Operational elements include those skills that are needed to become a competent meaning maker and communicator, with the ability to use various modes and tools in different contexts. In the context of science and scientific literacy, the operational dimension includes being able to engage in scientific process, such as making observations and inferences, and using various scientific tools for experimentation, including measurement tools.

The cultural dimension focuses on understanding scientific literacy as a cultural practice with its own rules, values, signs and practices (see also Snow and Dibner, 2016). In addition, the cultural dimension of scientific literacy includes science that occurs in people's living cultures and social ecologies: scientific phenomena, science-related texts and conversations.

The critical dimension refers to critical engagement with science-related texts and communication, as well as being able to recognise those power relationships that are evident in all literacy practices. For instance, the ability to ask questions about scientific processes, and to question the results, is a vital critical thinking skill in the context of scientific literacy and understanding the intentions behind different kinds of communication and texts. Table 4.1 demonstrates how these three dimensions of literacy relate to children's scientific enquiry during their maker activities, as identified in our research work (see Vartiainen and Kumpulainen, in press). It is worth noting that these practices are not restricted to those presented in the table, as they will change and evolve, and new ways of participation will arise in different contexts.

Introduction to the Poetry Science maker project

The maker project discussed in this chapter took place in a Finnish ECE centre and included 28 children aged 3–5 years old and their teachers. The maker project was embedded in the recently introduced national ECE curriculum framework, which emphasises integrated, multimodal and playful STEAM learning activities. The conceptual dimension of the maker project was built around those chemical and physical phenomena that are directly observable in children's everyday lives, in this case, air resistance.

The maker project is deeply rooted in Finnish ECE and the latest curriculum reform. Its pedagogical principles encourage children to use their imagination, creativity and collaboration, the cornerstones of the Finnish ECE and of the maker philosophy in general. Finnish policy maintains that ECE should promote pedagogy that includes multimodal, multi-sensory and playful characteristics. Children are encouraged to explore, use and produce meanings in different environments, using different

TABLE 4.1 Children's scientific literacy practices in their maker activity

Scientific literacy	Operational	Cultural	Critical
Defining goals for an activity	Children form questions and hypotheses	Children bring their former experiences into their questions and aim-generation process Children use scientific concepts	Children challenge and/or question knowledge

Observation and data collection	Children describe and record observations
	    Children measure
		Children use scientific language, i.e. concepts and labels
		    Children describe observations by comparing them to examples from everyday life
			Children question observations and inferences

Extension, elaboration or revision of knowledge based on empirical data and observation	Children make inferences and predictions	Children suggest extensions or elaborations to science activity and work collaboratively to test new ideas
		    Children observe, imitate and build on each other's ways of working
			Children use previous observations to test their hypotheses, extensions and/or elaborations
			    Children challenge and correct each other's inferences

Communication about enquiry to others	Children describe their methods for deriving their results, artefacts or other outcomes	Children make connections between their everyday and scientific literacies (i.e. concepts and language)	Children evaluate how the results of their work can be applied across different situations and contexts

tools in and across activities and contexts. Opportunities for experimenting, making and producing, both individually and collaboratively, are valued, as these situations are recognised as promoting creative thinking, teamwork skills and literacy skills in children (Finnish National Agency for Education, 2016). Play, curiosity and imagination are central pedagogical principles in the operational culture of Finnish ECE, recognising play as a vital source of children's holistic development.

The children's ideas for their maker activity were fed through the Poetry Science approach (Vartiainen, 2017), developed as part of the Joy of Learning Multiliteracies (MOI) research and development programme (Kumpulainen et al., 2018b). Poetry Science Cards entail theme-related poems embedded with rich, aesthetic visual designs that motivate children to explore and make meaning from familiar scientific phenomena, such as flying. Engaging children in science processes is known to be beneficial when using approaches that harness fairy tales and poems as starting points for hands-on activities (Feasey, 2006; Kalogiannakis, Nirgianaki and Papadakis, 2018; Mutonyi, 2016). The Poetry Science approach also resonates with the 'maker philosophy', in that it embraces creativity and innovation through the design and construction of physical objects. Here, maker activities were enriched with both playfulness and whimsical characteristics of inventiveness, e.g. inventing ways in which fish could fly to a tree (Bevan, Gutwill, Petrich and Wilkinson, 2015). The pedagogical principles behind Poetry Science include shared story-reading and -telling that help children recall their previous experiences for joint interaction. Children's creativity plays a role in all phases of maker activity, from storytelling, to design, making and playing with artefacts. The socio-material environment of the maker project is collaborative and transformative; children can interact with other children in ways they find meaningful. Physical space is used in various ways and children are allowed to freely use floors, tables, chairs and other physical objects for their meaning-making processes.

The actual poem the children were introduced to at the beginning of the maker project was about two fish who wanted to fly to a tree and make a nest there. The fish made a plan. However, in the end, they realised that fish cannot fly (Figure 4.1).

After listening to and engaging with the poem, the children were encouraged to imagine what would happen if fish could fly to a tree. The children were invited

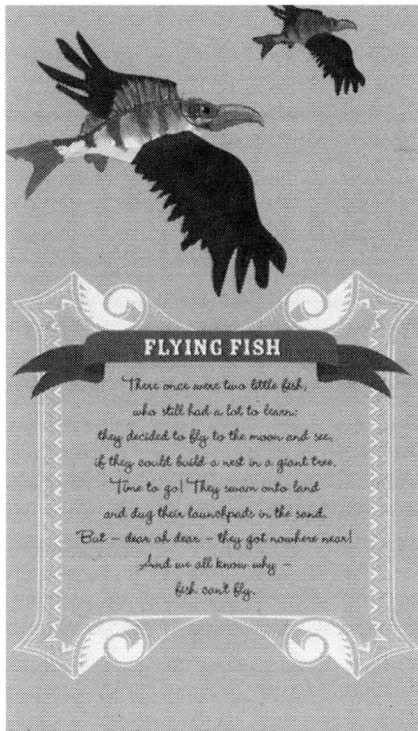

FIGURE 4.1 'Flying Fish' Poetry Science Card

to invent and suggest different ways in which fish could reach the tree: someone could lift them, they could use a helicopter or a hot-air balloon, or they could build an escalator. Allowing children to toy with impossibility at the beginning of maker activity sets a playful tone for the entire project.

Next, the children proceeded to design and make parachutes and skydivers with various tools and materials, including newspapers, string and playdough, and then experiment with and learn about air resistance via their self-made artefacts. The children had an active role in designing and making their parachutes – or whatever else the children imagined them to be. Once the parachutes were ready, the children tested how they worked, spreading around the ECE space. The children's making was supported by the teachers according to each child's needs.

Methods

The data collection included observation, video-recording and collecting children's artefacts over the whole maker project. Prior institutional and parental permission was granted for the children's involvement in the research. We also asked all participants, teachers and children, for their permission to record them working, and it was clarified that the opportunity to take part in the maker project was not dependent on their participation in the research. The children were told that they could ask us to stop filming or making notes at any point, and we were sensitive to non-verbal signs suggesting they would rather not be observed.

The analysis of video data, amplified by observational field notes, was grounded in a social semiotic framework (Bezemer and Kress, 2016), and the analysis process utilised characteristics of multimodal analysis methods (Norris, 2004). For the purposes of this chapter, we have chosen two representative situations from the whole data set to illuminate the children's maker activity, with a specific interest in the role of play and imagination in their making meaning of scientific literacies.

Children's meaning-making during maker activities

Vignette 1: Imagination as a fuel for meaning-making

A group of children sit or lie comfortably on a floor in a circle. They have just engaged with a poem about two fish that want to fly, read aloud by their teacher. In the preceding conversation with the teacher and each other, they have agreed that fish cannot fly, but birds can. 'Fish would need wings!' a child shouts cheerfully. 'Yes, wings,' a few children echo. 'Are there some other things the fish could use for flying?' a teacher wonders. The children look thoughtful. 'With the wings of flying fish,' a child ponders. 'And something else…' the teacher encourages. 'Air–' one child starts to vocalise his idea, '–plane,' another child joins in. 'A rocket,' someone shouts. 'And a helicopter!' a boy adds. 'I have been on a plane,' a girl says. 'Me too, it was fun! We went on a holiday.' Children speak enthusiastically over each other. A quiet moment occurs while the children think of other options. A boy whispers: 'A rocket can fly to the moon.' Playing with the idea of fish that can fly, the teacher continues: 'Let's imagine that the fish were able to manage to go to the tree. How could they come down in a safe way?' The teacher drums up the children's imagination. 'With a parachute,' a child suggests. 'Yes, a parachute,' other children approve the idea. 'The birds can dive,' a girl ventures. 'The fish can use an umbrella,' a boy suggests happily. Another boy is still thinking about the idea of diving birds: '…and they snatch a fish after diving,' he explains. 'Yes, that's the way it goes,' confirms the girl who initiated the talk about diving birds. 'I have seen it on my dad's smartphone,' she continues.

The children's conversation was meandering but at the same time built on each other's contributions. The poem invited the children to share their cultural experiences, memories and knowledge gained from their everyday lives, like flying in a plane on holiday. The children also related the poem to their earlier knowledge about flying objects, e.g. when a boy whispered that a rocket can fly to the moon. Obviously, the boy did not have direct experience of rockets, but this experience had nevertheless been mediated through some media, allowing the boy to build a knowledge structure about flying rockets. As Vygotsky argues, imagination is not the inner characteristics of young children; instead, it is built on children's prior experiences. Hence, children's imaginative mental actions are constructed based on connections to their earlier experiences and life-worlds. By drawing on previous experience and knowledge, the children created a social context for their joint meaning-making of flying and air resistance. By using their imagination, they showed skills in inferring from the poem and producing their own meanings for the events in the poem. Making inferences by using previous observations is one key skill related to the scientific process and is therefore connected to the operational dimension of scientific literacy (Vartiainen and Kumpulainen, 2019). The poem engaged the children in conversation enriched with imagination. It encouraged them to ponder and play with different possibilities. Creating these spaces for children's imagination, in the context of science, has been reported to significantly enhance children's engagement in science-related, problem-solving activities (Caiman and Lundegård, 2018).

A noticeable dimension of the children's poem-enhanced conversation about fish that wanted to fly to the tree was a shared commitment to imagination. The children agreed to pretend that it was possible for the fish to fly to the tree, despite the fact that they realised it would be impossible in the real world. Hence, they created a new emergent context for learning (Serafini and Gee, 2017), in which science and imagination combined in the process of playful meaning-making. This playful mental space offered the children possibilities to participate in the cultural and critical dimensions of dynamic literacies. For Vygotsky, imagination 'becomes the means by which a person's experience is broadened because he can imagine what he has not seen, can conceptualise something from another person's narration and description of what he himself has never directly experienced' (Vygotsky, 2004, p. 17). Together, the children extended the context of the poem through their collective imaginative activity (see also Caiman and Lundegård, 2018). Here, it was evident that imagination is a process (Dewey, 1980) that is affected by social interaction. The children needed to use their imagination to visualise other children's narratives about flying. Through imaginative activities, children could build on others' ideas and thus co-create the meaning of flying.

Vignette 2: Imaginative play as meaning-making

A group of three boys – Eemil, Alex and Joonas – have finished their parachutes. The boys are observing the parachutes in different locations. The teacher helps Joonas make observations by assisting him in dropping the parachute and draws his attention to how it floats. In the meantime, Alex's parachute strings get knotted up and he lays the parachute down on the chair. He picks up the parachute from the playdough skydiver. The parachute is hanging upside down while Alex comes to observe what Eemil is doing with the teacher. The teacher helps Alex get the strings straight, and they drop the parachute several times together. Joonas has observed the other boys' actions, and he turns his parachute upside down. He swings it carefully from side to side. He tries to catch Eemil's attention by swinging the parachute near Eemil's face. Eemil smiles and turns his parachute upside down, following Joonas's example. He starts swinging the parachute from side to side; meanwhile, he is carefully looking at the parachute. Eemil makes bigger swings and he spins around with the parachute so that the parachute arcs in a circular movement and fills up with air (Figure 4.2).

Meanwhile, Alex observes his parachute, which is upside down. He makes a pumping vertical movement. That causes the parachute to change its shape accordingly. He walks to Eemil and says, 'Look at this,' and he shows the pumping movement. Eemil repeats the pumping movement and lets his parachute fall. He laughs out loud when the parachute quickly falls down. Alex joins in. He drops his parachute several times, and after that, he goes to the teacher and shows his observation. Alex drops the parachute upside down and picks it up. He starts swinging it and adds a buzzing sound. He sprints to the other side of the room and makes a car-like sound. The parachute follows in a vertical movement behind him. He runs again but quickly stops and observes how the parachute is affected by the movement change. Next, he runs but dives to the floor to see how the parachute behaves. Joonas and Eemil join Alex. They start making an engine sound and whirling their parachutes. They spin around and make pumping movements. A boy, Niki, who has been experimenting with his parachute elsewhere, joins the three boys. Niki looks for a moment at what the other boys are

FIGURE 4.2 Eemil is swinging and spinning his parachute

doing, and then he joins them by starting the same spinning and pumping activity with his parachute (Figure 4.3).All four boys run to the next room. Then they run back. Eemil starts to run around the table while making his parachute fly. His parachute makes some wild spins in the air. Joonas walks round the table. He holds his parachute in front of him to see how it moves. Niki's parachute flies wildly in the air and spins many times (Figure 4.4).Eemil and Niki run in a small circle and then continue running round the table while shouting: 'Bang, bang!' Joonas stops running and sways his parachute slowly in the air. He repeats, 'Bang, bang.' Eemil says, 'This is spraying water.' Niki sways his parachute in the air and repeats after Eemil, 'Water.' Niki slams his parachute on the floor and says, 'I'm falling.' Then he continues running round the table, holding his parachute in his hand.

The previous vignette describes a moment from the latter part of the maker project. Here, the children have made their parachutes and have free time, no rush, to experiment with their parachutes. In this example, we can see a shift where the children's observations

FIGURE 4.3 Niki spins the parachute

FIGURE 4.4 Eemil and Niki are participating in imaginative play with parachutes. Eemil is making a pumping movement and Niki is spinning his parachute around

about the parachute and its properties turn into imaginative play. Making observations is one key skill needed to engage in science processes and to experiment. Thus, it is one of the operational domains in scientific literacy practices. The children made observations at the beginning of the vignette, seemingly independently of one another but, in fact, they were observing carefully what other children did. The children repeated the observation processes that others had engaged in. When the children started a shared play with the parachutes, they elaborated on the meanings they had been addressing for air resistance while observing the parachutes. The play constructed a micro learning environment wherein the children tested and elaborated their meanings of air resistance (Nicolopoulou, 1993). With respect to meaning-making processes, it is important that children are provided with opportunities to draw conclusions as a result of their active engagement. Hands-on activities that stimulate the imagination allow children to be active both mentally and physically.

In this vignette, the children's conclusions about air resistance formed a core part of how parachutes acted within the play. For Vygotsky (1978), the foundation of play is built on children's desires that cannot be met in the moment. Hence, to fulfil their motives, children invent imaginary situations, i.e. play activity, to meet their needs. Vygotsky also argued that children's play, although imaginary, is mediated by rule-based behaviour embedded in their everyday lives. Play therefore requires children to abstract and transfer the meaning of their real-life practice to their imagined scenario in the play activity. For Vygotsky, such abstraction from concrete to imaginary requires children's use of a pivot – an action or object that carries meaning from real life to imaginary play activity. In using such pivots, children begin to exert self-control by regulating their own activity according to the rules of their imaginary play. Parachutes were the bridges that allowed the children to move back and forth between concrete observations and imaginative play, which settled the children's conclusions into the context of their cultural experiences.

The children were able to adopt and use their newly constructed meanings for air resistance into their play activity. They did not vocalise their conclusions, but they did use them as part of their imaginative play. Imagination is thought to be at the core of the cultural development of a child, originating within social interaction and the cultural-historical moment of a child's development. Children's imaginative play can offer an important window into understanding children's science-related, meaning-making processes. Since science requires particular expressions, labels and words that are not used in everyday language (Evagorou and Osborne 2010), it is challenging for young children to put their conclusions into words. Play, then, can be used as a channel to communicate conclusions and place them in a wider context that stems from children's life-worlds.

Conclusions

In this chapter, we have shed light on children's meaning-making during maker activity in the context of playful, story-like and hands-on STEAM activities situated in Finnish ECE. Following the philosophy of making and the novel curriculum requirements set by the Finnish Agency of Education, children's agency and active participation were emphasised (Johnson, Adams Becker, Estrada and Freeman, 2015). The maker project allowed children to collaborate and interact in multimodal and playful ways, using space and artefacts in creative ways.

This case study points out that children's meaning-making about air resistance happened through a maker project by playing with objects – parachutes – they had made and sharing this play with other children. Through this playful meaning-making, the children not only participated in the process of science but also connected a scientific phenomenon to their own culture and experience by playing with it. As Elkonin (2005) argues, play is a key activity through which children gain skills, knowledge and understanding. With this in mind, we suggest that there is potential to widen the view of play in the early years of science activities beyond enquiry-based science instruction by viewing science through theories of literacy as a dynamic practice (Green, 1988).

This study widens the view of playfulness in science education within the context of maker education to include the idea of 'playing with science'. Playfulness and connecting science to stories and picture books have been found to enhance children's knowledge about scientific phenomena and support their positive experiences of learning about science (Kalogiannakis, Nirgianaki and Papadakis, 2018; Mutonyi, 2016). Young children make meanings by interacting with objects and phenomena, testing what it is possible to do with them and how they react to different manipulations.

Green's (1988) 3D model of literacy, amplified by a multimodal analysis, allowed us to assess children's meaning-making in science during their maker activities. In the making activity, it was observed that the children engaged in the operational dimension of scientific literacies by making observations, inferring and making predictions. They connected air resistance to their previous experiences of the phenomenon. The children also engaged in the critical dimension by evaluating and suggesting different viewpoints on flying, plunging and hovering. With regard to the key dimensions of operational, cultural and critical scientific literacy, the children engaged in a process that we call 'playful meaning-making' (Figure 4.5). We define this as a multimodal activity that stems from children's self-motivated inspiration to play with artefacts they have made. From the vignettes presented in this study, we can identify the children's processes of engaging in play for meaning-making in the context of science.

This study highlights children's social, cultural and playful processes while they are participating in maker activities. Playful maker-oriented science activities offer child-centred approaches, providing children with opportunities to translate science into their culture and life-worlds and, through that, to use available tools and materials to construct meanings. Connecting the philosophy of making to imaginative and playful approaches underscores children's agency and active participation, as well as their self-initiated play with artefacts. Playful meaning-making brings together the skills that multiliterate individuals need: the abilities to produce texts, infer, refine and critically evaluate them, and enrich these processes with imagination. The children's shared process of making and playing with parachutes in their maker activity provided them with an opportunity to make meanings about air resistance. Here, the children's everyday literacies and practices intersected with scientific literacies. It was in these

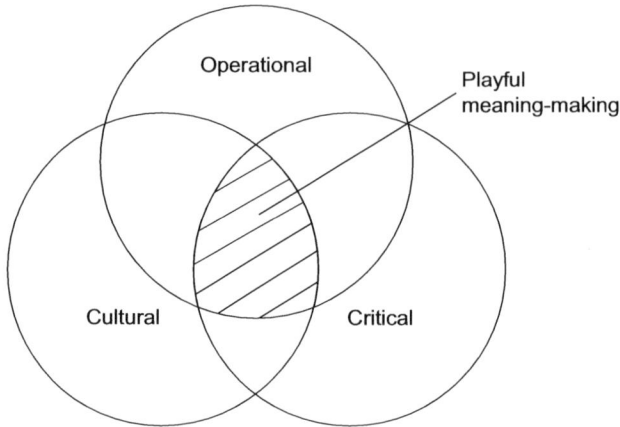

FIGURE 4.5 Position of play within children's cultural, operational and critical scientific literacy practices

hybrid interactions that the children co-created meanings via play. We hold that such a playful approach to early science education can lead to learning and relationships that stick and foster children's personal curiosity and interest in science.

Acknowledgements

We are grateful to the *Makerspaces in the Early Years: Enhancing Digital Literacy and Creativity (MakEY) project* (EU Commission H2020 No: 734720) and the *Joy of Learning Multiliteracies (MOI) research and development programme* (OKM/29/240/2016) for their support in conducting the work reported in this paper.

References

Akman, B. & Özgül, S. G. (2015). Role of play in teaching science in the early childhood years. In K. Trundle & M. Saçkes (eds), *Research in early childhood science education* (pp. 237–258). Dordrecht, the Netherlands: Springer.

Baram-Tsabari, A., Sethi, R. J., Bry, L. & Yarden, A. (2006). Using questions sent to an Ask-A-Scientist site to identify children's interests in science. *Science Education*, 90(6): 1050–1072.

Bevan, B., Gutwill, J. P., Petrich, M. & Wilkinson, K. (2015). Learning through stem-rich tinkering: Findings from a jointly negotiated research project taken up in practice. *Science Education*, 99(1): 98–120.

Bezemer, J. & Kress, G. (2016). *Multimodality, learning and communication: A social semiotic frame*. London: Routledge.

Bulunuz, M. (2013). Teaching science through play in kindergarten: Does integrated play and science instruction build understanding? *European Early Childhood Education Research Journal*, 21(2): 226–249.

Caiman, C. & Lundegård, I. (2018). Young children's imagination in science education and education for sustainability. *Cultural Studies of Science Education*, 13(3): 687–705.

Connery, M. C., John-Steiner, V. & Marjanovic-Shane, A. (eds). (2010). *Vygotsky and creativity: A cultural-historical approach to play, meaning making, and the arts*. Vol. 5. New York, NY: Peter Lang.

Dewey, J. (1980). *Art as experience*. 2nd ed.New York, NY: G. P. Putnam's Sons.

Elkonin, D. B. (2005) The psychology of play. *Journal of Russian & East European Psychology*, 43(1): 11–21.

Eshach, H. & Fried, M. (2005). Should science be taught in early childhood? *Journal of Science Education and Technology*, 14(3): 315–336.

Evagorou, M. & Osborne, J. (2010). The role of language in the learning and teaching of science. In J. Osborne & J. Dillon (eds), *Good practice in science teaching* (pp. 135–157). Maidenhead, England: Open University Press.

Feasey, R. (2006). Using stories and poems in science primary. *Science Review*, 92: 8–10.

Finnish National Agency for Education. (2016). *National Core Curriculum for Early Childhood Education and Care*. Retrieved from: www.oph.fi/fi/koulutus-ja-tutkinnot/varhaiskasva tussuunnitelmien-perusteet, 29 October 2018.

Green, B. (1988). Subject-specific literacy and school learning: A focus on writing. *Australian Journal of Education*, 32(2): 156–179.

Halverson, E. R. & Sheridan, K. (2014). The maker movement in education. *Harvard Educational Review*, 84(4): 495–504.

Johnson, L., Adams Becker, S., Estrada, V. & Freeman, A. (2015*). NMC Horizon report: 2015 K-12 edition*. Austin, TX: The New Media Consortium.

Kajamaa, A., Kumpulainen, K. & Rajala, A. (2018). A digital learning environment mediating students' funds of knowledge and knowledge creation. *Studia Pedagogica*, 23(4): 49–66. https://doi.org/10.5817/SP2018-4-3

Kalogiannakis, M., Nirgianaki, G. M. & Papadakis, S. (2018). Teaching magnetism to preschool children: The effectiveness of picture story reading. *Early Childhood Education Journal*, 46(5): 535–546.

Krapp, A. & Prenzel, M. (2011). Research on interest in science: Theories, methods, and findings. *International Journal of Science Education*, 33(1): 27–50.

Krishnamurthi, A., Bevan, B., Rinehart, J. & Coulon, V. (2013). What after-school STEM does best: How stakeholders describe youth learning outcomes. *After-school Matters*, 18: 42–49.

Kumpulainen, K. (2017). Makerspaces: Why they are important for digital literacy education. In J. Marsh, et al. (eds), *Makerspaces in the early years: A literature review* (pp. 12–16). Sheffield: University of Sheffield, Makey Project. Retrieved from: http://makeyproject. eu/wp-content/uploads/2017/02/Makey_Literature_Review.pdf

Kumpulainen, K. (2019). Promoting the joy of learning multiliteracies from early years onwards: An educational reform initiative in Finland. *Media Education Research Journal*, 8(2): 83–94.

Kumpulainen, K., Kajamaa, A. & Rajala, A. (2018a). Understanding educational change: Agency-structure dynamics in a novel design and making environment. *Digital Education Review*, 33: 26–38.

Kumpulainen, K., Sintonen, S., Vartiainen, J., Sairanen, H., Nordström, A., Byman, J. & Renlund, J. (2018b). *Playful parts: The joy of learning multiliteracies*. Helsinki: Kiriprintti Oy.

Litts, B. K. (2015). Making learning: Makerspaces as learning environments. Unpublished doctoral dissertation. University of Wisconsin, Madison, Wisconsin, US.

Marsh, J. A. (2016). The digital literacy skills and competences of children of pre-school age. *Media Education: Studi, Ricerche, Buone Practice*, 7(2): 197–214.

Marsh, J., Kumpulainen, K., Nisha, B., Velicu, A., Blum-Ross, A., Hyatt, D., Jónsdóttir, S. R., Levy, R., Little, S., Marusteru, G., Ólafsdóttir, M. E., Sandvik, K., Scott, F.,

Thestrup, K., Arnseth, H. C., Dýrfjörð, K., Jornet, A., Kjartansdóttir, S. H., Pahl, K., Pétursdóttir, S. and Thorsteinsson, G. (2017) *Makerspaces in the early years: A literature review.* Sheffield: University of Sheffield, MakEY Project.

Marsh, J., Arnseth, H. & Kumpulainen, K. (2018). Maker literacies and maker citizenship in the MakEY (Makerspaces in the Early Years) Project. *Multimodal Technologies and Interaction,* 2(3): 50.

Mutonyi, H. (2016). Stories, proverbs, and anecdotes as scaffolds for learning science concepts. *Journal of Research in Science Teaching,* 53(6): 943–971.

Nicolopoulou, A. (1993). Play, cognitive development, and the social world: Piaget, Vygotsky and beyond. *Human Development,* 36(1): 1–23.

Norris, S. (2004). *Analyzing multimodal interaction: A methodological framework.* London: Routledge.

Osborne, J., Simon, S. & Collins, S. (2003). Attitudes towards science: A review of the literature and its implications. *International Journal of Science Education,* 25(9): 1049–1079.

Potvin, P. & Hasni, A. (2014). Interest, motivation and attitude towards science and technology at K-12 levels: A systematic review of 12 years of educational research. *Studies in Science Education,* 50(1): 85–129.

Roth, W.-M. & Jornet, A. (2016). Perezhivanie in the light of the later Vygotsky's Spinozist turn. *Mind, Culture and Activity,* 23: 315–324.

Serafini, F. & Gee, E. (eds). (2017). *Remixing multiliteracies: Theory and practice from New London to new times.* New York, NY: Teachers College Press.

Snow, C. E. & Dibner, K. A. (eds). (2016). *Science literacy: Concepts, contexts, and consequences.* Washington, DC: The National Academies Press.

Stornaiuolo, A. & Nichols, T. P. (2018). Making publics: Mobilizing audiences in high school makerspaces. *Teachers College Record,* 120(8): 1–38.

Vanderhoof, C. M. (in press). Multimodal analysis of decision making in elementary engineering. In G. J. Kelly & J. L. Green (eds), *Theory and methods for sociocultural research in science and engineering education* (pp. 48–72). New York, NY: Routledge.

Vartiainen, J. (2017). *Poetry Science.* Retrieved from: www.monilukutaito.com/en/blog/39/poetry_science, 26 October 2018.

Vartiainen, J. L. & Kumpulainen, P. K. (2019). Promoting young children's scientific literacy as a dynamic practice. In K. Kumpulainen & J. Sefton-Green (eds), *Multiliteracies and Early Years Innovation: Perspectives from Finland and beyond (pp. 77–94).* London: Routledge.

Vossoughi, S. & Bevan, B. (2014). Making and tinkering: A review of the literature. Commissioned paper for Successful Out-of-School STEM Learning: A Consensus Study, Board on Science Education, National Research Council, Washington, DC. Retrieved from: http://sites.nationalacademies.org/cs/groups/dbassesite/documents/webpage/dba sse_089888.pdf, 29 October 2018.

Vygotsky, L. (1976). Play and its role in the mental development of the child. In J. S. Bruner, A. Jolly & K. Sylva (eds), *Play: Its role in development and evolution* (pp. 537–554). New York, NY: Penguin Books.

Vygotsky, L. (1978). Interaction between learning and development. *Readings on the Development of Children,* 23(3): 34–41.

Vygotsky, L. (1986). *Thought and language.* Revised edition. Cambridge, MA: MIT Press.

Vygotsky, L. (2004). Imagination and creativity. *Childhood Journal of Russian and East European Psychology,* 42(1): 7–97.

Wohlwend, K. E., Scott, J. A., Yi, J. H., Deliman, A. & Kargin, T. (2018). Hacking toys and remixing media: Integrating maker literacies into early childhood teacher education. In S. Danby, M. Fleer, C. Davidson & M. Hatzigianni (eds), *Digital childhoods* (pp. 147–162). Singapore: Springer.

5

MAKERSPACES AND VIRTUAL REALITY

Dylan Yamada-Rice, Deborah Rodrigues and
Justyna Zubrycka

Introduction

As part of the wider EU MakEY project on 'enhancing digital literacy and creativity', the study reported on in this chapter explored how makerspace-style workshops can provide opportunities for children to play and make in relation to emerging virtual reality (VR) technologies and software. The literature review outlines two areas: first, what is known about VR in children's lives, and second, how making can be used as a means of knowledge generation. These two areas set the context for our study, which explored children's engagement with a variety of experimental ideas created to allow them to make and play with physical and virtual materials and spaces. The findings provide insights into how the children learnt about the affordances of VR and also how the experience of making with physical materials proved to be as much of an immersive experience as that of VR. The outcomes of the project make a contribution to the very limited amount of research that has been undertaken on children's use of VR for entertainment, play and creativity.

We represent the German team in the EU MakEY project. Within this wider network of projects, we chose to focus specifically on how to include VR in makerspaces and other public facilities, such as schools and museums, in order to enhance children's creativity and digital 'literacy' skills, specifically in relation to this emerging technology. The initial idea to focus on VR arose from our individual interests in technology in relation to children's current use and potential possibilities for future creativity and play.

Deborah Rodrigues' interest in VR relates to her own art practice, which includes that for child audiences. She is also interested in how VR can be used with children as part of the practical workshops she runs on technology and play for children. Justyna Zubrycka's interest arose from her background as a designer of connected toys, as well as the work she does with children to understand their play and creativity as a means of informing her design processes. Dylan Yamada-Rice is a researcher specialising in children's play and design. Her interest in children's use of VR emerged from the findings of the 'Children and Virtual Reality' (CVR) study that she undertook just before the start of MakEY (Yamada-Rice et al., 2017). In particular, Yamada-Rice was interested in how the child participants in the CVR study desired a tangible means of crossing from the physical environment into VR in order to help them feel comfortable. Given that all three of us were interested in the connection between physical and virtual play and making, we designed a series of hands-on workshops to allow children to explore the crossover between the two domains in ways that had not been tried before.

This chapter is structured first to consider the wider literature on children and VR, followed by a section on what is known about learning through making. This sets the context for the study's methodology, which was based on making as a means of understanding VR. Finally, the chapter is divided into two sections that showcase the ways in which the workshops allowed children to understand the affordances of VR and how creating with physical materials proved to be as immersive, if not more so, than VR.

The chapter makes a contribution to what is known about children's use of VR for entertainment and begins a unique exploration of how they use this technology for making and creativity, which is an entirely new field of enquiry. Knowledge of children's VR use, as well as ideas on how children can understand the affordances of the technology, is needed because 'VR is fast becoming a reality, with estimates that over 200m headsets will have been sold by 2020, [with] the market value for VR hardware and software reaching well over $20bn by then' (Yamada-Rice et al., 2017, p.4). Further, research on children and VR has predominately focused on those with medical needs or learning difficulties (Blascovich and Bailenson, 2011). This chapter takes a step forward in our understanding of how children use VR for creativity and play.

Children and virtual reality

A white paper produced by WEARVR (2018), an app store for VR, shows the extent to which VR is growing. For example, they list the current state of play (in mid-2018) as having 14 companies manufacturing headsets, 6,000 VR content developers and 3 million VR app downloads (p.6). This statement illustrates the extent to which manufacturers of devices and content, as well as users, are investing in virtual technology. In relation to children specifically, the CVR report contains market research that illustrates that, in spring 2017, more than half of children interviewed in surveys in the UK and the US (sample sizes 1,300 and 2,000, respectively) aged 8 to 15 years said they were familiar with what VR was and/or had used it (Yamada-Rice et al., 2017). Despite this, information on children and VR for entertainment is predominantly limited to the commercial sector, such as that being used by the company Skylights, which has produced VR content to entertain children on long-haul flights (Horwitz, 2018, n.p.); academic research on the topic appears thus far to be unpublished. In part, this is probably due to the age barriers applied to children using VR, first, by headset manufacturers and also by the PEGI rating system applied to content. Most HMDs (head-mounted displays) for VR come with restrictions that range from 13+ to not to be used at all. It is hard to find evidence about why this decision was made, but one explanation is that Oculus Rift set an age limit of 13+ when the company was bought by Facebook and the existing age restriction of the social-media platform was then applied to their newly acquired VR company.

Although academic research on children's VR use for entertainment remains unpublished, there is a growing body of literature that shows it is a beneficial technology for child health. For example, Arane et al. (2017) found VR can be used for pain and anxiety management in children, which they state works through:

> …audio and visual immersion [that] encourages users to interact with the content and that as a result of this the medium has affordances that increase the ability to use it for distraction beyond that which has been noted in relation to both passive distraction (e.g. watching television, listening to a book) and active distraction (e.g. interactive toys, electronic games).
>
> *(Arane et al., 2017, p.932)*

Although the focus of the research discussed in this chapter is about the use of immersive technology for making and play, the rapid expansion of VR into child health suggests that children might increasingly come into contact with VR by one means or another, and thus more needs to be known about children's use of the medium in general.

Other researchers have suggested that VR's success in managing health problems such as anxiety (e.g. Tarrant et al., 2018) lies in the medium's ability to engender a strong sense of presence within virtual content (Riva and Waterworth, 2014; Waterworth and Riva, 2014). The CVR report (Yamada-Rice et al., 2017) also showed how children's engagement with content for entertainment was directly linked to how immersive the experience was, which in turn is tied to both the quality of the HMD and the VR content. For example, cardboard VR headsets were not as engaging as top-end devices and 360° video was enjoyed less than interactive content. This means that whatever the intended purpose of VR, whether for play, education or health, more work needs to be done on how children engage with the technology and software so that products can be produced that fully engage them. This is further supported by Grimes' (2018) work on virtual worlds, which has demonstrated that the industry has placed age restrictions and bans on child players at various points, and this shows how restrictions that are not based on research should be critiqued. Particularly, she notes that the restrictions seem to arise from a 'child/adult dialectic that permeates much of how we organize our social structures' (p.638) and thus frames what is or is not suitable for children. This, Grimes says, can come with its own problems and thus warrants immediate attention. With this in mind we began to think of ways in which we could allow children to explore the properties of VR in the belief that this would provide an initial stepping stone enabling critical engagement with content. In doing so, we drew on the ideas of Ingold (2013) on the importance of making as a means of learning, and how this could potentially be used to enhance children's under-standing of VR. To this end, the next section describes the literature on making as a means of knowing better how to set the context for our study.

Making as a means of knowing

Marsh et al. (2018b) describe the MakEY project as being undertaken in order to explore 'the rising "maker" culture in the development of children's digital literacy and creative design skills' (p.3). In the MakEY literature review, Marsh et al. (ibid.) outline a range of studies that show how makerspaces can engage people in not only creative but also critical practices (e.g. Hughes, 2016; Ratto, 2011). Ideas around making as a means of understanding are not new. Ingold (2013) writes that the history of making as a means of understanding is almost as long as that of humankind and that the ways in which we think are altered by the means with which we do it:

> What is the relation between thinking and making? The theorist and the craftsman would give different answers. It is not that the former only thinks and the latter only makes, but that the one makes through thinking and the other thinks through making.
>
> *(Ingold, 2013, p.6)*

Making can also bring about criticality in thinking. In relation to this, Marsh et al. (2018b) draw on the work of Knobel and Lankshear (2010) to state that:

> …makerspaces are part of the move to a "DIY" culture in which citizens take the initiative and become more self-sufficient, made possible through the development of new digital tools and practices.
>
> *(ibid.)*

This echoes the work of Kress (2010), who describes how changes in multimodal communication practices come about in relation to social, technological and eco-nomic developments. Regarding design processes, to which the makerspace move-ment can connect, Julier (2013) writes that current 'design culture is thus both a product and description of the wider social and economic processes of this design turn within neoliberalism' (p.220). This theory provides an opportunity to reflect on the ideas put forth by Marsh et al. (2018a) with respect to wider historical changes so as to understand how making has a long history across many cultures and sectors. For example, Flood and Grindon (2014) show how critical thinking in relation to political activism has brought about a wide range of creativity in the form of design ingenuity that has been used as part of a long history of protest. As with political activism, makerspaces also build creativity through a collectivist approach to making, where knowledge and skills are shared. Thus, while the methods/ethos of making, crafting and hacking that are shared in makerspaces have a long tradition, the technologies and materials utilised in them, such as VR, do not. This provision of a wide range of new technologies and materials might be one reason why Sullivan (2015) writes that makerspaces have become places where creative practices different from those in schools can be practised. Further, Sullivan argues that, as a result, they allow intense thinking, not only making, to occur. In relation to this, we question why kits with a clearly defined product are often provided for children working in makerspaces, which is an observation we have made. As a group of designers, makers and artists, our own practices and those of the creative communities we engage with reflect the open-ended opportunities we have to experiment with raw materials and technologies, having less of a planned trajectory towards an end product. This informed our decision to create open-ended making opportunities in the research we planned to undertake.

Finally, knowing through making necessitates knowledge of materials, because each one has distinct affordances, i.e. what is possible to do with them (Gibson, 1977), and therefore directly relates to what can be produced with them. As a result, we also considered making as an important means for children to experience the unique affordances of VR. Further, given that VR content can be used for creativity and play, it is of related importance that various researchers have argued that the materials of play have as much agency as the child who uses them. For example, Carrington and Dowdall (2013) have considered this in relation to LEGO, Giddings and Kennedy (2008) with regard to videogames and Yamada-Rice (2018a) in relation to connected toys. This is of further importance, given that play and creativity are often combined in children's lives. Therefore, the materials of new technologies for play and/or making stipulate affordances for their use and thus have agency that affects how they are used. This suggests that in order for children to be able to fully critique VR, they must have knowledge of virtual materials and their possibilities. Therefore, one of the intentions of this study was to explore the ways in which providing children with access to VR technology in the content of makerspace workshops might allow them to understand and think critically about VR. How this was achieved is the focus of the methodology section, outlined below.

Methodology

The methodology we developed arose directly from one of the findings of the CVR study, which showed how children had questions about and suggestions for what they were experiencing virtually. Further, the study indicated that these questions often centred on a desire to have a better experience when transitioning from physical to virtual spaces (Yamada-Rice et al., 2017). Building on this finding, our objectives were:

1. To understand the similarities and differences between children's play and making with physical and virtual materials.
2. To see if making with physical materials could be used as a means of on-boarding children into virtual spaces.
3. To form an initial understanding of the extent to which making and play might allow children to understand VR technologies and software.

In order to achieve these objectives, we designed a series of five workshops that combined physical and virtual making with play. In this chapter, we draw on data arising from two workshops that took place in a makerspace in Germany and one in a UK museum. Further details of these workshops are included in the findings and discussion sections.

All workshops were video-recorded by whatever means were most appropriate for the context we were working in. Mostly this meant that video was recorded by a fixed camera mounted on a tripod combined with shorter, close-up footage shot on mobile phones or tablets. The intention in using these two types of video recordings together was to get an overview of what was happening in the entire workshops, as well as to capture more detailed child-to-child and child-to-workshop facilitators' (us, teachers, museum staff etc.) interactions. This was also a way of capturing the children's interaction with the materials of their play and creativity, whether this used analogue or virtual materials. Some videos were transcribed verbatim but many were not, because in most cases the children in the workshops had a different first language to our own. This was not problematic when conducting the workshops because we were able to illustrate our ideas by doing rather than giving verbal explanations. In these cases we watched the videos several times, studying non-verbal data, i.e. children's movement, gestures and the materials of the participants to draw out themes using a means of analysis outlined by Braun and Clarke (2006). In addition to this, all physical and virtual creations of the child participants were photographed and formed a data set that was later analysed using methods devised by Van Mechelen (2016) and visual content analysis (Bell, 2001). Findings that emerged from these processes of analysis are presented and discussed next.

Findings and discussion

The remainder of this chapter is divided into two sections that relate to themes that emerged from the data analysis. These are: (1) learning VR affordances and (2) physical making as an immersive experience. Each section provides vignettes from workshops that took place at a museum in the UK and a temporary 'pop-up' makerspace in Germany. The workshops that form these vignettes are described in as much detail as required to make it possible for them to be replicated by others working in the creative education of young children, and for the ideas to be built on by other researchers with the intention of understanding how emerging technologies affect children's play and creativity.

Learning VR affordances

In a workshop in Berlin, children were given a wooden doll known as Avakai to play with (Figure 5.1). Avakai is an established toy designed and made by Zubrycka and her business partner. The four child participants of this workshop were given paper, cardboard, coloured tape, pens and glue and asked to create something that might be of use for the doll who would be travelling into a virtual world.

FIGURE 5.1 Wooden Avakai doll

Before the workshop, Rodrigues drew an image of Avakai inside a virtual environment called *Tiltbrush* (Google), which is a VR platform for drawing and painting. The intention was that, by starting with physical materials and then transitioning into the virtual world, the child participants would have a chance to think about what they wanted to make before entering *Tiltbrush*. Then, each child would put on an HTC Vive headset and find themselves in front of the drawn Avakai in the virtual space, where they would try to recreate their physical creations with virtual tools. The physical to virtual flow was also designed to help prepare each child for the VR experience.

An Avakai doll was chosen for the way in which it was originally designed by Zubrycka and her business partner to promote both play and creativity, which tied in with the overall focus of our study. In an article on the design of the doll, Yamada-Rice (2018a) describes how Avakai's design is deliberately simple to allow children to customise it and use it in open-ended play with narratives and ideas of their own. Further, by including the Avakai doll in our workshop, we were able to provide a physical and virtual version of the same character in order to explore similarities and differences, as well as crossovers in how it was played with and came into children's making practices, in both spaces, with a toy that we were familiar with.

Three of the four child participants used physical materials to create an object that related directly to the Avakai doll and were able to articulate clearly how they did so:

RESEARCHER: "Do you have an idea?"

BOY (Aged 9): "I think I have got an idea…"

MAKERSPACE ARTIST: "You have got an idea?"

BOY: "Yes an abandoned rocket… so maybe I could make it like they [the Avakai] are on the roof."

MAKERSPACE ARTIST: "Then cool, do it."Following this exchange, the boy sat down at a table and produced a rocket made using cardboard, tape and marker pens (Figure 5.2).

In the image shown in Figure 5.3, the tape crosses placed on the cardboard rocket were used to signify that it was abandoned. The boy also used the Avakai

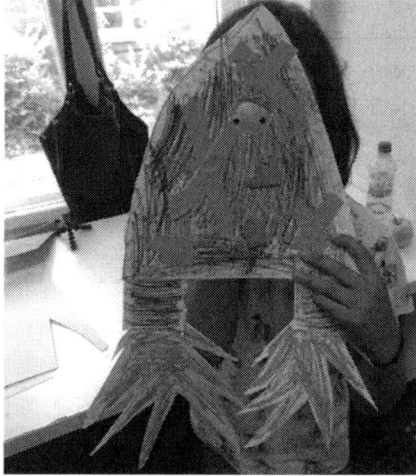

FIGURE 5.2 Avakai rocket made from physical materials

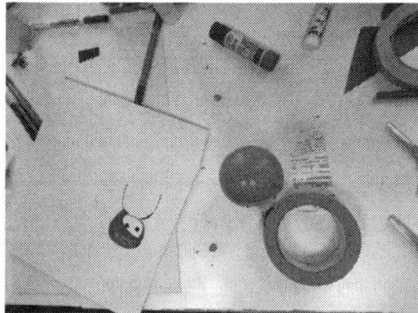

FIGURE 5.3 Drawing the Avakai's reflection

doll to judge the size needed for the window and ensure the rocket was big enough for the doll. These were activities that would be harder to do in VR. That said, one boy showed an awareness that the virtual space would be three-dimensional in his physical making. He had decided to make a mirror for the Avakai and started by drawing the doll's reflection (Figure 5.3).

He then set this idea aside and began to make the mirror and reflection three-dimensional, which he saw as more fitting for a VR experience (Figure 5.4).

In the next stage, each child put on an HTC Vive VR HMD and used *Tilt-brush* software to replicate their Avakai creations on the virtual platform. All four participants spent time exploring the materiality of the virtual drawing tools and the marks they made. Everyone immediately noticed differences in how they differed from physical tools.

FIGURE 5.4 3D Avakai mirror

Creating in *Tiltbrush* uses properties completely different from those of physical materials. For example, because VR is an infinite space, there is no surface that provides resistance in the same way as can be felt when a pen touches paper or a brush canvas. This means that once a line is completed it is impossible to start another one where the last left off, as can be done when drawing with physical pens. Further, the colours for mark-making are different. *Tiltbrush* offers the option to paint with coloured light, and all marks have flawlessly even coverage. When the boy who had made a broken rusty rocket for the Avakai came to recreate it in the virtual space, he became frustrated at how hard it was to make his spaceship look dilapidated:

BOY (trying to create a broken and abandoned looking rocket): "You can't get black on here. It comes out like that [sparks of blue light shoot out everywhere]."

MAKERSPACE ARTIST: "Because it [the VR environment] is dark."

RESEARCHER: "How about yellow?"

BOY (in a frustrated voice): "Yellow? This is like orange."

RESEARCHER: "Oh OK. How about green? Remember how sometimes when metal goes rusty it goes green?"

BOY: "Yeah, like coins."

RESEARCHER: "Yep."

BOY (showing frustration): "You can't see it here."

MAKERSPACE ARTIST: "You can walk around, you don't need to stay in the same place always. Walk around."

BOY: "Yeah, but how would you make it [the rocket he has drawn] look more
   abandoned?"
MAKERSPACE ARTIST: "More abandoned?"
BOY: "Yeah, so it's got like more cracks in it."

The above quote also shows how the boy (aged 9) asked to be shown by the
artist how he could use the VR drawing tools to create the effects he wanted. This
highlighted the importance of the adult in facilitating this new experience. Such
findings allow us to see how, in order for children to understand creative content
in VR, they need time to explore how the properties of creating in physical and
virtual domains differ.

As in the example above, the two oldest child participants drew directly on
their knowledge of the affordances of physical drawing materials and tried to
apply this to their VR creations. In contrast, the two youngest children in the
workshop, aged 5 and 6 years, never moved beyond exploring the affordances of
the VR drawing tools. Another unique property of drawing in the VR space that
these two boys discovered was that because virtual space is infinite, the user is
able to walk in and around the marks they make. Each of these two boys spent
their time in VR exploring virtual materials with their entire bodies; how their
movement affected their drawing and then in turn how their next movement
affected their engagement with what they had drawn. This seems to relate to the
work of Longhurst et al (2009), who state that, in early childhood, the body, its
movement and related senses have been documented as a means by which children come to understand new experiences.

The small sample size of four children makes it hard to draw any conclusions
beyond speculation, but the split in the way these two younger and two older children went about the task illustrates an interesting difference between how the virtual
tools were experienced. The youngest took these at face value, while the older boys
took them in relation to the properties of the physical equivalents of the virtual tools.
This is an area worthy of further investigation. Indeed, the current findings already
suggest implications for both how to introduce children to VR, and ways in which
software for young children could be designed to provide better on-boarding into
the virtual drawing space. With regard to the former, this would require educators to
spend time explaining some of the differences of VR space and what children can
expect, as well as encouraging them to ask questions while in that space. Further,
educators should consider the length of time each child might need in VR. The
current recommended time for younger children is 20 minutes (CVR), but offering
less than this removes the opportunity:

> …to allow knowledge to grow from the crucible of our practical and observa-
> tional engagement with… things around us… the conduct of thought [that]
> goes along with, and continually answers to the fluxes and flaws of the materials
> with which we work. These materials think in us, as we think through them.
> *(Ingold, 2013, p.6)*

With regard to design, Gibson (1977) writes that particular objects and materials afford different ways of being used. In relation to drawing, pens are familiar materials in children's lives and therefore it is not surprising that it was confusing when the affordances of the virtual pen were not similar to those of a physical pen. In particular, in this study it was completely new for the children to be given light as a material rather than ink, and a 360° infinite space rather than a bounded 2D platform. Therefore, if we consider that 'materials come from the public world and so have qualities in common with the materials of other experiences' (Dewey, 1938, p.208), then designers of VR software for younger children might need to relate the look of virtual tools (in this case drawing implements) more to the marks that they produce. This would make the connection between tools and materials clearer, e.g. in *Tiltbrush* pen strokes can be lines of light. Physical pens don't draw with light and so perhaps there is a need to create a container for virtual drawing ink that relates more closely to light than ink. Perhaps something like a torch, which has a closer alignment to light and space, might allow children to make the connection more easily.

Physical making is immersive

This section describes how physical making is equally as immersive to younger children as VR. Examples are drawn from an open-ended workshop that took place at a museum designed for children in the UK. The workshops took place over a two-day period during which participants were free to come and go as they chose. This time, we designed a workshop that would provide an opportunity for children to experience and learn about how 360° videos are made. To do so, we created another activity that allowed children to create with physical materials ahead of trying the VR experience. To this end, children were given physical materials to make a structure of their choosing to be added to a collaborative city that would grow over the course of the two days that we were working in the museum (Figure 5.5).

Once each child had added their structure to the city, they and their families were shown how to download a 360° camera app to their parents' mobile phones. The app was used to take a 360° photograph from the centre of the city, which they could then view in a VR cardboard HMD. Like the workshop described in the previous section, the intention was that children would begin with physical

FIGURE 5.5 City made from physical materials

making that would lead into a VR experience. Further, the aim was that the child participants would come to understand more about the medium, and at the same time the activity would act as a transition between the two domains.

Due to the open-ended nature of the workshop design, across two days, the data showed very clearly that children (and in most cases their families, too) were equally invested in the process of building with physical materials as they were in the opportunity to use VR. Indeed, the data show that children spent much longer immersed in the physical making aspect of the workshop than they did on the 360° video. In the current climate, it is worth noting that children have much more limited opportunities to engage with physical materials for making or hands-on art activities than they do with screens and digital play:

> ...[there is] a persistent under-valuing of the educational force of art in education by governments around the world. In recent decades... the time allocated for art in schools has been cut significantly to allow greater emphasis upon what are often called STEM subjects — science, technology and mathematics — that are viewed as central to economic ambition and competition. [This is despite the fact that the force of art can take us beyond the human as is constituted into new modes of becoming.]
>
> *(Atkinson, 2018, p.1)*

Thus, while digital play was once a luxury, this now seems to have reversed and it is physical making that is exotic. In part, this was reflected in the enjoyment children showed in working alone, or with friends, siblings or wider family, to create unique structures that were entirely different from one another, such as hotels, schools with swimming pools, aeroplanes and monsters with mouths that could open etc. The intricacy of many of their artworks also illustrates the degree of time spent perfecting and adding to them.

The 'Technology and Play' study (Marsh et al., 2015) showed a strong connection between open-ended digital content and opportunities for play and creativity. This also appeared to be the case with the physical parts of the workshops that we ran. Onwuegbuzie and Seaman (1995) found that there is a direct connection between time limits and creativity, i.e. that the removal of time barriers positively affects creativity; it offers motivation and elicits greater attention.

Attention to the production of structures was illustrated in the level of detail of the creations and the uniqueness of the output, as shown in Figure 5.5. It was also noted in the quietness caused by concentration in the room. For example, it was not uncommon for children to sit side by side and work on the same idea. Although no verbal communication took place, the activity shown in Figures 5.6, 5.7 and 5.8 was both creative and social.

Further, rather than being a linear activity that started with physical making and progressed to viewing a 360° video, the participants went back and forth between activities,

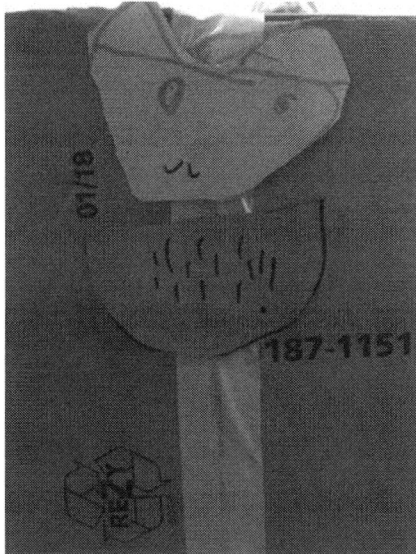

FIGURES 5.6, 5.7 and 5.8 Social activity

being motivated by how the experience changed at each stage. For example, once children discovered what their creations looked like in virtual space, they returned to modify their physical models. Further, encouraged by the crossover between the physical and virtual worlds, children asked for new 360° photographs to be taken, with the children themselves portrayed in the images. The discovery of themselves when viewed in the 360° headset caused great excitement, as shown by this example:

> "Aww [super excited voice]. I've found me… I look funny." (7-year-old girl)

As found in the CVR research (Yamada-Rice et al., 2017), the children mostly wanted to explore spaces and concepts that were familiar to them until they became comfortable with virtual space, when they would then venture off to try new things. Another study on Google Earth VR showed how children nearly always asked to visit their home in the virtual environment, before wanting any other experience (Yamada-Rice et al., 2017). This is consistent with findings of Kenner (2004), who shows that children acquire literacy skills in direct relation to the environments most familiar to them, such as their bedrooms, and then spiral out in layers from there.

Once they had viewed themselves in VR space, many of the participants went on to ask for more 360° to be taken via which they included themselves in the narrative of the city. They did this by pretending to tower over the building they had made like 'giants':

> "I'm in there, I am a giant." (6-year-old girl)

In addition, they did this by going inside the buildings they had made and peeking out. In some cases, buildings were modified to make this possible. Such examples show the connection between creativity and play and also appear to contest the nature of VR as either being or needing to be an isolated experience (Southgate et al., 2019); in contrast, VR in the workshops we produced for the MakEY project showed that the participants used it in very social ways. In general, the findings seem to suggest that the addition of physical materials as part of virtual play can aid both creativity and play and introduce a social element to the experience. This finding is a potential extension of the work undertaken by Marsh et al. (2015), which considered the importance of physical and digital play with augmented reality apps:

> This is a potentially rich format for the fostering of play and creativity. There has been little research in this area… What is of interest in this area is the extent to which such apps can blur the boundaries between offline and online and digital and non-digital play, particularly given the development of apps that interact with physical play objects.
>
> *(Marsh et al., 2015, p.2)*

Conclusions

The study described in this chapter sought to link physical and virtual making and play in a series of hands-on workshops for young children. The design of the workshops was experimental, as the technology was very new at the time of data collection and there were no previous studies we could find that had looked at the role of physical making in connection with children's use of VR. One of the initial objectives of the study was to understand the differences in young children's play and creativity inside and outside virtual reality and whether maker workshops, which include both physical and virtual tools, could combine these in ways would allow children to understand the basic affordances of VR. In this way, we can begin to build the tools needed to critique this technology and the content made for it.

The findings have only begun to touch on what is known about children's play and creativity in relation to VR. The project turned out to be a very rich area of study, with significant possibilities for children's play and creativity with new technologies. For example, some basic understandings of how a small group of children connected or not their understanding of the affordances of physical and virtual tools for creativity have emerged. Rather than providing a direct route from making into transitioning children into virtual space, children's physical making and play became entangled with one another. Indeed, when time constraints were removed, children enjoyed moving back and forth across the different domains and using both physical and virtual tools. This calls into question the very notion of what constitutes immersive technology in young children's lives, for the findings of this study seem to show that the children found the opportunity to make and create with physical materials as equal to, if not more of, an immersive experience than that of the virtual one. In other words, it was a loop in which creativity and making in both physical and virtual domains were seen as equally important as one another. As Yamada-Rice (2018b) argues:

> Beyond basic questions of health and safety, engagement and enjoyment, UI and UX, it's critical with this emerging medium to ask how children can learn to critique VR content. As with any medium, we should want young people across cultures to be critically literate—choosing and engaging thoughtfully across diverse VR content, but also to be content creators themselves.
>
> (Yamada-Rice, 2018b, n.p.)

Given how new forms of digital play are emerging that combine physical and digital play beyond Augmented Reality (AR), such as the Nintendo Switch Labo, which combines physical making with cardboard and digital gaming, or VR games such as VR Playroom, which combine players in VR with those outside the virtual world, more research needs to be undertaken that considers the crossover between children's physical and digital play to better understand how it promotes creativity and fosters social experiences. The enjoyment that children found in an activity that had a direct and much easier link between physical and virtual spaces also provides ideas for how VR experiences in general can be made more appealing for young children. Finally, another common theme across the studies was that VR was not a solitary experience; children played with one another, with one in the headset and one outside it. This is an important observation, as regulations may emerge in the future that try to prevent children from making contact with another child when in VR.

Overall, the chapter shows how makerspaces might be a good place for providing access to technology and also to workshops that allow children to do this. Makerspaces have staff that are familiar with the idea of making, and creating. It also calls for caution in applying pre-determined outcomes of workshops for children; instead we would whole-heartedly suggest that open-ended starting points are offered for children to familiarise themselves with the possibilities of the materials and tools:

> …real learning… is a process characterised by the idea of the not-known and that-which-is-not yet; it is a process of adventure… it has to be viewed as an adventure in which modes of learning and their outcomes may be unclear.
>
> *(Atkinson, 2018, p.2)*

References

Arane, K., Behboudi, A. & Goldman, R. D. (2017). Virtual reality for pain and anxiety management in children. *Canadian Family Physician*, 63: 932–934.

Atkinson, D. (2018). *Art, Disobedience, and Ethics: The Adventure of Pedagogy*. London: Palgrave Macmillan.

Blascovich. J. & Bailenson, J. N. (2011). *Infinite Reality: Avatars, Eternal Life, New Worlds, and the Dawn of the Virtual Evolution*. New York, NY: William Morrow.

Bell, P. (2001). Content analysis of visual images. In: T. van Leeuwen & C. Jewitt (eds), *Handbook of Visual Analysis*. London: Sage, pp.10–35.

Braun, V. and Clarke, V. (2006). Using thematic analysis in psychology. *Qualitative Research in Psychology*, 3(2): 77–101.

Carrington, V. & Dowdall, C. (2013). 'This is a job for Hazmat Guy!': Global media cultures and children's everyday lives. In: K. Hall, T. Cremin, B. Comber & L. C. Moll (eds), *International Handbook of Research on Children's Literacy, Learning, and Culture*. Chichester, UK: John Wiley & Sons Ltd, pp. 96–107.

Dewey, J. (2009/1938). *Art as Experience*. Los Angeles: Perigee Books.

Flood, C. & Grindon, G. (2014). *Disobedient Objects*. V&A Publishing.

Gibson, J. J. (1977). The theory of affordances. In: R. Shaw and J. Bransford (eds), *Perceiving, Acting and Knowing*. Hillsdale, NJ: Erlbaum, pp. 67–82.

Giddings, S. & Kennedy, H. W. (2008). Little Jesuses and fuckoff robots: On aesthetics, cybernetics, and not being very good at Lego Star Wars. In: M. Swalwell & J. Wilson (eds), *The Pleasures of Computer Gaming: Essays on Cultural History, Theory and Aesthetics*. Jefferson, NC: McFarland, pp. 13–32.

Grimes, S. (2018). Penguins, hype, and MMOGs for kids: A critical re-examination of the 2008 "boom" in children's virtual worlds development . *Games and Culture*, 13(6): 624–644.

Horwitz, J. (2018). SkyLights uses VR gear and Fox films to entertain kids on long flights. Venture Beat. Retrieved from: https://venturebeat.com/2018/08/21/skylights-uses-vr-gear-and-fox-films-to-entertain-kids-on-long-flights/

Hughes, J. (2016). Digital making with "at risk" youth. In: *Proceedings of the ICICTE*, Rhodes, Greece, 7–9 July 2016.

Ingold, T. (2013). *Making: Anthropology, Archaeology, Art and Architecture*. London: Routledge.

Julier, G. (2013). From design culture to design activism. *Design and Culture*, 5(2): 215–236.

Kenner, C. (2004). *Becoming Biliterate: Young Children Learning Different Writing Systems*. Stoke-on-Trent, UK: Trentham Books Limited.

Knobel, M. & Lankshear, C. (eds). (2010). *DIY Media: Creating, Sharing and Learning with New Technologies*. New York, NY: Peter Lang.

Kress, G. (2010). *Multimodality: A Social Semiotic Approach to Contemporary Communication*. London; New York, NY: Routledge.

Marsh, J., Plowman, L., Yamada-Rice, D., Bishop, J. & Scott, F. (2018a) Digital play: a new classification. *Early Years*, 36(3): 242–253.

Marsh, J., Arnseth, H. C. & Kumpulainen, K. (2018b). Maker literacies and maker citizenship in the MAKEY (Makerspaces in the Early Years) project. *Multimodal Technologies and Interaction*, 2(3): 50.

Marsh, J., Plowman, L., Yamada-Rice, D., Bishop, J. C., Lahmar, J., Scott, F., Davenport, A., Davis, S., French, K., Piras, M., Thornhill, S., Robinson, P. & Winter, P. (2015). *Exploring Play and Creativity in Pre-Schoolers' Use of Apps: Final Project Report*. Retrieved from www.techandplay.org/reports/TAP_Final_Report.pdf

Onwuegbuzie, A. J. & Seaman, M. A. (1995). The effect of time constraints and statistics test anxiety on test performance in a statistics course. *The Journal of Experimental Education*, 63(2): 115–124.

Ratto, M. (2011). Critical making: Conceptual and material studies. *The Information Society: An International Journal*, 27: 252–260.

Riva, G. & Waterworth, J. A. (2014). In: M. Grimshaw (ed), Being present in the virtual world. *The Oxford Handbook of Virtuality*. New York, NY: Oxford University Press, pp. 205–211

Southgate, E., Smith, S. P., Cividino, C., Saxby, S., Kilham, J., Eather, G., Scevak, J., Summerville, D., Buchanan, R. & Bergin, C. (2019). Embedding immersive virtual reality in classrooms: Ethical, organisational and educational lessons in bridging research and practice. *International Journal of Child-Computer Interaction*, 19: 19–29.

Sullivan, M. (2015). Maker, tinker, hacker? Active learning spaces in K-12 libraries. *Library Media Connection*, March/April 2015: 16–17.

Tarrant, J., Viczko, J. & Cope, H. (2018). Virtual reality for anxiety reduction demonstrated by quantitative eeg: A pilot study. *Frontiers in Psychology*, 9: 1280.

Van Mechelen, M. (2016). *Designing Technologies for and with Children: A Tool Kit to Prepare and Conduct Codesign Activities and Analyse the Outcome*. Mint Lab. Retrieved from: https://soc.kuleuven.be/mintlab/blog/wp-content/uploads/2017/01/CoDesign-Toolkit-Van-Mechelen-2016-highRes-II.pdf

Waterworth, J. & Riva, G. (2014). *Feeling Present in the Physical Works and in Computer-Mediated Environments*. Basingstoke: Palgrave Macmillan.

WEARVR. (2018). *ICO White Paper: Introducing WEAVE from WEARVR*. Leeds, UK: WEARVR. Retrieved from: https://weave.wearvr.com/whitepaper/weave-white-paper-en.pdf

Yamada-Rice, D. (2018a) Designing play: Young children's play and communication practices in relation to designers' intentions for their toy. *Global Studies in Childhood*, 8: 5–22.

Yamada-Rice, D. (2018b) Can making headsets teach children how VR works? The Medium. Retrieved from https://medium.com/kids-digital/can-making-headsets-teach-children-how-vr-works-ed7095b590bc

Yamada-Rice, D., Mushtaq, F., Woodgate, A., Bosmans, D., Douthwaite, A., Douthwaite, I., Harris, W., Holt, R., Kleeman, D., Marsh, J., Milovidov, E., Mon Williams, M., Parry, B., Riddler, A., Robinson, P., Rodrigues, D., Thompson, S. & Whitley, S. (2017). *Children and Virtual Reality: Emerging Possibilities and Challenges.* Retrieved from: http://childrenvr.org

6

MAKERSPACES IN FORMAL AND NON-FORMAL LEARNING CONTEXTS IN ICELAND

Kristín Dýrfjörð, Torfi Hjartarson, Anna Elísa Hreiðarsdótti, Sólveig Jakobsdóttir, Svanborg R. Jónsdóttir, Skúlína H. Kjartansdóttir, Margrét E. Ólafsdóttir, Svava Pétursdóttir and Gísli Thorsteinsson

Introduction

Icelandic schools provide, within the scope of the MakEY project, insights into an educational system that is small in scale in comparison to other national systems yet functions within a wider global context. The national government undertook a reform of the entire system with laws passed in 2008 for all school levels: pre-schools, compulsory education spanning ten grades at the primary and lower-secondary levels, upper-secondary education and universities (Jónasson and Óskarsdóttir, 2016). The government at the time may have been interested in deregulation, as well as both endogenous and external privatisation (Dýrfjörð and Magnúsdóttir, 2016), but the school system has, nevertheless, remained universal and open to the public to a great extent. Every child and young person has an equal right to education, more or less free of charge, at the primary, secondary and tertiary levels. Preschool is also considered universal, with parents paying fees on a sliding scale up to some 17 per cent of the real cost for an 8-hour school day (Dýrfjörð, 2018). The educational system is, overall, considered highly inclusive, with more than 99 per cent of all students at the primary and lower-secondary school levels attending mainstream schools. Private schools only make up around 7 per cent (12 out of 169) of schools at the compulsory level, and they educate only about 2.5 per cent of students (1,122 out of 45,195) (Statistics Iceland, n.d.).

The 2008 legislation on schooling was followed by curriculum guides that redefine pedagogical and educational roles across all subject areas and school levels, teachers' professionalism and the objectives of learning, based on six fundamental pillars: literacy; sustainability; health and welfare; democracy and human rights; equality; and creativity (Ministry of Education, Science and Culture, 2012, 2014). Creativity and critical thinking are to be promoted and integrated through study and play in everyday activities (Ministry of Education, Science and Culture, 2012). Thematic integration of learning across subject areas appears to be growing in most, if not all schools, at the primary and lower-secondary levels and is encouraged by educational policies at both municipal and national levels, in part through the introduction and application of digital technologies (Jakobsdóttir, Hjartarson and Thórhallsdóttir, 2014). Makerspaces are generally seen as an offshoot of this trend and considered to hold promise in relation to the convergence of knowledge that is expected to occur as a result of thematic teaching and learning.

Other aspects of educational practice relevant to the establishment of makerspaces in Iceland include an unbroken tradition since 1889 of arts and crafts education in state and compulsory schools (Ólafsson and Thorsteinsson, 2009; Thorsteinsson and Ólafsson, 2014); an attempt to implement innovation education and entrepreneurship in a national curriculum document published in 1999 (Jónsdóttir, 2011); the introduction of Fab Labs in 2008 by the Iceland Innovation Center; and the Nordic model of pedagogy prevailing at the preschool level, a model that tends to look at the mind and body as a whole. Art and crafts provide venues within the core curriculum guide from which to establish makerspaces, as well as specialised classrooms ready with tools and equipment for integrating digital fabrication into daily school practice. The innovation education approach provides teachers with an alternative pedagogy allowing work across subjects, possibility thinking and creativity as guiding principles. The introduction of Fab Labs, furthermore, paved the way for makerspaces in informal education. Fab Lab staff have, in addition, offered training options for teachers in formal education, as well as facilities for making and community building.

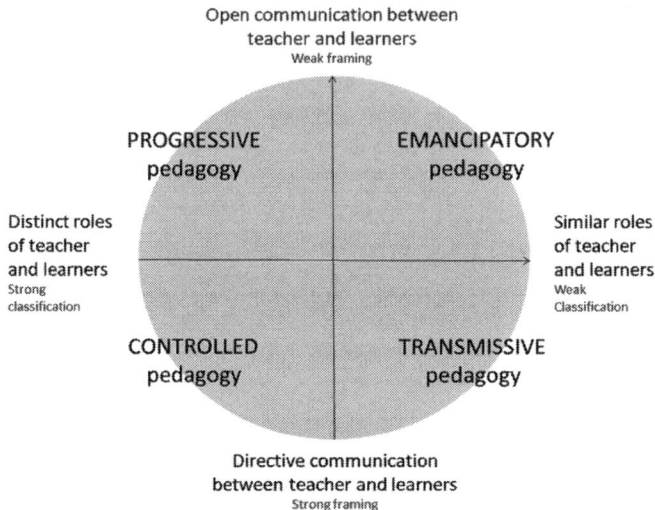

FIGURE 6.1 Pedagogies analysed with classification and framing
Adapted from Jónsdóttir and Macdonald (2013)

In this chapter we will provide an overview of case studies on the integration and use of makerspaces for young children in Iceland. The case studies are informed by work undertaken in Iceland on identifying and analysing the pedagogies applied in *Innovation and Entrepreneurial Education* (IEE) in schools. In the next section, we provide an overview of the key principles of IEE and the pedagogical model emerging from research on IEE.

Pedagogies supporting creativity and action

Creativity and innovation are both key to engagement in makerspaces, and the two concepts are closely intertwined. Innovation does not come about without creative thinking, and depending on how innovation is defined, it requires creative actions. Creative thinking does not necessarily bring about innovation; a novelty tends to require creative action. Some scholars, nevertheless, do not make a distinction between innovation and creativity (Georgsdottir, Lubart and Getz, 2003; Weisberg, 2003).

Innovation and Entrepreneurial Education (IEE) has been developing in Iceland since the early 1990s up to the present time. It is commonly coined Innovation Education at the compulsory school level, and Entrepreneurial Education or Entrepreneurship Education at the upper-secondary school level. It has, as a rule, also at preschool level, been effective in enhancing innovative capacities and an entrepreneurial spirit among learners (Jónsdóttir et al., 2008; Jónsdóttir and Macdonald, 2013; Ólafsdóttir and Jónsdóttir, 2016). In IEE the work is focused on using creativity and knowledge to solve problems that learners identify themselves, aiming to develop critical and creative thinking in design, science, technology, marketing and enterprise. The emphasis is on enhancing creative skills and actualising ideas through active participation, enhancing the competence of learners for action (Jónsdóttir and Gunnarsdóttir, 2017).

IEE requires work beyond traditional subject areas or school boundaries and has to acknowledge everyday knowledge (Jónsdóttir and Macdonald, 2013). Teachers need support to master the balance of freedom and structure required when integrating knowledge and crossing boundaries of various kinds. Other challenges involved can be found in informal relationships among teachers or between teachers and learners. Learners, teachers and administrators tend to see IEE as having characteristics that reflect weak boundaries, freedom and flexibility. The opportunities stemming from IEE have been seen to enhance learner creativity and innovativeness, as well as strengthen their capacity for social involvement. This resonates well with the aims of making as defined by scholars and the maker movement.

Jónsdóttir (2011) used criteria developed from Bernstein's (2000) concepts of *classification* and *framing* to analyse the practices of 13 IEE teachers. The findings revealed four types of pedagogy: *transmissive, controlled, progressive* and *emancipatory* (Jónsdóttir and Macdonald, 2013; Jónsdóttir and Gunnarsdóttir, 2017) (Figure 6.1). The weak framing advocated in IEE, as well as its weak classification of knowledge, can be particularly demanding for both teachers and schools that traditionally build on strongly classified subjects, clearly defined roles and strong framing.

TABLE 6.1 Overview of participants and data collection

Participants and data	Case 1: Innoent courses	Case 2: Preschool	Case 3: Virtual making	Case 4: VEXA team (suburban school)
No. of students	5–8[5]	9	10	17
Ages	5–10	5–6	7	6–8
No. of teachers	1–3 mentors	1+1 university student	1	1 (out of 7 in team)
No. of visits	5	9	3	9
Interviews with children + teachers	0+1	1+2	9+2	0+6
Hours of observation	15	9	6	10
Hours of video	0	6	60	87
No. of photos	155	293	107	422
Hours of audio		45 min.	6	7

The emancipatory type or mode is the one most in line with the ideology of IEE, and teachers working in the progressive mode could be viewed as being able to adapt or move into the emancipatory mode. The emancipatory pedagogy allows learners the most freedom and agency, representing a mode where teachers and learners can communicate as equals. The controlled mode allows the least learner agency and limited creativity but could serve as a starting point for some teachers to move towards progressive and eventually emancipatory modes. Teachers seem unlikely to apply the transmissive mode as it builds on a strong framing of communication and a weak classification of roles, but this mode may, nevertheless, constitute an interesting alternative considering recent trends in formal schooling as related above.

IEE teachers have to build upon or acquire approaches and views that are sometimes different from what they are used to (Jónsdóttir and Macdonald, 2013). Adapting an 'artistic approach' (Eisner, 2002) to teaching and a kind of holistic thinking that can easily override boundaries of subjects and social relations is clearly needed. Teachers need to know when to stand back while learners develop their ideas, and when to support and encourage. Some teachers tend to control too many aspects of their IEE lessons with strong and sometimes very strong framing. An awareness of this tendency to control can be acquired by reflecting on teaching practices, focusing on who controls and what they control (Jónsdóttir and Macdonald, 2013; Jónsdóttir and Gunnarsdóttir, 2017). The 13 innovation education teachers in Jónsdóttir's 2011 study were at different levels of adapting IEE pedagogy, depending on training, the school ethos and their personal and professional inclinations. An artistic orientation with mixed framing seemed to help some teachers find the balance needed between freedom and structure in the classroom, classrooms where teachers give value to the voice and position of each learner and situate his or her learning in a context specific to each

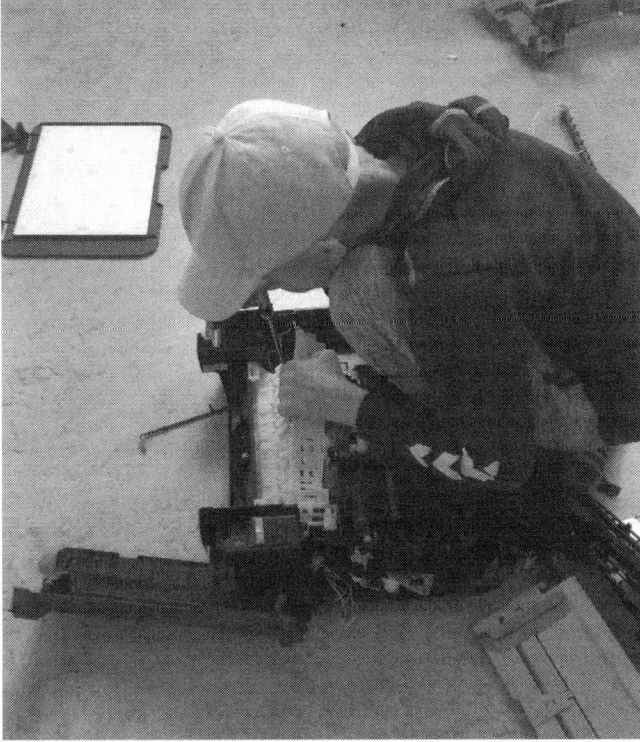

FIGURES 6.2 and 6.3 Children participating in an Innoent course, dismantling electrical devices

case. This capacity of teachers to allow enough freedom, accepting the role of a 'flexible teacher' in order to enhance learner agency and creativity within reasonable boundaries and different contexts, seems to make the greatest difference to realising the potential of IEE (Jónsdóttir, 2011).

What is expected of teachers working with children and young people and how those expectations fit their teaching philosophies does matter and needs to be understood by each and every teacher (Darling-Hammond, 1997). Helping teachers and mentors make their educational philosophies visible and face possible chaos and angst when assisting learners in creative spaces can be supported by having access to specialist support and/or peer consultation (Jónsdóttir and Gunnarsdóttir, 2017). Such an awareness seems likely to play a role when teachers and mentors organise and teach in makerspaces where creativity and action are expected and supported.

The analytical model of pedagogies presented above provides a strong framework for our work on makerspaces in the Icelandic MakEY project and helps us to detect how pedagogical approaches emerge in makerspaces aimed at younger children. Our four cases include formal and non-formal learning sites with permanent and temporary activities where a range of tools were applied. These include a project focusing on makerspaces in Innoent summer courses (non-formal, permanent),[1] a project on makerspaces in

FIGURES 6.2 and 6.3 (*Continued*)

preschool (formal, temporary),[2] a project involving the establishment of a virtual maker-space (Minecraft) in a primary school classroom (formal, permanent)[3] and, finally, a project aiming to establish and promote the use of makerspaces in primary schools (formal, temporary to permanent).[4] While these case studies were all very different in nature, they were united in their embedding of innovation and creativity into activities.

The research question posed in all four cases and addressed in this chapter is: What kind of pedagogy appears to be applied in makerspaces for young children in Iceland?

Makerspaces in Innoent summer courses

Innoent is a non-profit organisation offering training courses for teachers and courses for children. In this case, the focus is on the kind of pedagogy applied in Innoent summer courses offered to children in a community within the extended capital area. In its courses, Innoent offers learning spaces for children to work as inventors. The teachers or assistants in Innoent prefer to call themselves mentors rather than teachers, as their role is more in the spirit of mentoring rather than teaching in a traditional manner.

The Innoent courses in this case were held in an old but well-kept former school building in one of the towns neighbouring Reykjavik, Iceland's capital city. The courses took place on the ground floor in a large, bright classroom with two spacious corridors and an outside area for building and playing. Creative episodes were documented with learners deeply engaged in their creations working independently or in pairs. The social and physical surroundings were conducive to the tasks at hand, mentors guided and supported the children and were available when asked to help. Interactions were casual and the children often initiated conversations with their mentors, asking questions and telling the adults where they were heading or what they wanted to work on (Figures 6.2 and 6.3).

It is nine o'clock in the morning. I walk into the corridor, the main door is open and I continue into an open bright room. There are tables to one side, near the door, covered with a plastic sheet, with paintbrushes and paint in small yoghourt boxes, and the sheet is covered with strokes and dots in different colours. There is a big black bag on the floor over by the wall near the windows, it is full of old, electronic things, like phones, radios, organ keyboards, printers and other stuff. Three children, they look about 5 or 6 years old, are sitting on the floor with some discarded phones, taking them apart. Along another wall are placed three tables with orange-coloured, plastic cutters. Thordis, mentor and headmaster of the school, walks around putting things in their places. The atmosphere is relaxed and the children are focused on what they are doing.

(Researcher's notebook)

Various materials and tools were available and the children could choose what to work on, which materials and which tools to use. The children had ample agency to do what they wanted; at times, some of them seemed uninterested and idle, but usually not for long. They could also decide where within the makerspace to work, whom to work with and when, and whether or not they wanted to seek assistance. They were also allowed to take a break when they wanted, to play a game of cards, read a book or rest in a cosy corner:

It is ten past ten and a mother arrives with her son, who has a large book in his hand, and they walk into the big room where the main activities are taking place. There are now four boys in the room. Thordis is there and asks them what they want to do. They sit down at a table covered with different discarded, electrical things. She asks: "Do you want to tear these things apart? We have a toolbox here." She shows them a toolbox with screwdrivers and small pliers. The boys talk to each other and one of them starts singing. They start to pick out some tools and keep talking as they begin selecting stuff to dismantle.

Thordis is out in the inner corridor talking to a mother. A girl, about six or seven years old, walks towards the cozy corner with a book and sits down. A boy comes over to Thordis and asks: "What is this?" Thordis replies: "This is a screwdriver and you can use it like this." She shows him how to use the screwdriver. The assistant mentor, Tara, comes in and sits down by the boys at

FIGURES 6.4 and 6.5 Children collaborating, discussing and helping each other coding the Blue-Bot

the table. They continue exploring the stuff and experimenting with loosening screws as they talk amongst themselves, sometimes asking Tara's advice. "See Kalli, it's like this, it turns like this, try it Kalli," says one boy to another. The boy with the book sits down on the floor and starts to peruse it. Tara sits down on the floor beside him and chats to him.

(Researcher's notebook)

The mentors showed an interest in the children's projects and assisted when asked. They only occasionally talked to the group as a whole or initiated specific tasks and usually engaged with each child individually or with pairs or small groups working together. The mentors often bent down to be on the same level as the learners or sat down on the floor with them, talking to them like colleagues or collaborators. The atmosphere was in general very relaxed and had the gist of an open workshop.

An experimental makerspace at the preschool level

A preschool project in Akureyri, the largest township in the north of Iceland, focused on how children aged four and five years approached the use of digital technology to learn, create and play in a temporary makerspace within a preschool setting. A team of three researchers brought Blue-Bots and Cubelets to the maker-space, while the preschool provided drawing materials and Lego. The children were divided into two groups, led by a preschool teacher and a graduate university student. Each group had a floor mat as a delimited space for the Blue-Bot. The children could, however, move between mats, and make use of the classroom as a whole.

Nine children, four girls and five boys from a local preschool, worked in a temporary makerspace specially set up for the project's workshop. During the workshop, the children engaged in creative activities and coding with Blue-Bots and Cubelets, with the guidance of the teacher, who was assisted by the student. The children also had access to an iPad, fixed on a table located behind a partition in one corner of the room, and to a GoPro camera on a strap belt. Technological devices and traditional tools were used concurrently. The teacher had extensive experience of teaching and creative work, but no prior experience of working with robots. The aim was to observe how the children reacting to robots added to their familiar play world, to see how they engaged with the robots creatively, and to observe how their coding skills developed through the activities.

The data collection involved the use of video cameras, a GoPro camera, iPads, photographs and research diaries. In addition, the teacher asked the children towards the end of each session to evaluate the session, by asking them to choose an appropriate emotion sticker and answer follow-up questions. Follow-up interviews were also conducted separately, with the teacher, the student and the children, after the sessions had ended. The children attended six sessions, one period twice a week over a period of three weeks. The preschool teacher and the graduate student implemented the activities by following a curriculum plan drawn up by the researchers. The plan suggested that the children should begin the workshop by drawing and making

TABLE 6.2 Overview of key findings in interaction, gender similarities and differences, creativity and play, and coding

Themes	Between children	With robots	With teachers	With the space
Interaction	Rich. Children worked/played together in pairs and in bigger groups; all children at some point worked/played individually.	Robots travelled between children, from child A to child B. As an example of embodiment, children used their bodies as building material. Use of body to interact with robots.	Children did not look at the teacher for advice or information. The teacher showed encouragement and support. Sometimes the teacher was too quick to react and intervened too soon.	Children used all available space. Children moved freely in and through the space. The space put constraints on the children's play. Floor mats framed the play.
	Similarities	**Girls**	**Boys**	**Differences**
Gender – similarities and differences	Girls and boys showed interest, and their skills progressed; both girls and boys had problems interacting with technical devices. All the children made up stories while playing. All showed pride in their accomplishments.	Girls tended to stay in one place. Girls discussed plans in the preparation time, and they decorated their playing area.	Boys moved around the whole space (took ownership of it) and had a tendency to play in larger groups.	Girls prepared both the environment and their play. Boys approached the tools directly and started playing. No girl created a princess; some boys created superheroes and one cast himself in the role of a superhero.
	Creative	**Play**	**Design**	**Imagination**
Creativity and play	Drawings were used to create characters and settings. Lego bricks were used to create environments with buildings, animals, a forest and complementary objects. Characters were based on models.	Making stories and playing them out. Taking turns using the robots. Using the iPad and the GoPro freely. High level of imaginary play.	Building 3D Lego characters based on 2D drawings. Designing the play environment, staging.	Improvisation. Inventing trajectories, sceneries, obstacles etc. Personifying the robots.

Themes	Between children	With robots	With teachers	With the space
	Programming	**Planning**	**Experiments**	**Skill**
Coding	Children learned to give commands by counting and pushing buttons on the Blue-Bot. Learned the function of the X-button.	Planning different trajectories before programming the Blue-Bot. Making the plan fit a story. Adjusting the plan.	Experimenting with commands, observing the Blue-Bot not behaving as planned. Learning by making adjustments and repeating.	Being able to program a trajectory using available commands; using the grid and without the help of a grid.

characters. Then, the teacher introduced the children to coding and encouraged them to make stories, involving both characters and robots (Figures 6.4 and 6.5).

The work appeared relatively easy to integrate into the curriculum. Dýrfjörð (2018) points out that makerspace ideology, in general, connects well with the predominant pedagogy of the typical preschool in Iceland, a place where attention is paid to connectivity, creativity and sustainability; a place where spaces to be in and try out new things are provided; a place where the relations between humans, digital technologies, experimentation and creativity are allowed to grow.

There were rich and diverse interactions between the children, and between the children and the robots during the sessions. They made use of the classroom space as a whole and engaged in multifarious activities, with drawings, Lego blocks, robots and cameras being used in creative ways. The robots added a new layer to the play and, in some cases, the children interacted with the robots as if they were living beings. In all the activities, the children worked both individually and collaborated with each other in pairs and larger groups. All the children made up stories while playing with the robots. They used Lego bricks, either to build obstacles for the robots to pass by, gates to pass through, or structures as destinations. Some children tended to give up on the coding at an early stage and needed encouragement to continue. A few were quick learners, and other showed resilience. In Table 6.2, the main findings are outlined, with regard to the

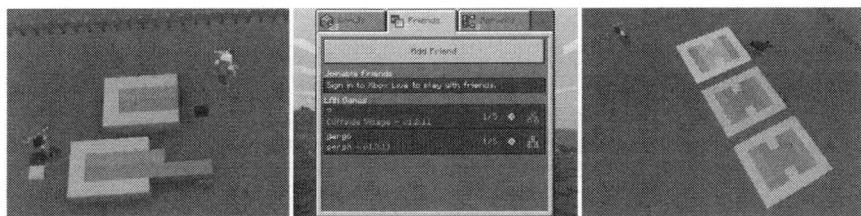

FIGURE 6.6 Collaborative activities: students resolving maths challenges in a Minecraft Virtual Learning Makerspace (MVLM)
Not official Minecraft product. Not approved by or associated with Mojang.

following themes: types of interaction; similarities and differences with regard to gender; creativity and play, and coding, as all of these were relevant to the work undertaken.

The benefits of setting up a makerspace within a preschool, and with a teacher and children who knew each other, was that the participants did not need time to become acquainted. The children were eager to participate, and open to the challenges of new tasks and new devices. The teacher guided the children through the assignments, interacted with them during the learning process, and paid attention to their questions and needs. Her role was to get the children started with the coding, but she tended to intervene when a child did not grasp the basics immediately. The teacher stated in an interview that she had been too keen on interfering in the process of learning coding. The graduate student made a similar evaluation, recognising that it was tempting to intervene too early, and not to give the children time to think before reacting to the input. Despite those interventions, the children had many opportunities to develop both their coding skills and creativity, and make use of these during their play (Table 6.2).

A virtual makerspace (Minecraft) in a primary school classroom

This case study focused on the use of a Minecraft Virtual Learning Makerspace (MVLM) on iPads to further mathematics teaching. It was carried out at a compulsory school in a coastal town in western Iceland. The participants were a group of ten 7-year-old students and their teacher. The aim of the study was to examine the context of teaching and learning in a conventional classroom where some of the learning activities were performed using a computer video game as an educational platform. A Virtual Learning Makerspace (VLM) is a place where people with shared interests, especially in computing or technology, can gather to work on projects while sharing ideas, equipment and knowledge (Oxford Dictionaries, 2018). It is based on an electronic system that allows collaboration of various kinds to take place between learners and teachers during online teaching and learning (Martin, 2007).

Computer video games, such as Minecraft, are emerging as an instructional medium offering strong cognitive efficiencies for active and experiential learning,

FIGURE 6.7 Teacher activities: introducing maths challenges, monitoring activities in the MVLM and discussing problems and progress in class

in part by building teams in a multi-player environment and enabling greater understanding of abstract concepts (Rice, 2007). Using a game-based application in the field of education is referred to as game-based learning, motivating students by using game-based elements in educational settings (Kapp, 2012; Shatz, 2015). Using a Minecraft VLM (MVLM) to support game-based learning is an ideal way to support students' learning (Figure 6.6), as it enables collaboration and sharing information in a playful manner (Hennessey and Deaney, 2004; Passey et al., 2004). Games can become a platform for playful learning, where students learn to make sense of the world around them through a variety of playful, physical or virtual activities (Resnick, 2004; Kangas, 2010; Whitton, 2018).

The key issues under consideration were the role of the teacher in an MVLM educational context and how the MVLM affected students' learning practices. Various data were used to triangulate the research and reinforce reliability. Information on participants and the data collected can be viewed in Table 6.1. The use of video invites the capture of multimodal data and enables access to fine details of conduct and interactions that are unavailable to more traditional science methods (Heath, Hindmarsh and Luff, 2010). GoPro videos portrayed human–computer interaction, design activities and group communication in the classroom, as well as in the virtual world, while students were completing their tasks. In-game videos also managed to capture the location and organisation of student activities in Minecraft.

The findings indicate that the MVLM provided the teacher with opportunities to assign interdisciplinary, project-based collaborative tasks. The study indicates the importance of the teacher as a technician, conventional instructor and pedagogical facilitator when preparing and guiding students in the MVLM. The teacher became an organiser of world elements within Minecraft, and a designer of learning settings and tasks. The teacher had to undertake multiple roles and be able to switch between classroom guidance, being an instructor and facilitator, and in the virtual educational setting, being an administrator and observer of learning activities. He had to prepare the game world, furnishing it with objects and guiding signs. He also had to step in when technical problems, such as a lost Internet connection, or reoccurring rain in the game world, affected learning.

Minecraft appeared to invite the teacher to enhance creativity with a variety of teaching methods. The teacher had to introduce the lesson plan and learning objectives, and guide students when they confronted difficulties, could not understand mathematical concepts or handle their tasks (Figure 6.7). This he often did by asking leading questions or withdrawing from assisting students in problem-solving and decision making, which encouraged students to reach their own conclusions. In doing so, the teacher made a transition from directive communication towards a more open communication. Moreover, during their work, the teacher ensured that the students had the flexibility needed to cooperate in a playful learning context.

Using the MVLM while learning mathematics appealed greatly to all the students. They enjoyed playing Minecraft; as one student expressed: "I wish we could always play Minecraft at school." They also felt motivated to learn about mathematics in a creative manner, which enabled an understanding of mathematical concepts and helped them solve mathematical problems. While students played inside Minecraft, they constantly communicated with each other, shared experiences and demonstrated to other students how they were getting on with their tasks. This flow of communication between students helped to improve their skills in mathematics and enhance their collaboration. Students of different abilities supported each other, for instance in reading in-game instructions and crafting objects, counting and designing. While playing, students were able to work on enhancing their understanding of factors such as geometry, measurements, mathematical expressions and general mathematics (Bos et al., 2014).

The MVLM is a cooperative playground for playful learning activities. It offers generative tools for co-creation, design and making. The world is flexible and adaptable to fit various pedagogical strategies and practices. The chance to create and customise an avatar enables the student to express his or her identity. Students are able to make their own choices when making objects, using multiple materials of different qualities and visual appearance. The biggest value of using MVLM in education might be to boost the motivation of students, harnessing their out-of-school experience for the purpose of learning. For the teacher, the MVLM might be an opportunity for professional development, to construct alternative learning paths and to experiment with new ways of teaching. In constructing an extended zone of proximal development, the teacher can further challenge students (Molin, 2017). New roles for the teacher are emerging, such as collaborative roles with game developers, where teachers are invited to help design educational games (Leinonen, 2010).

The VEXA team: Founded to establish and promote making in compulsory schools

This case study focused on the initiative and collective work of the VEXA team, a group of seven female educators, pioneers promoting making and makerspaces within the Icelandic compulsory school system and beyond. We have reviewed their attempt to establish makerspaces in a number of schools and provide pedagogical support to the wider community of teachers; we have considered the underlying

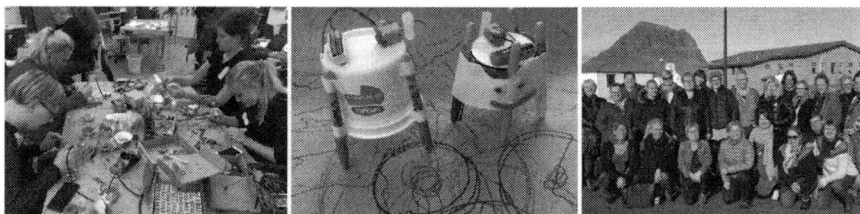

FIGURES 6.8 The VEXA group's professional training and learning camp at Snæfellsnes, Iceland, offered to teachers in September 2018 (#VEXAedu)

ideologies and motivations, and reflected on the agency and empowerment involved as the team ploughs the field of making in its effort to make makerspaces flourish as an integral part of compulsory education.

Data were collected in two group interviews with the VEXA group, as well as through field visits, interviews and observations at two different schools: a suburban school on the outskirts of Reykjavik, where a makerspace arrangement coined the 'Genius Lab' has been established, and a rural school in the west of Iceland where making has been taught and encouraged at three different school sites.

The all-women VEXA team represents a group of Icelandic educators who got together in 2017, created a plan and applied for a grant to further their own knowledge of makerspaces, as well as to inform and advise teachers all over Iceland about matters of making. Their aim was to foster interdisciplinary and technology-enhanced learning (Sheridan et al., 2014), creative collaboration (Sawyer and DeZutter, 2009; Nasciutti, Veresov and de Aragão, 2016) and technical literacy (Dakers, 2014) within primary and lower-secondary schools. Their initiative has, from the outset, been characterised by self-empowerment and knowledge-building among the women and other educators involved, mainly through tech meetings and Web dissemination, course development and practical activities in schools. Their ambition is to establish a network of different interest groups and public agencies in the educational sector to support and develop making in compulsory schools.

Professional development, in the case of makerspaces, is an important and multi-faceted process. Oliver (2016) outlines how teachers need to develop the abilities and means to design, resource and maintain the makerspace, as well as to facilitate and assess makerspace activities. The VEXA women have also found, coming from a country with a small language community, that their need for professional development could not be met without venturing abroad. This they have done by attending maker fairs and sharing experiences with makers in other countries, while providing peer support and information in Icelandic communities through work-shops and social media. The impact of these collective efforts has gradually become visible, most notably when the team organises and carries out successful workshops for teachers on making and maker pedagogy (Figure 6.8).

The VEXA women do, each and every one of them, have a long history of interest and active involvement in the advancement of ICT in the educational sector. They do, however, when asked, point out their interests in design thinking, communal learning and creativity as the driving elements behind their enthusiasm and efforts concerning makerspaces. There is a growing trend to integrate tasks in compulsory schooling, and the ideologies of making appear to echo or resonate with educational policies currently emphasising participatory learning, thematic work and digital skills.

Different models of makerspaces have emerged within school settings under the supervision of different teachers and consultants from the VEXA team. Here we relate four examples: an attempt to create the conditions for a makerspace in a school library in a suburban open-plan school, a peripatetic model where a teacher con-sultant in a rural school arranges or provides lessons in making for different age groups at three different school sites, a makerspace or class offered to teenage students

FIGURE 6.9 Students coding and solving problems: a plant development project in a genius workshop at Holabrekkuskoli compulsory school in Reykjavik, Iceland

as an elective at a school in one of the towns surrounding our capital, and finally the Genius Lab, established at a suburban school on the outskirts of Reykjavik, led by a project manager from the teaching staff and maintained across many grade levels.

Libraries have in recent years been embracing new technologies and redefining their role in that respect. A school library teacher from the VEXA group, working at the time in an open-plan school in the suburbs of Reykjavik, made an attempt to initiate making at her library by putting up a Lego wall and arranging a few other activities involving digital technologies. She did, however, find it difficult to get other teachers at the school involved in such efforts, as they appeared to be burdened with a tight schedule and too much teamwork in their open-plan settings to take on new obligations involving collaborative work. The school happens, nevertheless, to be an example of how traditional crafts and learning tasks can be integrated across subjects and digital technologies successfully applied in daily school practice. A somewhat different approach to digital making, more closely tied to class-based teams or art and crafts, might prove useful at this particular school. A teaching consultant at a rural school had more success, working closely with teachers in the same school at three different sites, facilitating or managing various activities and maker projects involving both teachers and students of different ages. Yet another member of the VEXA team offers elective courses on making to teenagers attending her lower-secondary school in a town close to Reykjavik. The model appears to work quite well for her and her students, but it is not offered directly to younger age levels where electives are usually not on offer.

Two of the VEXA women have, as consultants or project managers at a senior level in large municipalities, been able to promote viable ideas and digital tools applicable in makerspaces to municipal politicians, administrators, teachers and teaching consultants in their respective communities, as well as to encourage the provision of central support and services to teachers in the field. Another member of the team works at a municipal media centre that provides schools with professional and technical support for digital media and has of late, in addition, been lending programmable devices and technical sets of interest to makers.

Last but not least is a programme designed and implemented by one of the team members at a suburban school on the outskirts of our capital city, Reykjavik. The arrangement is called the Genius Lab and is based on the participation of two 'geniuses' carefully chosen from each class group, which amounts to four students from each grade level over a range of four grades (1st, 3rd, 5th and 7th). The geniuses meet their makerspace teacher every week to make decisions about lab activities and learn digital skills required for making. They need to learn basic skills on a relatively strictly defined basis to begin with, but creativity and independent work are encouraged as they become better acquainted with different tasks. They then move on to invite small groups of classmates to the lab and pass on knowledge and skills they have acquired in preparatory sessions. The idea is to introduce making and digital skills to the general school community through lab activities run by the geniuses. This dissemination of know-how and maker insights happens through lessons in the lab offered by the geniuses, as well as in so-called educamps, whole school events where geniuses showcase their learned wisdom and help others to tackle different tasks. Lab activities focus mostly on digital making with programmable tech sets like Arduino or littleBits, microcomputers such as micro: bits, or apps of particular interest to programmers and makers (Figure 6.9).

Enthusiasm and interest for making are evoked by the children themselves, students who have been chosen to serve as knowledgeable teachers, sometimes because they themselves needed support and attention. This is an empowering process that appears to have worked well, based upon our interviews with the project manager in charge, observations of peer-to-peer classes and visits to educamps arranged by the lab. Students have been making requests to attend the lab and they try not to act up in front of the project manager, hoping to be selected to join the team of geniuses or be picked out to attend lessons at the lab.

There appears to be relatively fertile ground for makerspaces within formal schooling, but the growth is only just starting. School leaders have not been putting any pressure of significance on their staff members to take on making or putting up makerspaces, while there seems to be growing interest flourishing at grass-roots level, in particular among educators enthusiastic about digital technologies. Some of the larger municipalities have been particularly supportive and are working on ways to promote making and makerspaces as one of many areas within the field of ICT in education that need to be cultivated for the school system to cope with a new era of technical invention. This movement also puts emphasis on fostering multi-literacies, creativity and democratic involvement embraced in the national curriculum.

Key enablers of innovation in the use of makerspaces include the kind of educators represented in the VEXA team, experienced pioneers deeply rooted in the teaching profession but in a position to have influence beyond their school or municipality. The fact that they are all women, as is the case with the majority of teachers at the compulsory school level, is furthermore of fundamental importance. Teacher education programmes could also be an enabling factor in this respect, with their ties to pioneers and the wider community of interested educators, and their recent involvement in the maker scene over the last few years, in particular through collaborative research efforts under the banner of the MakEY project. Introductory course units on the subject are bound to facilitate the introduction of making into compulsory school work and other educational settings.

The main barriers found in this study are somewhat harder to define, but an obvious challenge will be to find the institutional support and organisational space needed to maintain viable makerspaces within daily school practice over many years and across the compulsory school system at large. We have presented above a number of different approaches or models that may serve as valuable options for individual schools or communities to follow, but it will take both political and economic efforts, as well as organisational measures at different levels of school governance, to create the professionalism and means needed for the field to flourish in a sustainable way.

Conclusions

All four case studies are different in nature, but they all illuminate different aspects of the model proposed by Jónsdóttir and Macdonald (2013), and adapted by Jónsdóttir and Gunnarsdóttir (2017) to describe the modes of pedagogy underlying IEE.

Emancipatory pedagogy with weak framing and classification (Bernstein, 2000) characterised the mode and approach applied in the summer courses at Innoent. Learners could choose what to work with, which materials to use, the pace, location, social interaction and development of their ideas. The mentors often bent or kneeled down to be on the same level as the learners, sat down on the floor with young participants attending courses or workshops and talked to them like colleagues or collaborators.

The preschool case study applied a progressive pedagogy, where the roles of teachers and learners remained distinct during the initial stages. Communication was open from the outset and boundaries between learners and teachers became more blurred as participants became deeply involved in the activities. The workshops were led by a preschool teacher and her graduate assistant, while the children were offered time and space to explore, experiment and develop their coding skills through play and creative activities. All the children were able do as they pleased in the last sessions of the workshops, playing and creating with devices and materials of their own choice. Free play flourished, classification became weaker and the pedagogical approach thus more emancipatory.

The pedagogy applied in the Minecraft case was characterised by the distinct roles of the teacher and his learners, but also open communication between the participants. The teacher prepared the lesson plans and oversaw the world view of the makerspace, as well as the virtual objects and settings within it. He then introduced mathematical tasks laid out as the lesson began and divided students into groups. He acted in these preparations and the lessons under scrutiny as both a computer administrator and a pedagogical facilitator. The teacher relied on the prior knowledge and experience of his learners of using iPads and Minecraft, acquired both by playing at home and using game-based learning at school. This infused the lessons with a playful learning attitude and inspired action. The teacher gave the learners space to resolve the tasks in a collaborative context, supporting autonomy and self-reliance. The pedagogy applied can be considered progressive and at times emancipatory.

In the Genius Lab, led by one of the women making up the VEXA group, learners had been selected to become experts and disseminators of new technologies at their schools. The learning events were characterised by directive communication between the teacher and her learners, while the teacher was introducing computing and devices, coding kits and software used to complete defined tasks. These events were supported by Internet exploration on mobile phones, a search for tutorials and guidance, sometimes pointed out by the teacher. The pedagogic approach can be defined as transmissive, more often than not characterised by strong framing regarding technical tasks, but weak classification regarding guidelines and instruction. The students were empowered and emancipated by the fact that they were encouraged by their teacher to take on her role and introduce various digital technologies and newly acquired skills to their classmates in regular class sessions, as well as their parents and other students in the schools at educamp events. The overall goal was rooted in an emancipatory pedagogy encouraging students to have more agency in their own learning.

All four case studies point to the rich potential for makerspaces in both formal and non-formal settings for young children's learning and development. So far there have only been a few instances of making as an explicit or integral part of schooling in Iceland, but interest has been growing and appears to involve increasing numbers of teachers around the country. Changing school practice is an extensive process and a demanding challenge involving different elements or forces at work in manifold ways. The desire to blend or merge traditional and digital making was evident in the choice of location used for some of the lab activities described above. This sentiment, however, is not always the case and previous attempts by school authorities to merge digital innovation studies and traditional crafts have suffered setbacks in the past (Macdonald, Hjartarson and Jóhannsdóttir, 2005). It remains to be seen to what extent makerspaces will be integrated into daily school practice and how making will fare in the Icelandic school system over time.

Notes

1 Researcher: Svanborg R. Jónsdóttir.
2 Researchers: Kristín Dýrfjörð, Anna Elísa Hreiðarsdótti and Margrét E. Ólafsdóttir.
3 Researchers: Skúlína Kjartansdóttir and Gísli Thorsteinsson.
4 Researchers: Torfi Hjartarson, Skúlína Kjartansdóttir and Svava Pétursdóttir.
5 *Different numbers of children in different workshops.

References

Bernstein, B. (2000). *Pedagogy, symbolic control and identity* (2nd ed.). Lanham, MD: Rowman & Littlefield Publishers.

Bos, B., Wilder, L., Cook, M. & O'Donnell, R. (2014). iSTEM: Learning mathematics through Minecraft. *Teaching Children Mathematics*, 21(1): 56–59.

Dakers, J. R. (2014). *Defining technical literacy* (2nd ed.). New York: Palgrave Macmillan.

Darling-Hammond, L. (1997). *Doing what matters most: Investing in quality teaching.* New York: National Commission on Teaching & America's Future.

Dýrfjörð, K. (2018). Early childhood education and care in Iceland: The origin, influences, curriculum reforms and possible paths. In S. Garvis, S. Phillipson and H. Harju-Luuk-kainen (eds), *International perspectives on early childhood education and care* (pp. 103–113). London: Routledge. doi:10.4324/9780203730553

Dýrfjörð, K. & Magnúsdóttir, B. R. (2016). Privatization of early childhood education in Iceland. *Research in Comparative and International Education,* 11(1): 80–97. doi:10.1177/1745499916631062

Eisner, E. W. (2002). *The educational imagination: On the design and evaluation of school programs* (3rd ed.). Upper Saddle River, NJ: Prentice Hall.

Georgsdottir, A. S., Lubart, T. & Getz, I. (2003). The role of flexibility in innovation. In L. V. Shavinina (ed.), *The international handbook on innovation* (pp. 80–190). Amsterdam: Elsevier Science.

Heath, C., Hindmarsh, J. & Luff, P. (2010). *Video in qualitative research: Analysing social interaction in everyday life.* London: Sage Publications.

Hennessey, S. & Deaney, R. (2004). Sustainability and evolution of ICT supported classroom practice: Short report to BECTA/DfES. Retrieved from: https://pdfs.semanticscholar.org/cf87/a01df5c95202591a48a0a590f09127b2738a.pdf

Jakobsdóttir, S., Hjartarson, T. & Thórhallsdóttir, B. (2014). Upplýsingatækni í skólastarfi [ICT in school practice]. In G. G. Óskarsdóttir (ed.), *Starfshættir í grunnskólum við upphaf 21. aldar* [School practice in Icelandic compulsory schools at the beginning of the 21st century] (pp. 277–321). Reykjavik: Háskólaútgáfan.

Jónasson, J. T. & Óskarsdóttir, G. (2016). Iceland: Educational structure and development. In T. Sprague (ed.), *Education in non-EU countries in Western and Southern Europe* (pp. 11–36). London: Bloomsbury Academic.

Jónsdóttir, S. R. (2011). The location of innovation education in Icelandic compulsory schools. PhD thesis. University of Iceland, Reykjavik.

Jónsdóttir, S. R. & Gunnarsdóttir, R. (2017). *The road to independence: Emancipatory pedagogy.* Rotterdam: Sense.

Jónsdóttir, S. R. & Macdonald, A. (2013). Settings and pedagogy in innovation education. In L. V. Shavinina (ed.), *The Routledge international handbook of innovation education* (pp. 273–287). London: Routledge.

Jónsdóttir, S. R., Page, T., Thorsteinsson, G. & Nicolescu, A. (2008). An investigation into the development of innovation education as a new subject in secondary school education. *Cognition, Brain, Behavior: An Interdisciplinary Journal,* 12(4): 453–468.

Kangas, M. (2010). Creative and playful learning: Learning through game co-creation and games in a playful learning environment. *Thinking Skills and Creativity,* 5(5): 1–15. doi:10.1016/j.tsc.2009. 11. 001

Kapp, K. (2012). *The gamification of learning and instruction: Game-based methods and strategies for training and education.* San Francisco: Pfeiffer.

Leinonen, T. (2010). *Designing learning tools – methodological insights.* PhD thesis. Aalto University, Helsinki.

Macdonald, A., Hjartarson, þ. & Jóhannsdóttir, þ. (2005). "Við vorum ekki bundin á klafa fortíðarinnar": tilurð og gerð aðalnámskrár í upplýsinga- og tæknimennt ["We were not tied to the burdens of the past": the development of the ICT national curriculum in Iceland]. *Uppeldi og menntun,* 14(2): 71–92.

Martin, W. (2007). *Virtual Learning Environments: Using, choosing and developing your VLE.* Oxford, UK: Routledge.

Ministry of Education, Science and Culture. (2012). *The Icelandic national curriculum guide for preschools*. Reykjavik: Ministry of Education, Science and Culture.

Ministry of Education, Science and Culture. (2014). *The Icelandic national curriculum guide for compulsory schools – with subject areas*. Reykjavik: Ministry of Education Science and Culture.

Molin, G. (2017). The role of the teacher in game-based learning: A review and outlook. In M. Ma & A. Oikonomou (eds.), *Serious games and edutainment applications: Volume II* (pp.649–674). Cham: Springer International Publishing.

Nasciutti, F. M. B., Veresov, N. & de Aragão, A. M. F. (2016). The group as a source of development: Rethinking professional development in a collaborative perspective. *Outlines. Critical Practice Studies*, 17(1): 86–108. Retrieved from: https://tidsskrift.dk/out lines/article/view/24207

Ólafsdóttir, S. M. & Jónsdóttir, S. R. (2016). Nýsköpunarmennt í leikskólastarfi: Hugmyndir barna um hönnun leikskólalóðar [Innovation education in preschool: Children's ideas about redesigning their preschool playground]. *Netla – Veftímarit um uppeldi og menntun*. Retrieved from: http://netla.hi.is/greinar/2016/alm/01_alm_arsrit_2016.pdf

Ólafsson, B. & Thorsteinsson, G. (2009). Design and craft education in Iceland, pedagogical background and development: a literature review. *Design and Technology Education: An International Journal*, 14(2): 10–24. Retrieved from: https://ojs.lboro.ac.uk/DATE/article/view/246

Oliver, K. M. (2016). Professional development considerations for makerspace leaders, part one: Addressing "what?" and "why?". *TechTrends*, 60(2): 160–166. doi:10.1007/s11528-016-0028-5

Oxford Dictionaries. (2018). Oxford: Oxford University Press. Retrieved from: http://oxforddictionaries.com

Passey, D., Rogers, C., Machell, J. & McHugh, G. (2004). *The motivational effect of ICT on pupils*. Lancaster: Department of Educational Research, Lancaster University.

Resnick, M. (2004). Edutainment? No thanks. I prefer playful learning. Retrieved from: https://dam-prod.media.mit.edu/x/files/papers/edutainment.pdf

Rice, J. W. (2007). New media resistance: Barriers to implementation of computer video games in the classroom. *Journal of Educational Multimedia and Hypermedia*, 16(3): 249–261.

Sawyer, R. K. & DeZutter, S. (2009). Distributed creativity: How collective creations emerge from collaboration. *Psychology of Aesthetics, Creativity, and the Arts*, 3(2): 81–92.

Shatz, I. (2015). Using gamification and gaming in order to promote risk taking in the language learning process. In *Proceedings of the 13th annual MEITAL national conference* (pp. 227–232). Haifa, Israel: Inter-University Center for e-Learning.

Sheridan, K. M., Halverson, E. R., Litts, B. K., Brahms, L., Jacobs-Priebe, L. & Owens, T. (2014). Learning in the making: A comparative case study of three makerspaces. *Harvard Educational Review*, 84(4): 505–531. Retrieved from: www.makersempire.com/wp-con tent/uploads/2018/02/Learning-in-the-Making-A-Comparative-Case-Study-of-Three-Makerspaces-Sheridan-14.pdf

Statistics Iceland. (n.d.). Private, public and special compulsory schools 1998–2018. Retrieved from: https://px.hagstofa.is/pxen/pxweb/en/Samfelag/Samfelag__skolamal__2_grunnskolastig__2_gsSkolahald/SKO02202.px/

Thorsteinsson, G. & Ólafsson, B. (2014). Otto Salomon in Nääs and his first Icelandic students in Nordic Sloyd. *History of Education*, 43(1): 31–49. doi:10.1080/0046760X.2013.835451

Weisberg, R. W. (2003). Case studies of innovation: Ordinary thinking, extraordinary outcomes. In L. V. Shavinina (ed.), *The international handbook on innovation* (pp. 204–247). Amsterdam: Elsevier Science.

Whitton, N. (2018). Playful learning: Tools, techniques, and tactics. *Research in Learning Technology*, 26(2035). doi:10.25304/rlt.v26.2035

7

MAKERSPACES IN THE MAKING

Reconfiguring cultures of facilitation across the kindergarten and the science museum

Alfredo Jornet, Hans Christian Arnseth and Ole Smørdal

Introduction

During the past decade, makerspaces have become very popular across the world. In Norway there are currently approximately 60 makerspaces across institutional and non-institutional settings. In these spaces, participants can design and create artefacts and solutions using a whole range of digital and material tools, thereby engaging in creative forms of enquiry-based learning that align well with current progressive education values and principles. In the education literature, the blending of the digital and the physical world, for instance through 3D printing or laser-cutting, and the engagement opportunities such blends bring about, are often emphasized (Blikstein, 2013). Unlike other enquiry-based forms of education, however, makerspaces are inspired by cultural movements that emerged outside of education and which involve, in addition to those enquiry-based qualities, values of democratic empowerment, autonomy and community building (Halverson and Sheridan, 2014). In contrast to learning in formal education, makers have historically been characterized by having agency in deciding what they want to make, shifting their common role as consumers of ready-made products to become producers of their own products and learning. Local manufacturing, repairing and tinkering – which signal both autonomy and creative dimensions – have been an important part of the ethos of the maker movement.

When making is brought into formal institutional settings, what making is, and what it should be, becomes contested. As makerspaces have made their way into diverse educational institutional settings, such as schools, museums and libraries, research has only begun to emerge documenting the challenges and impacts of their implementation in these types of settings (Marsh et al., 2017). Particularly little is known about how maker practices can support young children's creativity and engagement with science and technology topics (Britton, 2012) and how the agency- and community-oriented aspects of maker culture may translate into spaces where young children are the makers. Although we may accept a broad definition of making and argue that making has always been an important part of children's everyday lives, and integral to the practices of early childhood education (Marsh et al., 2017, p.26), we still do not have a clear idea of what changes or reconfigurations makerspaces might bring about in young children's already existing forms of engagement. Moreover, as the boundaries between formal and informal settings become increasingly blurred in modern societies, a question remains as to whether and how makerspaces can transform or reconfigure young children's learning trajectories across diverse learning settings.

In this chapter, we are interested in the issue of agency as a central feature of makerspaces, and the challenges and opportunities that may emerge in that regard when such spaces are designed targeting young learners. Taking a cultural–historical theory perspective, according to which the "inner regulation of purposeful activity originates in external regulation" (Vygotsky and Luria, 1994, p.164), we conceive of children's agency as a developmental manifestation of the ways in which social (including maker) activities are organized, and how these afford distinct forms of autonomous exploration, mastery and engagement. In this regard, research on making in museums and in schools has demonstrated that facilitation is a key issue when accounting for learners' engagement (McCubbins, 2016). A central question in this chapter concerns, therefore, how different cultures of facilitation may afford different forms of agency and engagement in making.

We explore the question above in the context of a research-practice partnership between our university research team, a kindergarten and a science museum. Though seldom the focus of educational research literature on making, such inter-institutional partnerships bring with them tensions and transformational opportunities that are important to consider when designing innovative spaces for learning (Jornet and Jahreie, 2013). Our research on cultures of facilitation and agency thus connects with the issue of learning across contexts, and it brings with it a concern for the ways in which efforts to implement makerspaces come to reconfigure already existing social and cultural facilitation practices. More specifically, we explore how the work of designing and implementing makerspaces elicits new design concepts as well as ways of constructing time–space configurations or *chronotopes* (Bakhtin, 1982; Ritella, Ligorio and Hakkarainen, 2016) as part of which new understandings of what counts as learning emerge through social praxis.

To do so, we take and discuss a *design-based research* approach (Barab and Squire, 2004; Penuel, Cole and O'Neill, 2016). From this perspective, the making of makerspaces becomes itself a site of and for enquiry, where the task of designing and implementing innovative learning environments becomes an opportunity to disrupt, restructure and reconfigure already established norms, routines, values and time–space configurations.

Makerspaces as disruptive spaces

Recently, the education potential of makerspaces has been emphasized and making has become a recurrent way of creating interest in STEM subjects for children and young people in both formal and informal learning settings (Bevan et al., 2016).

Educational research tends to emphasize how makerspaces offer engaging and interesting activities that children find motivating. For instance, makerspaces have been shown to support experiential and constructionist pedagogies, where children can develop their abilities to design and produce things (Shrock, 2014). As a practice and global phenomenon, however, making and makerspaces first emerged outside of institutions, precisely as a way to contest the consumerist established ethos of modern culture and its tendency to undermine autonomy and creativity. It emphasizes agency and auto-determination; it involves community building but also, and at the same time, the subverting of mainstream culture (Dougherty, 2016). Connections between these socio-historical roots and the relevance of making in/for education are often highlighted to emphasize the creative and motivational potential of makerspaces as places for learning and education. But the extent to which it can be assumed that making in educational (formal and informal) settings brings with it some of the qualities that characterized that original social movement is of course an empirical question. There is a risk that the entrepreneurial spirit, creativity and culture of sharing that characterize makerspaces will be "domesticated" when they become part of institutional school-like practices (Dougherty, 2012). Making may be particularly difficult to reconcile with the types of activities tightly structured by curricular goals, procedures and institutional rules that characterize formal schooling, where issues of assessment often come to the fore.

There exists the possibility, however, that rather than simply becoming "domesticated" when educators attempt to implement making, designing makerspaces may work as a *boundary practice* (Wenger, 2000), i.e. as something that might expand, challenge and disrupt established educational practices. Prior research has shown how interdisciplinary, multi-professional collaborations that aim to design novel spaces for learning become contested places in which the very notion of learning and the practices that aim to support it become transformed in and through design work (Jornet and Jahreie, 2013; Jornet and Steier, 2015; Smørdal, Stuedahl and Sem, 2014). In this regard, the idea that makerspaces may act as *disruptive* places that shake up established forms of teaching and learning practice has been advanced in the literature (Blikstein, 2013, p.6). This idea stems from the notion of *innovative disruption*, initially formulated in market research but more recently used in education as a means to theorize ways in which technological and pedagogical innovations work as disruptive devices that – often unintentionally and in unforeseen ways – destabilize established norms and values. As a result, "what were valuable improvements before the disruption now are less relevant. And dimensions… that had been unimportant become highly valued" (Christensen, Horn and Johnson, 2011, p.44).

In studies investigating makerspaces, the idea of disruption has been explored with regard to the social materiality of given technologies such as electronic textiles (Kafai, Fields and Searle, 2014). In this regard, Kafai and colleagues document how "bringing maker activities like e-textiles into schools disrupts the notion of 'right'" (p.535) as well as gendered expectations with regard to engagement with technology. Though not directly using the notion, other ethnographic studies sensitive to makerspaces' cultural-historical dimensions conclude that, in makerspaces, "who can make and who cannot, whose knowledge matters and whose does not, are all a part of making itself' (Barton, Tan and Greenberg, 2017, p.2). Such studies make visible some of the cultural tensions and transformational potential that come into play when makerspaces are implemented as part of educationally oriented projects.

Yet, a significant amount of the design and research literature on making is inspired by constructionist ideas (Papert, 1993), where the focus is on learning and creativity affordances, and where cultural tensions are rarely addressed. With regard to agency and creativity, researchers have been concerned with the development of models that enable us to identify the learning happening in makerspaces. For example, Bevan et al. (2010) identified engagement, initiative and intentionality, social scaffolding and the development of understanding as crucial elements of such a model. Research also demonstrates how previous interests can occasion engagement in making, and explicit orientations to STEM topics by adults can result in more positive attitudes towards STEM (Davis and Mason, 2016). Sheridan et al. (2014) also found that makerspaces could be beneficial for STEM education, because they allow participants to actively seek knowledge they need to complete their tasks. In all cases, how adults (facilitators, educators) and institutional tasks frame activities is highlighted as a relevant, though often unexplored, feature (Barton, Tan and Greenberg, 2017). These studies, therefore, are relevant to our quest to understand how agency and creativity may develop as a function of facilitation practices in makerspaces. However, a problem with constructionist accounts is the lack of orientation to how engagement, learning and facilitation dynamically interact with one another (Arnseth and Krange, 2016).

There is, therefore, a need for studies to document and account for the tensions and potential for cultural transformation that lie at the intersection of established and yet-to-be established practices, and how these tensions play out at different levels, including the personal, the social and the institutional. This need is particularly acute in the case of young learners, where achieving the pedagogical values of autonomy and creative agency recognized in maker cultures may require reconsidering the implicit and explicit assumptions embedded in existing social and cultural forms of facilitation. Moreover, there is a need to adopt methodologies that are suitable to understand not just the educational opportunities that emerge in makerspaces but also the opportunities that emerge for social and institutional change in the making of such spaces. In this study, we explore and exhibit the use of design-based approach methods as a suitable method, where the development of design concepts that emerge as a means to deal with the emerging tensions becomes the analytical focus. Accordingly, our research questions are as follows:

- How does the design and implementation of makerspaces disrupt and reconfigure cultures of facilitation in a multi-disciplinary group of educators at the intersection of the kindergarten and the science museum?
- What design concepts and tools emerge through such reconfiguration?

Spaces in the making: A design-based research approach and its cultural-historical framework

Cultural-historical framework

In this chapter, we pursue a cultural-historical approach to designing and analysing making for young children. A cultural-historical approach shares with social cognitive theory the view that "people are producers as well as products of social systems" (Bandura, 2001, p. 1). Human agency is a function of ways of organizing activities. It distinguishes itself from other frameworks, however, in that it posits a *genetic* relation that unites often-thought-of-as individual psychological features with collective historical, societal objects. This genetic relation becomes the focus of analysis, thereby defining personal motivation as being an emergent function of the collective and historical *motives* that organize cultural contexts of practice (such as the school, the home) (Leontiev, 1977/2009). It is by participating in concrete, action-oriented collective activities that learners develop understanding along with agency and identity, all of which are central to engagement (Lave and Wenger, 1991). From this perspective, learning phenomena are not either individual or social, but rather *cultural-historical objects* that develop in and through human practices. It is therefore possible to address makerspaces as historical objects, and to attempt to understand how these objects develop and transform in and through becoming appropriated by other already existing practices, such as the practice of running educational programmes in science museums or of educating children in kindergartens (the two settings examined in this study).

In relation to making, language and action are interrelated and both contribute to the emergent character of making as a process and product. In contrast, the main idea in constructionist pedagogies is to see these processes as distinct. The process in fact starts with developing and articulating an idea either individually or together with others and then creating an external representation or model of that idea (Kafai, 2006; Kafai and Resnick, 1996). It is in the concrete and material work of pursuing that idea that not only the idea, but also new embodied and conceptual orientations, emerge in the participants, such that the very understanding of the object of the joint activity changes (Jornet and Jahreie, 2013; Jornet and Steier, 2015). In this regard, a cultural-historical framework focuses on the development of practical and discursive cultural resources as a means to deal with emerging tensions and understandings. In the context of design, this involves focusing on the *design concepts* that emerge as members from different backgrounds and with different interests work out ways of achieving a common project and object of activity.

In line with the overall MakEY project approach exhibited throughout this book, one of the main implications of a cultural-historical approach to making and the making of makerspaces is that learning phenomena are investigated as existing across multiple historical levels of analysis. Thus, the changes and conceptual development discussed above do not only involve those learners participating in the designed makerspaces, but also the designers and the very physical and institutional settings as part of which makerspaces are appropriated as a form of pedagogy. As a cultural and historical phenomenon, makerspaces, as they are appropriated in contemporary educational agendas of different institutional contexts, are phenomena that develop at personal, interpersonal and institutional levels. At the personal level, we are concerned with investigating how issues of agency, interest and engagement play out in social interaction. Children's previous participation in practices inside and outside of school, which in many ways is sedimented in their subjectivities, is also made relevant, oriented to and has an impact on present activity (Holland et al., 1998). An interest in the personal level also means that we are interested in the values and beliefs that educators bring to the setting, as actual courses of action, and how they bring about new and projected identities for possible future participation in making. We also focus on the personal meanings children make in these spaces and whether their motivations are facilitated through interacting with educators and through using the tools made available to them in the space.

At the interpersonal level, the focus concerns how issues of creativity and agency are constituted socially and relationally in and through the planning and implementation of a makerspace. This level is often referred to as socio-genesis in sociocultural theorizing. This is where people and tools come together in practices, and it is here that they get their actual sense and function for the participants involved. With regard to tools, a main focus in our study is how participants deal with and formulate design concepts as they tackle emerging tensions and contradictions. Heterogeneity is an integral feature of any social practice. This is also the case for makerspaces, which is a space where multiple ideologies, ideas and interests become visible. The actual outcomes of practices in makerspaces are the result of complex negotiations between the identities and interests of children, of educators and other stakeholders.

The institutional level involves an interest in how institutional practices, where particular historically developed institutional roles and objectives are made relevant, impact on children's creative making in the museum. Our particular interest here relates to how the makerspace is situated in a museum and part of the museum's educational programme. Institutional histories, norms and interests have an impact on how the makerspace is realized in this particular institution. However, the institution is not a stable context for activity; institutions can also be transformed through practices. What is interesting with a design-based methodology is to investigate precisely how and if institutional practices can be changed and transformed and what impacts on change and transformation. In this study, we follow how the work of making a makerspace leads to the development and transformation of ways of conceptualizing and going about facilitation practice.

Design-based approach: Considering the making of makerspaces

The cultural-historical perspective taken has methodological implications that are grounded in the view that one way to understand a social practice is by *changing* it. That is, to understand how agency and creativity emerge as part of the implementation of makerspaces, we need to understand *the making of* makerspaces as purposeful intervention sites, themselves contested sites of creativity and imagination that involve change and disruption of existing forms of institutional organization and social participation. In this regard, a method that considers both the learning spaces designed and their designing as part of a unitary methodological process is design-based research (Barab and Squire, 2004). When approached from a cultural-historical perspective, design-based research methodologies approach learning research objects or phenomena not as merely existing out there to be researched, but also and at the same time as outcomes of purposeful design activity. The objects of learning research, then, are artificial; they are the outcome of human practices, and they are so in a double sense. According to Cole and Packer (2016), "design research must grapple with the *doubly artificial*, as the classrooms in which many educational designs are implemented are themselves already artificial and contingent—the products of design—and the learning that is the focus of investigation is already an adaptation to the classroom environment and so artificial" (p. 503).

A design-based perspective builds upon principles of participatory design in which partnerships are established between researchers, educators and other relevant stakeholders. In design-based research, theory-driven innovative educational environments are designed while experimental studies are simultaneously carried out to assess those innovations. Aspects of the environment are systematically manipulated, in order to observe and understand which practice works best (Barab and Squire, 2004). Typically, this involves iterative cycles of implementing, assessing and refining practice. Outcomes are thus of both theoretical and practical value. With regard to makerspace design and research, designing creative spaces while engaging in active conversation with other stakeholders can allow us to create relational patterns that support new conversations among children and educators. At the same time, designing and implementing makerspaces opens up opportunities for intra- and inter-institutional tensions that become visible when a new historical object emerges that requires different views and takes. Opportunities then open up for developing new design concepts that orient participants towards new forms of praxis.

Data collection methods and participants

This chapter reports on a case study deriving from a participatory research initiative involving a university, a science museum and a kindergarten in Norway, which collaborated to develop and explore design concepts for makerspaces targeting 5–6-year-old children. The research comprised an iterative and cyclical design involving

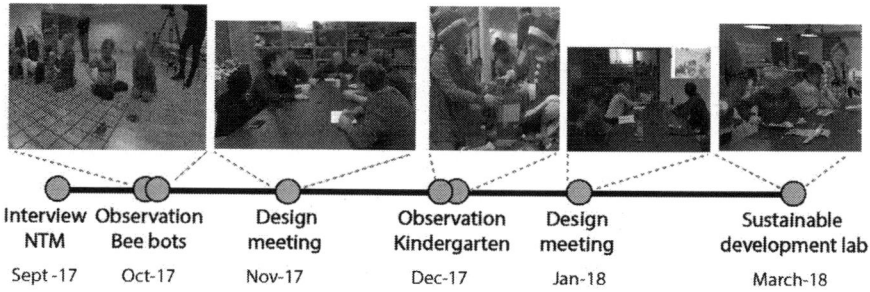

Interview   Observation   Design   Observation   Design   Sustainable
NTM   Bee bots   meeting   Kindergarten   meeting   development lab

Sept-17   Oct-17   Nov-17   Dec-17   Jan-18   March-18

FIGURE 7.1 Data collection milestones along the iterative design process

several data collection points, including initial ethnographic observations of children playing in their kindergarten and during existing activities at the museum. These observations and knowledge from prior experiences in both settings became input to exploratory design meetings where the goal was to design a making activity. Using a cultural-historical approach, we identified design *bridging concepts* and analysed the ways in which the socio-material conditions surrounding the design and implementation of the resulting activity supported and/or hindered opportunities for agency and creativity.

To analyse and develop cultures of creative making in and across the science museum and the kindergarten, from our design-based perspective we were mindful to follow a participatory design approach (Bang and Vossoughi, 2016). This would ensure that the research problems were grounded in the participants' interests and concerns. Although our efforts were inspired by design-based research, unlike typical studies within this tradition, we did not explicitly aim to test and develop specific design principles. Rather, the iterations were the result of negotiations of these interests and constituted an attempt to put them into practice. We focus on the challenges and opportunities when collaborating with practitioners, and how museums can facilitate creative making activities for young children. We also provide descriptions on a more institutional level concerning how making can be constituted very differently within the two settings, but also how connections between the settings can be made in regard to children's experiences with making activities. We analyse more in detail the different ways that practitioners support children's making and how the characteristics of their support influence the development of children's creative processes and practices.

Participants included (a) a team of researchers, including five educational researchers with different experience and focus but sharing a concern with the design and understanding of technology-enhanced spaces for learning; (b) a team of three museum curators and educators who have a specific responsibility for developing science enquiry experiences for young children in the science museum; (c) and four kindergarten educators from a kindergarten in the Oslo area, along with a group of 20 kindergarten children between 5 and 6 years old. The kindergarten was located close to the museum, which is situated in a typical middle-class area. We recruited the kindergarten through the museum. They had already signed up for an activity and we contacted them and asked if they would let us observe them when they visited the museum. All but one of the children assented to participating in the project.

Since September 2017, the participatory design process has involved design meetings, as well as observations in the science museum and the kindergarten. In addition, we have conducted interviews with museum and kindergarten educators during the process. All of the above were recorded using traditional zoom-lens cameras, as well as wide-angle action cameras, to ensure adequately capturing embodied interaction in both the design and the designed spaces. Data collection milestones during this process are detailed in Figure 7.1. We started by observing an existing activity in the museum. Then, we arranged a design meeting with museum staff where the goal was to design a making activity. After that, we observed children involved in arts-based activities in the kindergarten, in order to document the participants' native "maker-like" competences. Finally, we observed children engaging in a new making activity in the museum. As part of our participatory research, we held three exploratory design meetings with partners in the project.

Building on the insights gained and observations made, we developed an activity where we aimed to foster children's creative making in relation to the issue of sustainable development. Based on a series of workshops in which we collected data and created concepts for designs, we ran an intervention in March 2018. Taken together, the data collection comprised five workshops.

Case study: Making a makerspace for kindergarten children in the science museum

In the sections below, we summarize the results of our ethnographic observations and interviews documenting the process of designing and implementing a makerspace at a science museum targeting kindergarten visits. We show how, through a process of confronting the task of developing a makerspace activity for young children, established but otherwise tacit assumptions about and the practice of facilitating children's agency and creativity become visible, workable and contested. Tensions and disruptions become visible in actual interactions between adults, as they discuss and formulate challenges and possible solutions, but also between adults and children during the implementation of actual facilitation practices. When, through the iterative design process, adults reflect back on their experiences, a transition from the personal to the interpersonal (relational) takes place. A change in the design concepts then becomes a means to deal with the emerging tensions on the interpersonal plane, orienting participants towards new horizons of (pedagogical) activity.

We present the development trajectory described above in terms of a summary narrative that intertwines three levels of analysis (personal, social, institutional). The narrative approaches the emergent object of design, i.e. the yet-to-be makerspace, as a transforming object that changes and is changed by the social relations involved in its making (hence the chapter title *Makerspaces in the Making*). More specifically, as the work of designing a makerspace for young children in the science museum unfolds, tensions and contradictions emerge with regard to a practical and sensuous aspect of facilitating agency and creativity in making for young children. These tensions manifest in the participants' struggles to find a balance between providing the children with enough *structure* while at the same time providing them with an open frame allowing them to gain agency and develop a creative stance.

A need/motive emerges

As a historical and global object, makerspaces have grown in popularity in recent years. In Norway, too, makerspaces have become more popular and are being increasingly planned and implemented as part of diverse public cultural spaces, such as libraries and museums. The Museum of Science and Technology (NTM in Norwegian abbreviation) in particular has been a leading actor in this regard, having organized and hosted the first Maker Fair in Norway, as well as having established a dedicated makerspace in the museum. At the weekend, the space is open to visitors of all ages, but on weekdays and during special events, the makerspace is most often offered and reserved for older children and adults. At the moment our research began, there were no activities offered for children of kindergarten age.

An interest in makerspaces has simultaneously grown in educational research, as reviewed in previous sections. As an academic area of interest, this focus does not only manifest in the increasing number of research articles published about the topic, but also in the stimulation of research-practice partnerships where makerspaces acquire new meaning not only as sites for learners' experimentation but also for experiments concerning the pedagogical (teaching-learning) potentials embedded in such spaces. The MakEY project is but another manifestation of this interest as it concerns extending research into the early years. And it is as part of this experimental concern and orientation that we, a group of educational researchers from the University of Oslo, approached NTM to learn about and discuss their approach.

Facilitation emerges as a challenge/focal concern

A challenge concerning facilitation emerged as a central challenge and focal concern of the research-practice partnership very early in the trajectory. Thus, during an initial meeting/interview with Carl (pseudonym) – one of the museum curators in charge of the museum's educational programmes – as the researchers (Jan and Audun) were articulating "their" interest in exploring maker-like activities, the issue of facilitation emerged as a key factor in achieving a common understanding of the emerging task.

Fragment 1

01   CARL: but were you thinking that you would like to test out a set-up that is already offered or more like a free…

02   JAN: perhaps a bit free, yes,

03   CARL: but which is not organized?

04   JAN: no. It needs to be facilitated in one or other way, be supported.
05   CARL: uhum.

In Fragment 1, we observe how a turn (01) seeking to clarify whether what had been said before about the researchers' goals involved testing something "like a free…". We do not hear the speaker fully articulate the statement, but Jan, one of the researchers confirms that this is "a bit free", possibly as opposed to a set-up that is already organized as part of the museum's offer. Yet, Carl requests further clarification, "but which is not organized?" to which Jan responds in the negative, arguing that "it needs to be facilitated" (turn 03).

In this exchange, facilitation is jointly articulated as a key feature that requires repair and clarification work during the initial work of establishing a common project. Throughout this and further conversations, there is a need to address to what extent and in which ways the target maker activity should be facilitated, particularly given the group's age. Soon after, during the same conversation, the curator clarifies that they "do not currently offer something in the makerspace, as far as I know, for that age group" (Interview, September 2017). The conversation moves on to discuss which age group is the lowest for which activities in the makerspace are offered (grades 4–5), and the type of activities that are indeed offered to younger children. The question of facilitation is thereby taken up again, but becomes further elaborated as one involving a challenge to find an adequate balance between providing young visitors with enough structure, while at the same time giving them enough freedom and agency to pursue their own goals and creativity. Carl mentions a particular activity (Strawbees[1]) that had recently been re-designed precisely to address this challenge:

> …the reason that it was re-made was that you had a completely free set-up that did not work so well, because children became frustrated. They did not know what they should do… such that they faded out or just sat there cutting straw without any goal…
>
> *(Interview 1, 27 September)*

The concern Carl articulates characterizes not only issues the museum deals with, but is also shared among most studies on learner-centred, progressive pedagogies. When Carl articulates it as part of a conversational repair, this is immediately taken up by the researchers, who clearly are sensitive to and familiar with the issue. The tension between structure and freedom, guidance and self-direction, is also a concern present in creativity research, where the question of whether and to what extent structure and constraints enable or hinder creativity has long been posed (Sawyer, 2012).

In the context of our research, this concern – with historical roots outside our research project and the specific settings involved – increasingly becomes a need and a motive in the sense that, for the shared object to evolve, the issue of facilitation needs to be addressed. The very idea of having a makerspace activity for young children begins to be built around a definition of whether and to what extent a maker activity is supported, and how. As we shall see, it is through developing discourse and tools in order to deal with this concern that the work of designing a makerspace becomes disruptive and leads to the possibility of (personal, social, institutional) change.

Making in the kindergarten and in the science museum: Different chronotopes and cultures of facilitation

As part of our participatory design-based approach, we enlisted as active partners a kindergarten that had already signed up to join one of the educational activities in the museum offered to kindergartens. As described in the methods section, following a group of children and educators from this kindergarten allowed us to document already existing practices in both the science museum and the kindergarten. Such observations allowed us to characterize the different settings involved.

One way to characterize the agency and creativity facilitation practices in the museum and in the kindergarten is by describing how these are organized differently in terms of time and space orientations or *chronotopes* (Arnseth, Silseth and Hanghøj, 2019; Ritella, Ligorio and Hakkarainen, 2016). In this regard, the organization of time and space in the kindergarten may be best described as being somewhat circular in that activities tend not to be limited by time – any creative activity can go on for a long time and may always be continued the day after – and by space – where kindergarten spaces are places to be in for children, not just to visit or pass through. It is the daily routines that provide rhythm and structure to practices, and not an orientation towards given outcomes. It is a place where they are gradually gaining agency and developing ways of being in the world throughout a broad spectrum of skills, including everyday conduct skills, but also intellectual, literacy and artistic competences.

Most relevant to our focus on making, when children engage in creative making in the kindergarten, there appears to be no rush to create a final product, nor is there any prominent orientation towards that product. The social organization of activities and the facilitation that goes into them is not oriented towards making *something*, but towards the *making* itself. In this sense, the kindergarten exhibits what in the design and creativity literature has been referred to as an *intransitive* approach to making (Jornet and Roth, 2018). The latter approach emphasizes the fluid, processual nature that verbs such as to make, to draw or to read mark when they do not have a grammatical object. Thus, when a verb like "to make" takes a transitive form, it always brings an object with it: "I make *this thing*" or "I read *this book*". In the intransitive form, there is no object and all the emphasis goes into the verb. "I *make*" or "I *read*" then become ends in and of themselves as form-giving processes.

We observed the latter orientation in every creative activity in the kindergarten, including an artistic painting activity that had been offered as an option along with three other possibilities (playing with play dough, playing with Lego bricks,

FIGURES 7.2 and 7.3 Children painting in the kindergarten. At the top, children begin with a blank canvas; the lower image shows the same activity a little later, most children having painted a Christmas tree.

composing stories on a digital tablet). Only those children who chose painting joined the drawing table, suggesting a quite open form of agency in which children are led into an environment in which they are supported to feel safe and confident and are invited to make choices with respect to the types of activities that they want to engage in. Once they had gathered, they were given a blank canvas and

FIGURE 7.4 Two kindergarten girls building a tower with blocks

the instruction: "We will now paint something having to do with Christmas" (Kindergarten Educator, December 2017). Fragment 2 illustrates the ensuing conversation.

Fragment 2

CHILD 1: reindeer?
TEACHER: if you want to paint a reindeer you can paint a reindeer,
CHILD 2: or nissen[2]?
TEACHER: or nissen.
CHILD 3: or Santa's hat,
TEACHER: or Santa's hat,
CHILD 1: or a Christmas tree,
TEACHER: or a Christmas tree

FIGURE 7.5 Bee Bot activity at the science museum
The floor has been enhanced with a grid to structure the children's activity of counting

CHILD 1: I will paint a Christmas tree…
TEACHER: but we will paint something having to do with Christmas, so perhaps you will choose yourself what to paint.

Fragment 2 displays a form of facilitation in which an overall goal is given, namely painting something "having to do with Christmas", as it is that time of the year. They are given a clear, yet broad enough frame as part of which the children are able to suggest a diversity of motives. For each suggestion, the teacher simply repeats the child's suggestion and then restates the general frame, i.e. that it must be something to do with Christmas. Interestingly enough, although the children come up with a diversity of suggestions, as the paintings begin to take form, we can see that all but one child ends up painting the same motif (a Christmas tree). Yet, the fact does not become an issue during the session, and a new canvas is provided after each child is done, so that further works can be produced (Figures 7.2 and 7.3).

The interaction above nicely illustrates how practices of making and facilitation that are present in the kindergarten focus on the doing of things as opportunities for gradually building agency in and through making, such that this and other aspects of social competence grow while making. This orientation to making in the intransitive form is also illustrated in Figure 7.4, where two children spend a substantial part of the morning building a tower together, one that grows indefinitely, without limit, until the children somehow randomly decide it is tall enough.

Rather than working with an "end in mind", it seemed that simply working, letting the emergent sensuous activity lead without an end in mind, was at stake.

By contrast, the types of activities in which young children engage in the museum as part of visiting groups are very different. The motive or object in the centre as an activity system is to provide young people with engaging and fun experiences of science, offering a variety of materials and installations, the value of which is that they are not accessible in other educational and/or everyday settings. Again, describing the type of chronotype involved helps. The organization of time and space in the museum, because of constraints inherent to the nature of the activities, is very structured. Museums need to accommodate given numbers and diversity of visitors, and they need to schedule activities and projects accordingly. Groups of students visit for short periods of time and follow tightly scheduled activities, which are supported by the museum educators.

One example of such scheduled activity for young children is a Bee Bot[3] based activity in which children learn to program a bot such that it moves through space to reach a target, often a toy flower. This activity can be done on any surface, and the bot constraints consist of a set of fixed front, back, right or left movements that can be programmed in advance by pressing the bot's control buttons. In many ways this is a toy-based version of Semour Papert's "Logo Turtle". The aim is for children to learn computational thinking. In the museum activity targeting children, the task has been further structured by inscribing a grid on the floor (Figure 7.5). Each square in the grid has been marked out as the length of each move that the Bee Bot makes. This makes it easier for the children to keep track of how many steps. In addition, adults (kindergarten teachers and museum educators) are present to further facilitate the children's task.

As the description above suggests, the form of facilitation here is tightly organized to ensure that an end goal is reached, here getting the Bee Bot to reach the flower and avoid obstacles in its way. The task requires an intensive structure for various reasons connected to the young age of the participants, including the fact that some of the literacies required are still being learned, but also the fact that the frames for participation and goals are very unlike those in the kindergarten, and they need to be built quickly within the short timeframe of the visit. One of the kindergarten educators noted this gap in an interview following the activity:

> [in situations like Bee Bots,] you can see that there is great diversity… some get it very quickly and some don't really understand. A bit more of time would help… It is when the kids have got some time to master something that they begin to be creative.
>
> (Interview with Kindergarten Educator, October 2017)

Although clearly hands-on and engaging, the creative and agency-related qualities of making are here absent. The goal was not creative making but to learn to solve a very procedural task. Thus, the structural set-up of the activity and the task did not require any creativity on the part of the children. They only needed to infer the

FIGURE 7.6 Educational researchers and museum educators during Workshop II, where images and observations from the kindergarten were displayed and discussed

relation between the grid and the buttons they needed to push on the Bee Bot. In a sense this was a very instructional task, one characteristic of school practices but with which the children from the kindergarten were not necessarily very familiar. As we collaborated with the museum, the joint goal of designing a maker activity was still one where the structuring frames would allow the children to participate meaningfully while also supporting creative and agency engagement.

Jointly defining a makerspace (between the kindergarten and the museum)

Once we established the initial shared goal of exploring possible set-ups for maker-like activities at the museum targeting young children, we arranged a series of design meetings as part of our participatory design-based approach. In a first meeting (November 2017), initial ideas around and difficulties with defining what a makerspace is and what it may look like when it comes to engaging young children was at the centre. It is in that sense interesting to explore how maker-spaces, as historical objects, make their way into other settings and historical purposes through joint collaboration.

One of the things that characterize the maker movement as part of which makerspaces emerged as promising arenas for formal and informal education is the fact that ordinary people, indeed anyone, may become an agent and builder of her own products, hence leading to less consumerist and more democratic forms of production and consumption. The fact that something is produced is important. In the context of our design-based research, this historical aspect of makerspaces as a societal form of organization manifested as the participants began formulating what a makerspace may mean as a space for learning in science museums.

The interdisciplinary group (three educational researchers, two museum curators/educators and a museum technician) was in the midst of discussing to what extent technological and digital components were desired or required as a feature, with arguments being raised that low-tech solutions might be more solid and retain just as much pedagogical value (Figure 7.6). At that point, the question was raised, "What would be the required criteria for this to be a makerspace activity?" (researcher, WP1). The curators then began formulating what a space or activity should include to be a makerspace. Summarizing here, the group jointly articulated that, "Something must be created", "which they [the visitors] can take home", and "must be open-ended to some extent". Moreover, the object produced must be "something you think gives you something positive" that "has a value". The idea that the activity needs to include some electronic or digital element, on the other hand, was discarded as a criterion. And as the group kept discussing these ideas, it became more difficult to discern how what goes on in kindergartens could not also be considered a form of making. This was before we had conducted observations at the kindergarten, and it was then agreed that we needed to get to better understand creativity and agency practices at the kindergarten.

Observations from the kindergarten were shared and discussed during the second design meeting.[4] Among other cases, the painting example discussed above was taken up in the meeting. A positioning emerged in which the fact that the children had ended up painting the same image despite having been given the space and agency to choose – an issue that was never marked as problematic at the kindergarten – came to be seen from a deficit perspective: there had not been more creativity because the frame the kindergarten educator had given was too broad. A possibility for more clearly differentiating between the type of "making" that goes on in kindergartens and the type of making that the museum could offer began to be articulated around the idea of further stimulating creativity in the sense of a diversity of unique products (i.e. as opposed to almost everyone painting the same thing).

Constraints for creativity as a design concept

As discussed above, during the second design meeting, the need to address the tension between structure and freedom that had already emerged as a focal concern in the first interview began to be intertwined with the task of defining what a makerspace activity for children in the museum might look like. If earlier on during the design trajectory there had been doubts about the extent to which kindergartens were themselves makerspaces, now the role and place of the envisioned makerspace activity for children in the science museum began to be formulated precisely by articulating how the planned activity could offer an alternative way of facilitating the creative process.

Against this background, the museum educators recalled and presented during the meeting an activity called (in Norwegian) "Kreativt Klimaverksted" (Sustainable Development Lab). The idea was based on the fact that makerspaces generate lots of rubbish, and this rubbish could be re-used as material for other making activities. In those activities, recycled materials could be used as a means to address environmental issues (hence thematic sustainability). The activity was particularly interesting and pertinent for the ongoing conversation for, unlike a blank canvas that may end up serving to paint the same Christmas tree, using bits and pieces from a trash bin made it virtually impossible for two children to create the same thing, for each bit and piece is uniquely different. Furthermore, and also in line with what the discussions had been revolving around, the activity had been designed to stimulate creativity by forcing participants to choose two words (a noun and a verb) laser-printed over small wooden planks. Children would then use those combinations of verbs/nouns randomly put together (e.g. work, store) as "constraints" (curator, design meeting II).

The notion of *constraints for creativity* was quickly taken up and functioned as a bridging concept to address the tensions between the need to offer open and exploratory opportunities and scaffolding young children's participation in making. Considering the age group that was the target, participants quickly agreed that there would be a need to adjust the activity for kindergarten visitors. One idea was to use pictures instead of words, in case some of the participants could not yet read, as a means "to scale down" the activity for the target age. The materials for the activity were generated during the following weeks, including pictures as stimuli[5] for ideas and creativity. One stack of cards contained pictures related to pollution and the environment, while another contained pictures of things like tractors, bulldozers, policemen or nurses. The children could combine pictures from each stack and use them as inspiration to come up with new, creative solutions. As a task, the children would be given the mission to create an invention that would address the issue of sustainable development.

Refining the concepts, reconfiguring the spaces

The scaled down "Sustainable Development Lab" was tested out with the same kindergarten students that had been followed throughout the design trajectory. The task was run twice as the children were divided into two main groups. Students were first introduced to the problem or challenge – inventing something to collect plastic from the sea – in plenum, and then, in smaller groups, they were given the chance to choose images as stimuli for ideas. Then they would get a box with trash, scissors and glue and, helped by an adult in each group, they went into making things – boats, machines etc. – that would help to clean up plastic from the sea.

After the hands-on activities, museum staff, researchers and kindergarten educators got the chance to reflect back and further develop the emerging concepts and ideas. Overall, the experience had been positive for everyone, including the children who built artefacts and had fun. But there were some difficulties too. A consensus among the museum educators and kindergarten educators was that the pictures as "constraints for creativity" had not worked as planned: "...the pictures, I don't think they understood what they were... how should one put them together", "they were concerned with getting a picture... not about listening to what was coming… as soon as [they get the pictures] they disconnect from what is being said" (Kindergarten Educator, March 2018). There were complaints that these were too abstract. The museum staff specifically were concerned that, in addition, there was a constant need to facilitate the activity; the children needed guidance or else were off-task, a situation that may be unrealistic with respect to the museum's resources during normal operation.

Throughout the evaluation, new opportunities emerged to re-conceptualize the goals and ideas that had been developed so far, including the concept of "constraints for creativity". These opportunities came up along with personal experiences confronting the very historical objects that had been the object of the design work all along: the challenges of facilitation and of finding a balance between structure and freedom. One museum curator expressed having felt that the situation was "very difficult" and that on several occasion he sensed how "the children just wanted to experiment with how they could use this straw and things like that" but he also felt this might destroy the activity flow. He wondered "whether it was the children's creativity or the adults' leading that becomes visible through the children's work" (Museum Curator, March 2018). A more decided reflection came from the kindergarten teacher, who argued:

> It is the creative process that is important, it is not the product that is impor-tant… so it is us, the adults, who have the biggest problem. Because we want it to become something… The process, it is then when they have fun. They forgot before they came out of there that there was something they had made.
> *(Kindergarten Teacher, March 2018)*

Apparent in the reflections is a sense that formulating the concept of "constraints for creativity" in terms of pictures as stimuli was too narrow a formulation, and that further work was need to elaborate on the concept, as that work could further transform the personal and institutional experiences and relations of the members involved, including those of the children.

Discussion and concluding remarks

In this chapter, we have exhibited a design-based perspective as a means to address the disruptive and transformational character of makerspaces targeting agency and creativity in young children as this develops across different levels of analysis (per-sonal, interpersonal and institutional levels). We have shown how tensions and opportunities for change that are brought about by the actual design and imple-mentation of makerspaces across diverse institutional settings can be understood as historical tensions that unfold across multiple levels. By making these tensions and the emerging concepts that participants generate to deal with them the focus of our analyses, our findings contribute to the literature on makerspaces as generative places for pedagogical innovation, and not as ready-made teaching solutions that can unproblematically be appropriated in formal educational contexts.

We have argued that to explore how makerspaces can offer new learning experiences for children and the mechanisms that facilitate the development of children's digital literacies and creativity, it is not enough to look at how different designs lead to different learning experiences. Whereas much of the existing literature on makerspaces in/for learning has focused on constructivist/constructionist premises and has been limited to looking at the learning happening or failing to happen in designed environments, research also suggests the need to approach makerspaces as sites of cultural disruption by means of which established values and meaning-making practices can be challenged and potentially transformed (Blikstein, 2013). Therefore, it is also critical to examine and explore pedagogies and forms of social organization that can enable us to develop children's digital literacies, and how these pedagogies build upon institutionally supported frameworks. Understanding how agency and creativity may develop as a function of facilitation practices in makerspaces, therefore, requires not only looking at already established activities, but also at the process of *making* those activities actually happen.

In our study we have taken a cultural-historical approach to account for the way makerspaces are making their way into education, and how these intertwining contexts for learning are reconfiguring each other in and through personal and interpersonal experiences, which are, in turn, mediated or facilitated by given institutional practices. But our study also shows how these very institutional practices, in turn, also change. Historical tensions and contradictions become transformative forces as they, as historical practices, are appropriated in new contexts is through the concrete labour in which members engage to make sense and develop concepts and tools to address the newly emerging conditions that this very work creates. In this study, we have exhibited how ways of conceptualizing "making" with respect to both established and emerging facilitation practices have been transformed in and through the work of design. Specifically, we have described how the concept of *constraints for creativity* emerged and how its meaning changed throughout the collaborative design trajectory. We have also shown how different cultures of facilitation can be best characterized with respect to how the notion of an object or end-product is approached as an orienting feature in actual interactions.

One of the main features of the approach exhibited here consists of a multi-level approach to learning and change. We have through our analyses shown how the aforementioned tensions manifest not only as abstract concepts but also as particular, individual ways of experiencing at the personal level (e.g. feeling tension between the need to give guidance towards producing a thing and the need to let children enjoy the creative process), while the same tensions also exist at the societal level (Engeström and Sannino, 2011). Connected to this, a general issue that emerged across the different phases in our data collection was the need for connecting constraints with children's experiences. In many ways this is a critical dilemma for educators working with children in makerspaces, that is to say, the need for structure and support while maintaining children's agency and sustained interest in making. Furthermore, it is a challenge to balance these concerns with institutional constraints.

We have explored models of making where we have built on arts and design-based play in kindergarten and from that introduced particular materials and tools for facilitating creative making. As we have demonstrated, whether such materials and tools become part of creative making processes is very much dependent on the guidance and facilitation of adults, but these very practices are also part of the "makerspaces" phenomenon and need to be understood as concrete, historical processes inherent to the learning phenomena of interest. In this chapter, we have reported findings from an investigation into what making might be for very young children, thus adding to existing *repertoires of practice* (Gutiérrez and Rogoff, 2003). Our findings most clearly show that maker practices, as these have developed in informal spaces through interest-driven activities, hold promise for disrupting and changing formal educational practices, but making change on a larger scale requires systematic work over time.

Notes

1 Trade Mark: https://strawbees.com/about-us/
2 Wikipedia defines a "Nissen" as a "mythological creature from Nordic folklore today typically associated with the winter solstice and the Christmas season".
3 Bee Bot is a trade mark: www.bee-bot.us
4 Three educational researchers and two museum educators participated in that meeting. A teacher from the kindergarten who had been invited and had agreed to participate could not come in the end.
5 Readers familiar with cultural-historical theory may recognize an inspiration in Vygotsky's theory of double stimulation (Vygotsky, 1978). In the classical formulation, a second stimulus is introduced into an activity and this can function as a mediation device for the relation between the first stimulus and the object of the activity. Providing apparently unrelated stimuli is also a stimulating technique well known in the literature on creativity (Sawyer, 2012).

References

Arnseth, H. C. & Krange, I. (2016). What happens when you push the button? Analyzing the functional dynamics of concept development in computer supported science inquiry. *International Journal of Computer-Supported Collaborative Learning*, 11(4): 479–502.
Arnseth, H. C., Silseth, K. & Hanghøj, T. (2019). Time-space configuration and experiences of continuity and transformation across formal and informal sites for learning. Manuscript in preparation.
Bakhtin, M. M. (1981). *The dialogic imagination. Four essays.* Austin, TX: University of Texas Press.
Bandura, A. (2001). Social cognitive theory: An agentic perspective. *Annual Review of Psychology*, 52, 1–26.
Bang, M. & Vossoughi, S. (2016). Participatory design research and educational justice: Studying learning and relations within social change making. *Cognition & Instruction*, 34(3), 173–193.
Barab, S. & Squire, K. (2004). Design-based research: Putting a stake in the ground. *Journal of the Learning Sciences*, 13(1): 1–14.
Barton, A. C., Tan, E. & Greenberg, D. (2017). The makerspace movement: Sites of possibilities for equitable opportunities to engage underrepresented youth in STEM. *Teachers College Record*, 119(7): 1–44.

Bevan, B., Ryoo, J. J., Shea, M., Kekelis, L., Pooler, P., Green, E., … & Hernandez, M. (2016). *Making as a strategy for afterschool STEM learning: Report from the Californian tinkering afterschool network research-practice partnership.* San Francisco, CA: The Exploratorium.

Blikstein, P. (2013). Digital fabrication and 'making' in education: The democratization of invention. In: J. Walter-Herrmann & C. Büching (eds), *FabLab: Of machines, makers and inventors* (pp. 203–222). Bielefeld, DE: Transcript Publishers.

Britton, L. (2012). *The makings of maker spaces.* Retrieved from: www.thedigitalshift.com/2012/10/public-services/the-makings-of-maker-spaces

Christensen, C. M., Horn, M. B. & Johnson, C. W. (2011). *Disrupting class. How disruptive innovation will change the way the world learns.* New York, NY: McGraw-Hill.

Cole, M. & Packer, M. (2016). Design-based intervention research as the science of the doubly artificial. *Journal of the Learning Sciences,* 25: 503–530.

Davis, D. & Mason, L. L. (2016). Behavioral phenomenological inquiry of maker identity. *Behavior Analysis: Research and Practice,* Advance online publication. Retrieved from: doi:10.1037/bar0000060

Dougherty, D. (2012). The maker movement. *Innovations,* 7(3): 11–14. doi:10.1162/INOV_a_00135

Dougherty, D. (2016). *Free to make. How the maker movement is changing our schools, our jobs, and our minds.* Berkeley, CA: North Atlantic Books.

Engeström, Y. & Sannino, A. (2011). Discursive manifestations of contradictions in organization change efforts. *Journal of Organizational Change Management,* 24(3): 368–387.

Gutiérrez, K. & Rogoff, B. (2003). Cultural ways of learning: Individual traits or repertoires of practice. *Educational Researcher,* 32(5): 19–25.

Halverson, E. R. & Sheridan, K. M. (2014). The maker movement in education. *Harvard Educational Review,* 84(4): 495–505.

Holland, D., Lachicotte, W., Skinner, D. & Cain, C. (1998). *Identity and agency in cultural worlds.* Cambridge, MA: Harvard University Press.

Jornet, A. & Jahreie, C. F. (2013). Designing for hybrid learning environments in a science museum: Inter-professional conceptualisations of space. In: M. Childs & A. Peachey (eds), *Understanding learning in virtual worlds* (pp. 41–63). London: Springer.

Jornet, A. & Roth, W.-M. (2018). Imagining design: Transitive and intransitive dimensions. *Design Studies,* 56: 28–53.

Jornet, A. & Steier, R. (2015). The matter of space: Bodily performances and the emergence of boundary objects during multidisciplinary design meetings. *Mind, Culture, and Activity,* 22(2): 129–151.

Kafai, Y. B. (2006). Playing and making games for learning: Instructionist and constructionist perspective for game studies. *Games and Culture,* 1: 36–40.

Kafai, Y. B. & Resnick, M. (eds) (1996). *Constructionism in practice: Designing, thinking, and learning in a digital world.* London: Routledge.

Kafai, Y. B., Fields, D. A., & Searle, K. A. (2014). Electronic textiles as disruptive designs: Supporting and challenging maker activities in schools. *Harvard Educational Review,* 84(4): 532–556.

Lave, J. & Wenger, E. (1991). *Situated learning: Legitimate peripheral participation.* Cambridge, UK: Cambridge University Press.

Leontiev, A. N. (2009). *Activity and consciousness.* Pacifica, CA: Marxists Internet Archive. First published in 1977.

Marsh, J., Kumpulainen, K., Nisha, B., Velicu, A., Blum-Ross, A., … Thorsteinsson, G. (2017). *Makerspaces in the early years: A literature review.* Sheffield: University of Sheffield, Makey Project.

McCubbins, S. (2016). *Using a visitor based framework to observe engagement in a children's museum makerspace*. (Doctoral dissertation), Illinois State University.

Papert, S. (1993). *The children's machine: Rethinking school in the age of the computer*. New York, NY: Basic Books.

Penuel, W. R., Cole, M. & O'Neill, K. (2016). Introduction to the special issue. *Journal of the Learning Sciences*, 25: 487–496.

Ritella, G., Liborio, M. B. & Hakkarainen, K. (2016). Theorizing space-time relations in education. *Frontline Learning Research*, 4: 48–55.

Sawyer, K. R. (2012). *Explaining creativity: The science of human innovation*. Oxford, UK: Oxford University Press.

Sheridan, K. M., Halverson, E. R., Litts, B. K., Jacobs-Priebe, L. & Owens, T. (2014). Learning in the making: A comparative case study of three makerspaces. *Harvard Educational Review*, 84, 505–531.

Shrock, A. R. (2014). "Education in disguise": Culture of a hacker and maker space. *Inter-Actions: UCLA Journal of Education and Information Studies*, 10(1). Retrieved from https://escholarship.org/uc/item/0js1n1qg

Smørdal, O., Stuedahl, D. & Sem, I. (2014). Experimental zones: Two cases of exploring frames of participation in a dialogic museum. *Digital Creativity*, 25(2): 224–232.

Vygotsky, L. S. (1978). *Mind in society: The development of higher psychological processes*. Cambridge, MA: Harvard University Press.

Vygotsky, L. S. & Luria, A. R. (1994). Tool and symbol in child development. In: R. van der Veer & J. Valsiner (eds), *The Vygotsky reader* (pp. 99–174). Cambridge, MA: Blackwell.

Wenger, E. (2000). Communities of practice and social learning systems. *Organization*, 7(2): 225–246.

8

TYPES OF ENGAGEMENT IN MAKERSPACES

Anca Velicu and Monica Mitarcă

The introduction of makerspaces to Romanian schools is still at an early stage. To date, we have identified only a few such initiatives that have openly assumed the name of *makerspace*, and these are in their infancy. For example, Babel Makerspace, organised in a private school in Timişoara, opened in the summer of 2018;[1] it values hands-on activities and the way in which foreign languages can be learned through makerspace-induced social interaction. Some others, to be opened in state and private schools in autumn 2018, according to the association that provides them with the necessarily tools (in the form of a kit) for building a makerspace,[2] are more inclined towards digital fabrication, robotics and coding activities, preparing children for Industry 4.0 (Velicu and Mitarcă, in press).

Nonetheless, in a survey conducted for the MakEY project (Lahmar et al., 2017), some Romanian teachers reported being involved in activities that are specific to these spaces (most of them as part of art projects) or having a pedagogical approach resembling that of a makerspace; likewise, robotics courses are being organised in some schools, in general paid for by parents (Velicu and Mitarcă, in press). Moreover, when arguing for the need to implement makerspaces in schools (especially for young children under 8 years old), both Romanian respondents to the MakEY survey, and staff from makerspaces with whom we conducted interviews during the project, mentioned schools' excessive focus on a theoretical and abstract approach to teaching being the biggest challenge of the Romanian educational system, especially true for science education. To the best of our knowledge, there are no available statistics or studies describing Romanian young children's attitudes towards science or their level of scientific knowledge, but older Romanian children score lower than the European average on science education, with 38.5 per cent of 15-year-olds underachieving in science, against 20.6 per cent at the European level (European Commission, 2018).

Meanwhile in kindergartens, assignments are still seen as play, so that when entering school, children switch from playing to learning – from self-directed play to adult-directed learning (Samuelsson and Carlsson, 2008). We believe this play dimension should be put to work, for instance by introducing makerspace-type activities in school. Also, taking advantage of children's skills in videogames in such spaces makes it easier for them to engage in makerspaces.

In this context, within the design of the Romanian case study of the MakEY project, we aimed 1) to introduce young children to STEM subjects in a playful (as opposed to instructionist) way; 2) to create a learning context that mixes artistic and creative activities with scientific challenges; 3) to integrate activities involving traditional and digital materials; and 4) to offer this learning experience to children from various socioeconomic backgrounds. The research question that this chapter will address is: What are the main types of engagement of young children with materials and technology, when they participate in makerspace-like activities/settings that involve mainly robots and videogames?

Therefore, we came up with the concept of a Space Academy, a series of workshops in which making aspects were oriented towards both new technologies (videogames or robots) and hands-on activities, focusing on the idea of space exploration. We used Kerbal Space Program and Universe Sandbox, two videogame tools that allowed children to mimic on screen the physical assembly of a rocket, in a makerspace type of setting, out of given 'parts', which entails an in-game creation approach. Cubelets, the robots we used, had been introduced as part of space exploration, children being invited to create meaningful robots.

We undertake this work informed by the posthumanist paradigm (Barad, 2007). In a discussion of posthumanism, we agree with Kruger that one should discriminate between the posthuman present – which 'describes the radically hybridised world we presently inhabit' – and posthumanism – which, by relying on anti-humanist, post-colonial, anti-racism and material feminist theories, denounces the idea of human-centred action and criticises the Cartesian assumption of the foundational dualism of modern science (2016, p.78). Hence, we not only embraced the hybridised nature of makerspaces (i.e. with their mix of digital and non-digital, art/craft and technology etc.), but also refer to each particular situation in our project as a unique agentic assemblage (Jackson and Mazzei, 2016) formed through the intra-actions (Barad, 2000) of its components, which do not have independent and pre-existing agency that could be considered to be in a causal relationship with each other.

We draw on Barad's concept (2000) of 'agential reality', which is seen as a material-discursive phenomenon within which we intra-act and which does not have a fixed ontology, independent of human practices (including research practice). This frame not only repositions the researcher in the agential assemblage of doing and teaching science, but redefines the more fundamental concepts of 'objectivity' in science and refutes the traditional concept of 'causality', as 'intra-actions are constraining but not determining' (Barad, 2000, p.236). It also changes the meaning of science education, as we will explain in detail in the next section, moving from teaching 'scientific facts and methods' to teaching *agential literacy*', i.e. 'knowing how to intra-act responsibly within the world' (Barad, 2000, p.246).

In this chapter, we begin with a discussion of some of the challenges of science education and review some studies on the use of videogames and robots in education, including for STEM education. In the second part of the chapter, we describe the 'Space Academy', a Romanian project, and present and discuss six types of engagement by children that we extracted from the data gathered during the workshops. Anticipating this, we identified the following types: creative engagement, playful/gamer-like engagement, learning-driven engagement, assistant engagement, storytelling-driven engagement and versatile engagement (a give-it-a-try approach). In the final section of the chapter, we will discuss the findings within the theoretical framework of posthumanism.

STEM education

STEM education seems to be the panacea of the 21st century. With the advances in new digital technologies, there is a new narrative whereby science education (especially digital literacy) will directly improve the quality of people's lives, which leads to associating STEM education with citizenship; hence there is an attempt to consider it as one of the basic forms of literacy (Barad, 2000). On the other hand, STEM education is also associated with economic development, resulting in efforts to increase the rate of youth who choose a STEM-related career (European Commission, 2015).

Although nowadays nobody argues against the importance of STEM education, nor against the necessity to engage children from an early age in STEM-related subjects (European Commission, 2015), a consensus is far from being reached on how to ensure a successful approach to science education. Thus, whereas some argue that in order to successfully engage students with science one has to make science relevant for youth by placing it in the context of their interests (Marginson et al., 2013), Barad (2000) shows how the attempt to contextualise science in science education introduces a false and limited understanding 'of science, of culture, and of their heterogeneous and multiple interactions' (Barad, 2000, p.222), by referring to a dualism of nature vs culture and reifying one or the other. Although supported in public discourse, even the idea of making science enjoyable and entertaining for students is criticised in the literature, because what is usually taken to be students' enthusiasm could in fact be them feeling disempowered (Barad, 2000). This 'excite and engage' type of approach to STEM subjects also runs the risk of a high rate of abandonment once failure or difficulties are encountered, already described as a 'bait and switch' approach to science (Banks, 2018).

In a case study of the functioning of a school makerspace, Tan (2018) notices the existence of alternative methods of learning STEM subjects that occur in the makerspace, but sees them as complementary to the school's approach and not as a replacement for it. He also argues for adding a societal dimension to form a triangle of science, technology and society education, in an attempt to recognise other-than-human agency in science and reconfigure the assemblage of scientist-nature-technology. Moreover, Tan (2018) understands the kind of knowledge students acquired in the school makerspace he studied as a new layer of more intimate knowledge ('ephemeral' knowledge that comes through performative interaction with science), which adds to the abstract knowledge that official school education provides. In Tan's words (2018), to the representational way of learning science in school, makerspaces add a performative way. Or, if we proceed with Tan's idea and reframe the performativity of science within the posthumanism concepts of assemblage and intra-activity (Barad, 2000), knowledge is not only ephemeral, but an always adjustable outcome of a never-ending reconfiguration.

Using videogames in education

Creating videogames as a makerspace-linked activity is well documented in the literature (Rusk, 2016). It is also common to use videogames (especially Minecraft) in educational makerspaces as a way to have in-game creation and development of worlds, but also as a proxy for creating your own game or hacking into a game. The recent turn is interesting if we consider the public discourse, where videogames have generated a moral panic comparable to those generated by other, more physical addictions (see Young, 1996, but also Markey and Ferguson, 2017 for a debunk of such panics) or other violent media (see Markey and Ferguson, 2018). Recent years have seen an abundance of studies trying to probe the likelihood of establishing a positive connection between videogames and aspects such as education, development and health (Gee, 2003; Harrington and O'Connell, 2016). There is also a recognition of videogames' educational value at an institutional level. With the introduction of videogames in libraries, they started to be seen as valuable, 'just like any other library service' (Levine, 2008, in Brown, 2014, p.447). Yet, the most important shift the last decade saw was in videogames being perceived as a valid academic subject, with journals dedicated to the subject.[3]

Despite the claim that videogames have the potential to be used as educational tools (a claim that supports a whole industry of 'serious games') and although there are some studies that have proved their efficacy in learning, a systematic literature review only partially supports this claim. After reviewing more than 300 studies, Young et al. (2012) found some evidence for the effects of videogames on language learning, history and physical education, but little evidence for the academic value of videogames in science and maths. But even those researchers who did not find evidence of a connection between academic achievement and the use of videogames are not prepared to discard this possibility. They either nuanced the benefits of videogames in terms of students' engagement, and not of students' scores on standardised tests, or explained the lack of evidence by the limited time of the experiment (Harris, 2008). In their attempt to understand the lack of efficacy of using videogames in teaching science, Young et al. speculate about the fundamental disconnection between 'doing' science and the instructional use of videogames, mentioning 'the direct result of continued content disassembly and the lack of cohesive reassembly for the purposes of a spiral curricula' (2012, p.72). This disconnection could be overcome by adding a backstory 'that includes the narrative of science history and its future potential. These strategies may ultimately reduce the current trend of presenting science as an exercise in mastery of isolated facts' (ibid.). With this proposal, Young et al. (2012) meet Barad's (2000, p.243) ideas, as she argues against the 'cookbook laboratory' approach to teaching science, which misleads students so that they see science as linear progressively accumulated knowledge, and not as a 'changeable, open-ended set of practices', pleading instead for a variant of the 'history of physics' approach.

Using robots in education

The use of robots in makerspaces is already a common practice (Chou, 2018), as they bring together two of the distinctive elements of a makerspace, namely, digital coding skills and hands-on creation. Also, the need to introduce and use robots in schools seems not to be questioned, the variations from country to country being only represented by divergences regarding what grade they should be introduced at in the curriculum, and the financial resources available to implement them. In current Romanian curricula, references to robots only appear around the 7th grade,[4] yet in the UK they are introduced from the very first year of schooling (Marsh et al., 2017). There are other countries falling in the middle, such as Austria, where pilot tests are being undertaken to introduce robots in early-years education (Trültzsch–Wijnen, 2017). However, in most cases, robotics is part of informal, extra-curricular education or after-school programmes (Eguchi, 2017).

The most important shift that robots in education bring is a change in children's status, from being merely technology consumers, to producers (Eguchi, 2017). Other benefits of studying robots are: a hands-on approach to programming, a visual approach (assessing accuracy and correcting coding errors is done via visual stimuli) and a pupil-centred approach (Chetty, 2017). Engaging with robots helps children to develop fine motor skills and collaborative skills (Benitti and Spolaôr, 2017); it also allows physical movement, an activity that is limited while in class (Marsh et al., 2017). A systematic review of the literature on the uses of robots in early childhood education puts these benefits into four classes: cognitive, conceptual, language development and social/collaborative (Toh et al., 2016). Referring specifically to the connection between using robots in education and the increase of STEM knowledge/learning, Benitti and Spolaôr (2017) show that one of the challenges of these studies remains the problem of evaluating the STEM knowledge acquired by using robots. Despite the fact that some of the concepts in STEM are being introduced to pupils during robotics activities, the assessment of the efficiency of such an approach remains problematic (Marsh et al., 2017). In this context, most studies assess and focus on the general knowledge acquired, such as teamwork and problem-solving skills (Benitti and Spolaôr, 2017).

The Romanian project

The workshops organised by the Romanian team were given to first graders (6–8 years old) from three different schools in Bucharest. The schools were chosen to represent the socioeconomic diversity of schoolchildren. The three series, each one comprising at least six workshops, were each offered to ten children. The design of the workshops included many layers of simultaneous activities on the principle of modularity.

Each series was focused on the idea of space, but we did not provide a unifiying narrative for the sessions in a series, nor a gamified approach that would link them together. Instead, we aimed to get the children to engage and intra-act with the matter(materiality) of what they were offered, following their own points of interest in opting for the topic (artistic and creative, robotics or videogames), more akin to how adults or older youth would find their way into a makerspace. Thus, in line with our posthumanist approach, children's engagement with 'things' was considered intrinsically relevant, avoiding 'children's relations to their material surroundings… [being] reduced to instrumental activity the significance of which is predetermined and known by adults' (Rautio, 2014, p.461).

Each session lasted for 2–3 hours, during which children were offered a combination of the following: two videogames, Cubelet modular robots, 3D pens and various arts & crafts materials (beads, crayons, paper, scissors, glue, plasticine etc.). The latter resources were present at all times on the tables, while the others were introduced gradually, during the workshops, robots being introduced last. Not least, children had cameras at their disposal which they were encouraged to use to document their own activities or to record and understand the activities of their peers, simulating a journalistic approach. A GoPro chest or frontal camera was also used for getting the child's point of view (Chalfen, 2014). The four types of activities were structured on the Playshop Model (Peppler and Bender, 2013; Wohlwend et al., 2016), which 'brings together childhood strengths with school curricula in four quadrants: play, collaboration, new technologies, and a content area' (Wohlwend and Peppler, 2015, p.24). In our case, the content area was science, leading to a Science Playshop. Hatch Atelier suggested two games and the types of robots to be used during the workshops.

Kerbal Space Program (KSP) is a videogame developed by Squad Company that allows users to build their own rocket (using a variety of elements that are realistically designed and proportionate) and launch it. The game perfectly simulates the laws of physics. Although the official rating of Common Sense media is +8 for this game (Chen, 2011), we considered it for two main reasons: first because we deemed it appropriate for introducing children to physics, technology and engineering, and second because playing it supposes a similar approach to makerspace activities, by trial and error, with a big failure rate, which also requires a great degree of commitment. Although highly acknowledged for its educational potential (Yang, 2015), to the best of our knowledge, only one article goes into depth with an analysis of the use of KSP, specifically in a parent–child approach, assessing it as suitable for 'intergenerational play by providing roles for the knowledgeable parent and game skilled child' (Klopfer and Klopfer, 2016, p.116).

For technical reasons,[5] Universe Sandbox was only used in the first series of workshops. It aims to simulate the creation and functioning (also destruction) of a universe, by adding and letting collide various types of planets, stars and black holes and seeing their interaction. Cubelets feature three types of cubes (sensing, acting and programmable blocks) and brick adapters to link robots with Lego blocks. They are considered a good introduction to basic robotics challenges (basic I/O).

We prompted the children to use the cameras for three reasons: first, we wanted them to have a reflexive approach towards their activities, in the very moment of them (and not as an added layer). Second, as makerspaces, the literature shows (Wolf et al., 2014) that the documenting part of the process of making and the sharing part are key points in maker culture. Third, we wanted them to discover the object of the camera. We live in a culture where smartphones and web cameras are ubiquitous. Still, a dedicated video or photo camera is sometimes not familiar to children. Sometimes, as many as four cameras were handled by children recording in parallel, with children filming each other, while their full engagement was with cameras and their peers. In these situations, we were mostly interested in the assemblage, which includes the way children used them to interact with others and the things at their disposal. In this chapter, we did not set out to analyse the content of their stories but, within our posthumanist frame, we shall discuss their engagement with the cameras.

The data collected were field notes. As stated above, we also gathered video footage with one wide-angle camera that we tried to maintain in a fixed location and at least one mobile camera held by a pupil in a methodological shift involving adopting children as partners (data collectors) in the research (Marsh and Richards, 2013). The results we report in this chapter are mostly based on field notes and only confirmed or supported by video footage.

Engagement in makerspaces

The general idea of the Romanian case study was to offer children a general subject for thinking, playing and making with (the space), various materials (videogames as digital materials, non-digital arts & crafts materials, also robots and cameras) and support whenever they needed it. In the first part of each series, we gradually introduced the materials and games and some theoretical knowledge transfer (about gravity, orbits, space, atmosphere etc.) supported by YouTube videos from NASA. Then, in the second part of each series, we let the children freely choose what to do during the workshops, while having everything at their disposal.[6]

In our project, the main purpose of the workshops was to see if children would attain a genuine interest in the topic, interest that could take an artistic, scientific, creative, technical or communicational form (Wohlwend et al., 2016), or if they would find their own interests – or, as we also deemed possible, they would remain unengaged. With this objective in mind, the activities presented by the facilitators were merely an example of what they could do, and not mandatory. The findings we report here are mainly from the second part of the workshops in each series, when we could just follow their self-driven activities. We observed how the children approached things/materials, how they approached each other and how they related to the idea of learning and creating. From these observations, we identified the following six types of engagement, and illustrate some of them with extracts from field notes.

Creative-builder engagement (build-your-own approach)

> Laur sits still in front of the computer, staring at the giant rocket he has created (with too many fuel tanks on it and other elements with a purely decorative function). A facilitator, believing he needs technical help, offers to assist him. Laur rejects any idea he is pitched, saying that is not what he wants and, anyway, he wouldn't put his rocket to the test by launching it (if improperly assembled, the rocket might explode). The facilitator withdraws and Laur keeps adding other elements to it. In the end, he calls his friend over to boast about his beautiful rocket.

> While some children were playing with Cubelets, trying to create robots as multifunctional as possible (that can shine a light, sense obstacles, stop, move around) and negotiating useful cubes for these actions (black, transparent or navy blue), Mihai gathers all the brightly coloured cubes that cannot be used by themselves to make something useful, as they do not act, sense or prompt movement, creating a brightly coloured construction, symmetrical and grand, but totally non-functional. He rejects the facilitator's help, saying that is what he wants to create.

In this mode of participation, children aimed, first and foremost, to build new things, often based only on aesthetic criteria (colours, shapes and sizes). When children who play with robots manifest this type of engagement, they do not want to create a meaningful robot (one that will light up when meeting an obstacle), but probably a big, colourful one. Or, if they create a rocket in KSP, they will be more interested in adding many attractive elements to it, rather than launching it (because, most probably, this would result in destroying it, as the elements will not have been chosen to accommodate the laws of physics). The rule here is: the bigger, the better. In this mode of engagement, children are not interested in how things function or if they function; they approach them strictly as materiality that will support their vision. If not successful, children will finally abandon them. Although they seek social recognition as well, anything that is felt to be limiting them will be rejected. In this kind of engagement, the children want to be in control of the situation (including objects/materiality, or other people with whom they enter an assemblage), as they have their own vision of the output that is not easy to put into words (as opposed to where the product can be described by its functionality). Interactions with the adult facilitator are difficult as, in this engagement mode, children's criteria are personal, so there is no common ground where adult and child can meet.

When engaged in this way, children may look for collaboration with other children, but with the purpose of attracting them to their way of playing (i.e. to build as much, tall or large as possible). Yet, if resources are limited, these situations can become conflictual, as the 'constructor' will try to seize as many of the resources as possible, their aesthetic criteria being quantity-related. The most important idea in this kind of engagement is the novelty of the outcome. Rautio (2014) talks about imitation as a key element in children's engagement with things, but we found that, in a makerspace setting, sometimes children approach things in total opposition to this general pattern, with the wish to just do things differently.

Gamer-like engagement

> After creating his first rocket and successfully launching it, Sorin started to explore the options of the game by opening various menus and closing them quickly, as they were text-based. At one moment, he finds the possibility of also using a plane (not only a rocket, as they were told). He lets his friend (sitting at another desk) know that, by saying, "I found a plane, come and see!" After asking for help with it and not receiving what he expected, he applied himself, by trial and error, going back and forth and trying all the commands that he already knew or those that he discovered on the spot. In the end, he made his plane move and proclaimed his victory loudly.

Best described as 'playing mode', this type of engagement emulates children's approach to videogames, by trial and error, with little or no interest in any 'just-in-case information'. When children become familiar enough with a general 'modus operandi', they will just jump into the activity, figuring out how things work while or after they operate them. If they get stuck, they can ask for help, but usually they ask how to do something (e.g. 'How can I control the rocket?', or 'How do I make my robot work?'), and not why it did not work. Many times, children who manifest this kind of engagement also exhibit some game literacy. As for their interaction with other children, they manifest an individualistic approach to the materials they play with; occasionally there is some transfer of information between peers (especially if they are friends), in a scaffolding paradigm; also, there is a joyful sharing of their achievements with their peers. When in this mode, children ask for adults' help only if they have a specific question; they dismiss long explanations and try to figure things out by trial and error.

Learning-driven engagement

When in this mode, children primarily want to learn (to play the game better, to accumulate knowledge for making things better etc.) and to understand different things. The presence of a knowledgeable adult is mandatory for this type of engagement and children stick around this adult figure, acquiescing to his/her explanations and help. Children give up control of an object to the adult, and frequently do not engage themselves directly with an object, but via an adult's mediation. They willingly absorb not only just-in-time knowledge, but also just-in-case knowledge (Gee, 2003). In this mode, children acquire basic language and are able to use it and reflect on some of their activities in the game ("I did this because of that"). They tend to monopolise the facilitator and sometime become emotionally attached to her/him.

By learning-driven engagement, we are not referring to a situation in which children observe an adult doing something and then try it themselves. In our description, children are satisfied with a 'theoretical' understanding; therefore, they want to go further and further with their questions. In different situations, a boy and a girl happily listened to the facilitator's explanations for 15 minutes, not touching the mouse of the computer, but prompting him with questions for more complex constructions and in-depth explanations. In relation to intra-acting with other children, these children generally want to attract them to their knowledge exploration/adventure.

> Theodora, who was very skilled in playing KSP and managed to launch her rocket, was seen at some point by the researchers writing something on small pieces of paper. She was rather embarrassed to admit she was briefly describing how the game was played (which would be seen as cheating at school), for her less-skilled friend, who was in fact not very attracted by the game. We assured her we were glad she took the initiative of sharing knowledge.

Subsequently, we reflected on the way the Romanian school system imprints children's behaviour, promoting individualism and punishing collaboration, which is seen as cheating. In another situation, two boys were negotiating what mode of KSP they should play, after having discovered the training mode. One of them, with a learning type of engagement, wanted to go into training mode, while the second one, with a creative type of engagement, pleaded to go straight to creating a spaceship. Each of them pleaded, in fact, for the benefit they valued most, the benefits of learning ('We must learn') versus the benefits of an intuitive approach to novelty creation ('Learning, it's not fun. We cannot build what we want').

Storytelling-driven engagement

The children's interaction with the cameras around them was mostly playful. While camera-mediated interaction was constant during our workshops, storytelling-driven engagement was sporadic. It mostly appeared in two forms: the first was somewhat spontaneous, aiming to put some narrative flesh on the meanings, characters and actions the child was performing while filming. This narrativisation process required an audience (be it the researchers or other children or both), and the audience's interest boosted the complexity of the story. In contrast, when audience interest was missing, the story faded away. In this situation, the presence of a camera in the assemblage did not play a significant role in the story. Interestingly, if the audience was formed only by children, they did not feel the need to bring a camera into interaction based on telling a story. They would just listen to the initial story, perhaps intervening and starting their own story, but the story itself did not trigger camera use. Alternatively, as we will show in the second form of the storytelling engagement, the cameras did trigger the story. When approached by the researchers to explain what they did in their activities, the children explained, in either a school-like discourse (self-explanatory one) or in a storytelling discourse.

> In the last workshop at the Finnish-Romanian school, Dan transformed his making of plasticine characters into a trans-media performance: out of

plasticine he recreated characters from his favourite game, *Bendy and the Ink Machine*, then he told the general story of the cartoon-based videogame to his peers and searched on YouTube to show them an episode of it.

The second type of storytelling engagement appeared when the story was built around the camera, with the purpose of being filmed – notably, when the pupil with a camera in hand was hunting for a story. When he/she could not engage his/her peers, he/she entered into a new assemblage with the objects around him/her, exploring them through the lens of the camera. At other times, the child and camera left the classroom to catch a story: be it filming something out of the window, or leaving the classroom, in an attempt to explore other spaces, as though they were convinced the camera would find the story by itself. Two or three children would team up with a camera, trying to 'stage' a story. Importantly, in this second sub-type of engagement, not only were the camera and its own technical affordances revealed to children, via such exploration, but also their own bodies. Thus, for instance, when a boy discovered the camera viewfinder, another child he was trying to interview pretended to bite the lens. The cameraboy discovered how fascinating the mouth of his friend was, as seen through the lens, and they started to explore each other's mouths with the help of the camera.

Assistant/side-observer type of engagement

This type of engagement can take many forms; one should avoid assimilating it with a lack of engagement. Thus, as part of an assemblage, the child's engagement is mediated by a person (situation in which the child is engaged by observing the others) or materials (when the child engaged with the materials only in the preparatory activities for a creative act that somebody else will perform). Sometimes, in the case of prior friendships, we noticed a situation where a child refused to personally engage with objects or actions his friend was using, thus preferring the role of observer. In so doing, they were acting as supportive friends, not showing a lack of interest. Another form of this engagement appeared when, lacking self-confidence, a child would ask another to do something for him/her. Then, they would offer their help to the one engaged in creating, for instance, by selecting tools or materials for them, but stayed away from the actual making. The interesting thing is that the same child was not restricted to this type of engagement, but took turns in making afterwards.

Versatile engagement (give-it-a-try approach)

Although during the workshops children migrated from one activity to another, we only considered as versatile engagement those situations when the movement between workstations was at that moment the main activity. The children in this engagement mode would enter a different assemblage, sometimes driven by the agency of the things around them. Thus, they would pick up some robots and play with them for a few seconds because they happened to be there, at hand, or they would be hanging around in a game left open by another child, just because they sat for a moment in an empty chair in front of that particular computer. As in the previously described mode, this approach is often dismissed, not seen as a valid form of engagement on the adult's part, and considered instead a manifestation of a lack of attention, or a lack of engagement. But in our observation of children, this engagement is important for two reasons. First, it occurs as a relaxing or pausing mode, a sort of stand-by moment that allows children to switch to another form of engagement (which is more meaningful from the adults' point of view). Second, it is an exploration mode, in which a genuine encounter with materiality may happen. By lowering/diminishing their own agency and allowing things to 'come' to them, children enter a privileged mode to discover things. Inspired by the participation modes, Ito et al. (2010) considered this a first step towards 'messing around', in which one just 'looks around' in an attempt to later engage with new media.

Conclusions

In this chapter, we have analysed the data from three series of workshops that were held as part of the Romanian case study of the MakEY project, in an attempt to understand the main types of young children's engagement in them. The Romanian project aimed to create an alternative educational space to school in which, via maker and hacker types of activities, children were introduced to science. Hence, in partnership with our colleagues from Hatch Atelier, we created a 'Space Academy'. From this work, we found six types of engagement or participation modes children manifested during our workshops: creative-builder engagement (build-your-own approach), gamer-like engagement, learning-driven engagement, storytelling-driven engagement, assistant/side-observer type of engagement, and versatile engagement (give-it-a-try approach).

These types of engagement are more like Weber's 'ideal types' and not to be seen as the singular engagement of a child at a given moment. Most of the time, we witnessed a combination of more than one type of engagement. Moreover, like Ito et al. (2010), we also warn against taking these types of engagement as representing types of individuals, as we do not aim to categorise individuals in relation to practices, but to understand their engagement with technology and materiality in a certain space/setting. During our workshops, children manifested fluid engagement, switching from one activity to another, depending on the assemblage they entered at a given time. Also, we do not pretend here that these are the only forms of engagement young children may display in a makerspace, nor that these types of engagement are only to be found in young children and not in adults; we also do not claim that these are universal forms of engagement. This limitation is due to both our qualitative exploratory approach and our posthumanist frame that is situational-centred/sensitive (Barad, 2000).

Moreover, we have chosen to distinguish between types of engagement and the outcomes of these engagements. A short episode will illustrate this distinction. While playing with Cubelets, Vera, a girl in the last group, was short of wheel Cubelets for her robots and came up with a solution that stunned the facilitators: she linked her robot to a cube, which entailed a rotation movement of the cube attached to it, and added another cube, which in this assemblage acted like a wheel. Basically, she hacked a wheel because of the limitation of available tools. Starting from this episode, we considered whether we should add another form of engagement, hacking oriented, but finally chose not to do so, as her hack was the result of gamer-like engagement (by trial and error) combined with learner-driven engagement (as for her it was very important to understand how each cube functioned and how she could link them together). Last but not least, we want to dismiss an axiological reading of these types of engagement, as we do not consider one type of engagement superior to others in a makerspace setting. If, in school, learning-driven engagement is primarily valued, and in the arts creative types rule, we think that a successful approach in a makerspace should rely on some combinations of these ideal types.

Overall, despite these caveats, we would argue that these types of engagement have implications for early childhood educators. If kindergartens and schools are to introduce makerspaces, then educators need to provide space and time for a range of types of involvement, instead of assuming that, for example, learning-driven engagement will be the primary mode of participation. This means adopting an approach in which teachers become facilitators of learning, and are able to step back and watch what types of engagement emerge in the makerspace, supporting children when necessary. In this project, the children learned much about STEM, including robotics, through active but also some passive forms of engagement across the workshops. There are implications here for further work on the role of adults in supporting learning in such spaces, and at a theoretical level, on what learning means and occurs in a posthumanistic and materialistic approach.

Notes

1 In an interview with the school's principal, we learned that their makerspace is inspired by the experiential learning movement and project-based learning theory.
2 Inspired by the MIT movement LifeLong Kindergarten (Resnick, 2017) and Seymour Papert's (1991) concept of constructionism (as opposed to instructionism).
3 Such as *Videogame Studies, Game Studies* (International Journal of Computer Games Technology), *Games Culture*, and *Simulation and Gaming*.
4 It is true that 'using a virtual environment for programming didactical use robot' (Ministerul Educației Naționale, 2017, p.10) is at an abstraction level far above the introductory level.
5 The game was a big resource consumer and if played in an exploratory (but also chaotic) manner by children led to ruining the videocards of the laptops.
6 Some constraints existed nevertheless, in terms of available materials, constraints that triggered a continuous negotiation of the available resources among them.

References

Banks, D. A. (2018, January 24). Engineered for dystopia. Retrieved 16 November 2018 from: https://thebaffler.com/latest/engineered-for-dystopia-banks
Barad, K. (2000) Reconceiving scientific literacy as agential literacy: Or learning how to intra-act responsibly within the world. In R. Reid and S. Traweek (eds.), *Doing Science +Culture*. New York: Routledge, pp. 221–258.

Barad, K. (2007). *Meeting the Universe Halfway: Quantum Physics and the Entanglement of Matter and Meaning*. Durham, NC: Duke University Press.

Benitti, F. B. V. & Spolaôr, N. (2017). How have robots supported STEM teaching? In M. S. Khine (ed.), *Robotics in STEM Education: Redesigning the Learning Experience*. Cham: Springer International Publishing, pp. 103–129. doi:10.1007/978-3-319-57786-9_5

Brown, R. T. (2014). A literature review of how videogames are assessed in library and information science and beyond. *The Journal of Academic Librarianship*, 40(5): 447–451.

Chalfen, R. (2014). "Your panopticon or mine?" Incorporating wearable technology's Glass and GoPro into visual social science. *Visual Studies*, 29(3): 299–310. doi:10.1080/1472586X.2014.941547

Chen, M. (2011) Review of the Kerbal Space Program. Common Sense Media. Retrieved 1 December 2018 from: www.commonsensemedia.org/game-reviews/kerbal-space-program

Chetty, J. (2017). Combatting the war against machines: an innovative hands-on approach to coding. In M. S. Khine (ed.), *Robotics in STEM Education: Redesigning the Learning Experience*. Cham: Springer International Publishing, pp. 59–83. doi:10.1007/978-3-319-57786-9_3

Chou, P.-N. (2018). Skill development and knowledge acquisition cultivated by maker education: Evidence from Arduino-based educational robotics. *Eurasia Journal of Mathematics, Science and Technology Education*, 14(10): 1–15. doi:10.29333/ejmste/93483

Eguchi, A. (2017). Bringing robotics in classrooms. In: M. S. Khine (ed.), *Robotics in STEM Education: Redesigning the Learning Experience* (pp. 3–32). Cham: Springer International Publishing. doi:10.1007/978-3-319-57786-9_1

European Commission. (2015). *Science Education for Responsible Citizenship*. Retrieved 1 December 2018 from: http://ec.europa.eu/research/swafs/pdf/pub_science_education/KI-NA-26-893-EN-N.pdf

European Commission. (2018). *Education and Training Monitor 2018. Romania Factsheet*. Retrieved 16 November 2018 from: https://ec.europa.eu/education/resources-and-tools/document-library/education-and-training-monitor-2018-romania-factsheet_en

Gee, J. P. (2003). *What Video Games Have to Teach Us about Learning and Literacy*. New York: Palgrave Macmillan.

Harrington, B. & O'Connell, M. (2016). Video games as virtual teachers: Prosocial video game use by children and adolescents from different socioeconomic groups is associated with increased empathy and prosocial behaviour. *Computers in Human Behavior*, 63: 650–658. doi:10.1016/j.chb.2016.05.062

Harris, D. (2008). A comparative study of the effect of collaborative problem-solving in a massively multiplayer online game (MMO) on individual achievement. *Dissertation Abstracts International Section A: Humanities and Social Sciences*, 69(6-A): 2117.

Ito, M., Baumer, S., Bittanti, M., Boyd, D., Cody, R., Herr-Stephenson, B. & Horst, H. A. (2010). *Hanging Out, Messing Around, and Geeking out*. Cambridge; London: MIT Press.

Jackson, A. & Mazzei, L. (2016). Thinking with an agentic assemblage in posthuman inquiry. In C. Taylor and C. Hughes (eds.), *Posthuman Research Practices in Education*. New York: Palgrave Macmillan, pp. 93–107.

Klopfer, E. & Klopfer, O. (2016). Intergenerational gaming in Kerbal Space Program. *Well Played: A Journal on Video Games, Value and Meaning*, 5(2): 116–129.

Kruger, F. (2016). Posthumanism and educational research for sustainable futures. *Journal of Education*, 65: 1–18.

Lahmar, J., Taylor, M., Marsh, J., Jakobsdóttir, S., Velicu, A., Arnseth, H. C., Blum-Ross, A., Dýrfjörð, K., Gissurardóttir, S., Hjartarson, T., Jónsdóttir, S. R., Kjartansdóttir, S. H., Kumpulainen, K., Mitarca, M., Ólafsdóttir, M. E., Pétursdóttir, S., Sandvik, K., Thestrup,

K. and Thorsteinsson, G. (2017). Makerspaces in the Early Years: Current Perceptions and Practices of Early Years Practitioners, Library and Museum Educators and Makerspace Staff. Sheffield: University of Sheffield, MakEY Project. ISBN: 9780902831513.

Marginson, S., Tytler, R., Freeman, B. & Roberts, K. (2013). *STEM: Country Comparisons.* Report for the Australian Council of Learned Academies. Retrieved 4 September 2019 from: https://acola.org.au/wp/PDF/SAF02Consultants/SAF02_STEM_%20FINAL.pdf

MarkeyP. M. & Ferguson, C. J. (2017). Internet gaming addiction: Disorder or moral panic? *American Journal of Psychiatry*, 174(3): 195–196.

Markey, P. M. & Ferguson, C. J. (2018). Teaching us to fear: The violent video game moral panic and the politics of game research. *American Journal of Play*, 10(1).

Marsh, J. & Richards, C. (2013). Children as researchers. In R. Willett, C. Richards, J. Marsh, A. Burn & J. C. Bishop (eds.), *Children, Media and Playground Cultures.* Basingstoke, UK: Palgrave Macmillan, pp. 51–67.

Marsh, J., Mascheroni, G., Carrington, V., Árnadóttir, H., Brito, R., Dias, R., Kupiainen, R. & Trueltzsch-Wijnen, C. (2017). *The Online and Offline Digital Literacy Practices of Young Children: A Review of the Literature.* COST ACTION IS1410. Retrieved 1 August 2019 from: http://digilitey.eu/wp-content/uploads/2017/01/WG4-LR-jan-2017.pdf

Ministerul Educaşiei Naşionale (2017). *Programa şcolară pentru disciplina INFORMATICş ȘI TIC. Clasele a V-a – a VIII-a. Anexa nr. 2 la ordinul ministrului educaşiei naȘionale nr. 3393 / 28.02.2017* [The curricula for Informatics and IT&C, 5th to 8th Grade. Annex No. 2 to the Minister of Education bill no. 3393/Feb. 28, 2017]. Retrieved 1 December 2018 from: http://programe.ise.ro/Portals/1/Curriculum/2017-progr/117-INFORMATICA%20si%20TIC.pdf

Papert, S. (1991). Situating constructionism. In I. Harel & S. Papert (eds.), *Constructionism.* Norwood NJ: Ablex Publishing. Retrieved 1 August 2019 from: www.papert.org/articles/SituatingConstructionism.html

Peppler, K. & Bender, S. (2013). Maker movement spreads innovation one project at a time. *Phi Delta Kappan*, 95(3): 22–27.

Rautio, P. (2014). Mingling and imitating in producing spaces for knowing and being: Insights from a Finnish study of child–matter intra-action. *Childhood*, 21(4): 461–474. doi:10.1177/0907568213496653

Resnick, M. (2017). *Lifelong Kindergarten: Cultivating Creativity Through Projects, Passion, Peers, and Play.* Cambridge, MA: MIT Press.

Rusk, N. (2016) Motivation for making. In K. Peppler & E. Rosenfeld Halverson (eds.), *Makeology.* Vol. II. New York: Routledge, pp. 85–108.

Samuelsson, I. P. & Carlsson, M. A. (2008). The playing learning child: Towards a pedagogy of early childhood. *Scandinavian Journal of Educational Research*, 52(6): 623–641. doi:10.1080/00313830802497265

Tan, M. (2018). When makerspaces meet school: Negotiating tensions between instruction and construction. *Journal of Science, Education and Technology*, 28(2): 75–89. doi:10.1007/s10956-018-9749-x

Toh, L., Causo, A., Tzuo, P. & Chen, I. (2016). A review on the use of robots in education and young children. *Educational Technology & Society*, 19: 148–163.

Trültzsch-Wijnen, C. (2017). School 4.0 – The introduction of robotics in Austrian primary schools by using BeeBots and Lego WeDo, XVth International Conference Cyberspace, Brno (CZ) [25. 11. 2017].

Velicu, A. & Mitarcă, M. (in press). MakEY Romanian report (unpublished).

Wohlwend, K. & Peppler, K. (2015). All rigor and no play is no way to improve learning. *Phi Delta Kappan*, 96(8): 22–26. doi:10.1177/0031721715583957

Wohlwend, K., Keune, A. & Peppler, K. (2016). Design playshop: Preschoolers making, playing and learning with squishy circuits. In K. Peppler, E. R. Halverson & Y. B. Kafai (eds.), *Makeology* (Vol. 1, pp. 83–96). New York: Routledge.

Wolf, P., Troxler, P., Kocher, P.-Y., Harboe, J., & Gaudenz, U. (2014). Sharing is sparing: Open knowledge sharing in Fab Labs. *Journal of Peer Production*, 5.

Yang, J. (2015). Video games for STEM learning: How does it work? Presented at the American Society Engineering Education Illinois-Indiana Section Annual Conference, Illinois. Retrieved 1 August 2019 from: http://ilin.asee.org/Conference2015/papers/Yang.pdf

Young, K. S. (1996). Pathological Internet use: A case that breaks the stereotype. *Psychological Reports*, 79: 899–902.

Young, M., Slota, S., Cutter, A., Jalette, G., Mullin, G., Lai, B., Simeoni, Z., Tran, M. & Yukhymenko, M. (2012). Our princess is in another castle: A review of trends in serious gaming for education. *Review of Educational Research*, 82(1): 61–89. doi:10.3102/0034654312436980

9

ASSESSMENT OF LEARNING IN STEAM-FOCUSED MAKERSPACES

Louise Kay, Jackie Marsh, David Hyatt, Liz Chesworth, Bobby Nisha, Beth Nutbrown and Bryony Olney

In this chapter, the work of the MakEY team based at the University of Sheffield is outlined. The focus for this chapter is the work the team undertook on the development of an assessment tool, which was used to identify the characteristics of effective learning that could be discerned as children engaged in making. In the first section of the chapter, issues relating to assessment in makerspaces are explored, before the chapter moves on to outline an approach used in the Sheffield project to assess Characteristics of Effective Learning (COEL). COEL underpin learning and development across all disciplinary areas, and are a key element in England's Early Years Foundation Stage (DfE, 2017). The MakEY 'Makerspace Learning Assessment Framework' (MLAF) is then outlined, in which children's learning and development across a range of areas of COEL can be mapped. Finally, the chapter considers other approaches to assessment in makerspaces based on documentation and the development of narratives. First, however, an outline of the Sheffield-based project itself is provided, and the concept of 'STEAM' (Science, Technology, Engineering, Arts and Mathematics) is explored.

The Sheffield case studies: STEAM in practice

In 2011 Google's executive chairman, Eric Schmidt, gave a lecture declaring that, beginning with education, the UK needed to 'bring art and science back together' and 'reignite children's passion for science, engineering and maths'. Traditionally, the Arts and Sciences have been perceived as 'disciplinary silos', and as a way of 'driving innovation and growth in the UK's creative economy' there have been calls to encourage schools and universities to bring the two disciplines together (Bakhshi & Mateos-Garcia, 2014). Jenlink (2015) argues that in the modern world we can no longer 'safely reside' in these 'disciplinary silos', and that the focus should be on the integration of experiences, academics and society aimed towards the future within which young people will exist (p.200).

The disciplines that make up STEM (Science, Technology, Engineering and Mathematics) are viewed as 'separate domains of knowledge' tied together for the role they play within the economies of the technological world (Isabelle & Valle, 2015, p.1). Conversely, STEAM is an 'interdisciplinary learning method where rigorous academic concepts are coupled with artistic works and cultural practices' and students apply their subject knowledge within contexts that 'make connections between school, community, personal interests, and the global marketplace' (Gaskins, 2014, p.79). The Organisation for Economic and Co-operative Development (OECD) (2012) acknowledges that, 'Today's workplaces demand people who can solve non-routine problems' (p.26). It is argued that the STEAM initiative is a useful vehicle for enabling students to use more creative skills to 'simultaneously decompose a complex problem using convergent thinking and then apply the corresponding solution to the real world' (Land, 2013, p.552).

As outlined in this book, a current and successful approach to STEM/STEAM is the 'makerspace' movement. A key factor of the movement is to provide a hands-on learning experience to encourage engagement in STEAM activities, particularly for girls and other under-represented groups in science, emphasising the idea that every child can be an innovator (Hughes, 2017, p.2). Julian and Parrott (2017) assert that 'the ideal "makerspace" session should provide opportunities to encourage students to 'think about things they may never have considered' (p.16).

The case studies in Sheffield were undertaken with two nurseries and two primary schools, and they each adopted a STEAM approach. The first setting was a nursery school that caters for 90 children aged 3–4. The nursery serves diverse racial and ethnic communities, and many children speak English as an Additional Language. As the project took place just before Christmas, the school wanted to focus on the topic of 'Light and Colour'. A key aim of the project was to introduce children to the concept of a circuit through a variety of activities which involved making circuits. The children undertook a range of activities, such as making light boxes with cardboard boxes that had clear tops, using cellophane and DIY torches. They then used the torches to create lightshows in a blackout tent, using the app *PABLO*. These were then created as calendars for parents using images of the lightshows. The lightshows were printed off as stickers, using the HP Sprocket printer. The children also used Play Doh with circuits to make models, and they created animated films using an overhead projector and coloured transparent shapes, a tablet and the app *iMotion*. Other activities including drawing pictures in which they incorporated circuits, using copper tape, LEDs and batteries, and then drawing on an interactive whiteboard and projecting lightshows onto the screen.

The second setting was a nursery unit with 45 children aged 3–4, which is part of a primary school in a primarily White, working-class area of the city that is one of the most socially deprived nationally. Again, related to the time of the year, the aim was to introduce children to the concept of a circuit through a variety of activities which involved making circuits to light up houses, streets and Christmas trees. Children made a box model of their homes with their parents (at home). They then created a light for inside their house, using copper tape and LEDs on a laser-cut base, and made street lights using similar resources. They constructed a Christmas tree shape using card triangles, which were laser cut by a local maker involved in the project, James Wallbank. Copper tape and flashing LEDs were then placed on the trees. Children moved on to create a green screen animated film of themselves singing Christmas songs in front of an image of a forest of their twinkling trees. Finally, some children made green screen animations with their houses and dolls.

The third setting was a Year 2 class in an inner-city Church of England (faith) primary school, with 28 children aged 6–7, the majority of whom were White. There was some diversity in the class with regard to socio-economic status, but many of the children came from middle-class families. The topic for the period in which the project took places was fantasy stories, and so the school stated that they wanted the project to feature the fantastical creatures, the Moomins (based on the books by Tove Jansson). The aim of the project was to develop imagination and creativity as the children respond to the story through maker activities. A range of activities was undertaken (outlined fully in Marsh, Nordström, Sairanen and Shkul, in press). The project began with the children watching a theatre performance with Moomin puppets. They drew Moomin characters, which were laser cut by James, and stuck on to wooden rods to create moveable characters for shoe-box theatres. The children then wrote play scripts for their theatres. They created clay Moomin models and scanned those using the app *Qlone* to create 3D digital models. The 3D digital Moomin figures were then printed out using a 3D printer, and the clay and 3D printed models were used alongside each other to make green screen animated films using the app *iMotion*. Finally, the children imported the 3D digital Moomin models into *Google Tilt Brush* to create a Virtual Reality Moominvalley.

The fourth setting consisted of two parallel Year 3 classes in a primary school, with 60 children in total, aged 7–8. The school was ethnically diverse, and located in an area of the city that has indicators of social deprivation. The topic chosen was 'Imaginary Playspaces', and the aim of the project was to create imaginary playscapes using Virtual Reality. This involved identifying favourite playspaces in the neighbourhood, using tablets and then printing off the images, and using them as a basis for collages of imagined spaces. The children then created 3D clay models of elements in their imagined playspaces and, scanning those using the *Qlone* app, created 3D digital representations of their clay models. Children were then able to import the 3D digital files into *Google Tilt Brush* and created a Virtual Reality imaginary playspace around them.

In all of the settings, whilst the emphasis was on activities that led to the production of a range of artefacts, there were also opportunities to play and experiment with materials. Tinkering and hacking are important elements of makerspaces (Peppler, Halverson and Kafai, 2016). The nurseries set up maker tables in the outdoor areas in which children were able to engage in open-ended play with the materials.

Data were collected in a number of ways. Observations were undertaken of sessions, recorded as field notes, and video recordings were made of them. Children could choose to wear Go-Pro Chestcams during the workshops in order to capture their activities. Finally, six staff were interviewed about the project (the head of Setting 1 and two of the nursery teachers, the head of Setting 2, the teacher of Setting 3 and one of the teachers of Setting 4), in addition to the artist and maker. Interviews took between 30 minutes and one hour. The teacher in Setting 4 could not be interviewed in person, and so submitted her answers to the interview questions via email. Table 9.1 offers a summary of the data collected.

The data were coded using a set of codes agreed between the MakEY team, in addition to inductive coding. In this chapter, data relating to the themes in the assessment framework developed in the project are discussed.

Assessment in makerspaces

At the heart of makerspaces are creativity, exploration and innovation, given that makerspaces are collaborative environments that encourage discovery and problem-based learning (Fleming, 2015). As with other constructivist-inspired approaches to learning, makerspace assessment must go beyond simply the evaluation of learner copying of a 'delivered' curriculum (Chuter, 2016). Standardised summative assessment runs the risk of squeezing the joy out of makerspaces – the essence of motivation/engagement can be strangled by teachers feeling compelled to train for the test (Kohn, 2000).

Standardised assessment struggles to capture the creativity and artistic benefits of makerspaces, including the difficult-to-measure, qualitative pedagogic and leadership skills that children regularly demonstrate during makerspace activities. Standardised assessment does not demonstrate the kind of measurable outcomes from makerspaces that, in a neo-liberal performative policy context, speak to policymakers. Chuter (2016) argues that much makerspace literature still relies on quantitative measurements (Davis et al. 2013) or focuses solely on technical skills (Blikstein et al. 2017) to evaluate the outcomes and effectiveness of makerspace pedagogies. Similarly, a study by Gahagan (2016) on how public libraries assess the outcomes of makerspaces argued that whilst efforts are

TABLE 9.1 Summary of data collected

	Number of Go Pro films	Number of hand-held and static camera films	Hours/ mins/secs of video data	Number of photo-graphs	Files of children's-work (.stl/ .obj./mov)	Number of days of fieldnotes	Number of interviews with prac-titioners	Number of inter-views with artists/ makers
Setting 1	51	97	17.56.51	73	25	5	3	1
Setting 2	55	75	18.38.57	101	17	4	1	1
Setting 3	31	26	9.05.56	336	245	5	1	1
Setting 4	93	80	28.38.31	149	319	2	1	1
Total	**230**	**278**	**74.20.15**	**659**	**606**	**16**	**6**	**4**

being made to assess the outcomes of makerspaces, the reporting of this relied solely on quantitative measurement, such as visitor or participant numbers, and she argues that this approach fails to capture the effects of the service on users. Chuter (2016) argues that, in order to focus on creativity and innovation, 'assessment strategies should focus away from marks as indicators and instead look towards more qualitative methods that demonstrate a maker's thinking and detailed progress' (para. 7). Indeed, the idea of applying a standardised model of testing to makerspace pedagogies may be centrally flawed given that, as Barniskis (2014) notes, children may not all be engaged in the same activity at the same time, which implies assessment needs to be individual and bespoke – the assumption of whole class assessment processes cannot be made.

Assessment has a strong impact on the way students learn. Biggs and Tang (2007) argue that if we wish students to learn particular skills and aptitudes, which, in the makerspace scenario, focus on creativity and innovation, then we should make sure that they know it will be assessed. In other words, assessment must not only be of learning but also for learning. They argue that we should align our teaching, our intended learning outcomes and our assessment design: a process they term 'constructive alignment'. (Biggs & Tang, 2007). Chuter (2016) offers three examples of constructively aligned types of assessment in design journals, reflective writing and digital badging (Fontichiaro, 2015), a form of micro-credentialing. Boud (2009) argues that if we wish to develop students' capability for making informed judgements, then we need them to practise using their judgement, and their efforts in this endeavour should be assessed. Boud further suggests that assessment should apply not only to the outcome of students' judgements, but also to the ways in which they reached their judgements. The processes by which learners arrive at their judgements are largely private to the learners themselves. This makes them better placed than others to assess these processes, through self-assessment.

Flores (2014) similarly argues that peer assessment, either in class or through online open-source sharing, models the formative development and collaborative approaches to evaluation of work that makerspace pedagogies also foster. Race (2001) suggests that peer feedback is often more meaningful to learners as the self-evaluation skills derived from peer assessment can have a significant impact on subsequent student engagement and activity. In order to properly assess the work of their peers, students need to have a good understanding of the assessment criteria and the assignment task, both of which promote a deeper approach to learning. One could, then, conclude that the only authentic, credible forms of assessment for makerspaces would be self-assessment and possibly peer assessment, of the work that learners do and the things they make in makerspaces. One way in which this could be realised is through the use of portfolios, as argued by Semour Papert (2001), described by Martinez and Stager (2013, p.5) as the 'Father of the Maker Movement'. In line with Papert's (1980) constructionist theory of learning, attempts could also be made to adopt an approach whereby criteria and objectives are negotiated between learners and assessors, with the goal of promoting collaboration and creativity (Beghetto, 2005).

Nevertheless, we would suggest that there is value in undertaking practitioner-led assessment in makerspaces, given that it is important to capture the kinds of knowledge and skills children develop in order to recognise fully their accomplishments. This process could focus on examining specific subject knowledge across STEAM disciplines, or looking at how knowledge was synthesised across these areas. The approach undertaken in the MakEY project was to examine the ways in which makerspaces develop transversal skills.

Curriculum reform in England for both the primary and secondary sector has given increasing significance to ICT, highlighting an 'explicit recognition of the increasing digitisation of the world' (Hague & Payton, 2010, p.15). However, it is argued that if education seeks to prepare young people to make sense of the modern world then it is important that the social and cultural practices of digital literacies, and the opportunities these provide, are recognised (p.3). Land (2013) states that, 'Progress does not come from technology alone but from the melding of technology and creative thinking through art and design' (p.548). As discussed previously, the integration of Art and STEM has been gaining momentum as research exploring 21st century workforce competencies has highlighted creativity, innovation, problem-solving, critical thinking, and collaboration as being critical to achieving a more productive and sustainable economy (Allina, 2018, p.80). Different terms have been used to encapsulate these competencies including 21st century skills, soft skills, core skills, basic skills, and non-cognitive skills (Care & Luo, 2016; ESCO, 2018). In 2012, the Asia-Pacific Education Research Institutes Network (ERI-Net) defined these skills as 'transversal competencies' (TVC) which refer to 'knowledge, skills, values, and attitudes that are integral to life in the 21st century' (Care & Luo, 2016, p.2). Recent research carried out by Blackley et al. (2018) which used a makerspace to engage Indonesian primary students with STEM found that in the workshop, students demonstrated the '21st century skills' of 'collaboration, communication and problem solving' (p.37) through a process of 'asking questions, explaining ideas, and applying knowledge' to the scientific activity (p.36).

In the Sheffield MakEY project, the focus for observations was on what are known in the English Early Years Foundation Stage as the 'Characteristics of Early Learning' (COEL). These characteristics fall across three areas, as follows:

- *Playing and Exploring:* finding out and exploring; playing with what they know; being willing to 'have a go'.
- *Active Learning:* being involved and concentrating; keeping on trying; enjoying achieving what they set out to do.
- *Creating and Thinking Critically:* having their own ideas; making links; choosing ways to do things and finding new ways.

Stewart (2014) asserts that 'Central to working with the characteristics of effective learning is the understanding that children, as the agents of their own learning, must be willing to actively expend mental and physical effort in the process' (p.54).

This aligns comfortably with the key characteristics of makerspaces as a space where children's problem-solving abilities are developed, and agency, persistence and self-efficacy are exercised (Bevan et al., 2016, p.2).

An assessment framework was developed for this purpose, based on COEL. The starting point was work undertaken by Bristol Learning City (2017), in which they developed an assessment tool that included prompt questions that practitioners could use to identify COEL in practice. For example, in relation to 'Playing and Exploring', the prompt questions includes the following:

- Do they use their senses to explore and make sense of the world?
- Do they transform resources?

The Active Learning section includes the following prompts:

- Are there times when they are absorbed in their own learning?
- Do they show persistence – not giving up, even if it means starting again?

The Bristol model was adapted for MakEY in that the third aspect of COEL identified in the Early Years Framework, 'Creating and Thinking Critically', was split into two elements, given the significance of both for work in makerspaces. Therefore, a section titled 'Creative Thinking' was identified, which includes the following prompt questions:

- Do they extend and challenge their own learning?
- Do they use strategies to solve problems or challenges in their design?

A separate section was also included, labelled 'Creativity and Design'. Some of the prompt questions used are as follows:

- Do they explore the properties of materials and use their understanding of them to achieve their design goals?
- Do they use materials in creative ways?

A final section was added to the framework, given the importance of social interaction in learning in makerspaces. This includes prompt questions such as:

- Do they listen to the ideas of others?
- Do they build on the ideas of others?

The framework includes a blank page for practitioners to record their observations, using the prompts as a means to guide this process. The prompt questions are not exhaustive, and other behaviours in each of the themes may be recorded.

In the following section, an example of learning in each of the five separate sections is outlined for illustrative purposes. Of course, learning in maker episodes

MAKERSPACE LEARNING ASSESSMENT FRAMEWORK	
Name:	**Age:**
Date of Observation:	
Details of Activity/Context:	

OBSERVING HOW A CHILD IS LEARNING	
PLAYING AND EXPLORING	**ACTIVE LEARNING**
PE1: Do they use their senses to explore and make sense of their world? **PE2:** Do they transform resources? **PE3:** Do they follow their interests and explore things which interest them? **PE4:** Do they demonstrate a 'can do' attitude? **PE5:** Do they use their knowledge of similar experiences to extend their play and learning? **PE6:** Are they unafraid to make mistakes and work outside of their comfort zone?	**AL1:** Are there times when they are absorbed in their own learning? **AL2:** Do they demonstrate a sense of purpose? **AL3:** Do they show persistence – not giving up even if it means starting again? **AL4:** Are they able to set their own goals? **AL5:** Do they demonstrate pride in their achievements? **AL6:** Do they enjoy meeting their own challenges?
CRITICAL THINKING	**CREATIVITY & DESIGN**
CT: Do they have their own ideas and use their own initiative when planning designs? **CT2:** Do they demonstrate curiosity, imagination, spontaneity and innovation? **CT3:** Do they use strategies to solve problems or challenges in their designs? **CT4:** Do they challenge and extend their own learning? **CT5:** Do they try something different rather than follow what someone else has done? **CT6:** Do they try out and repeat their ideas to see if they work?	**CD1:** Do they explore the properties of materials and use their understanding of them to achieve design goals? **CD2:** Do they use materials in creative ways? **CD3:** Are they confident in using a 'trial and error' approach and do they show or talk about why some things do or don't work? **CD4:** Do they use their previous experience and knowledge to develop workarounds? **CD5:** Do they adjust their goals based on feedback and evidence? **CD6:** Can they make suggestions as to how the artefact could be improved?
SOCIAL LEARNING	
S1: Do they listen to the ideas of others? **S2:** Do they build on the idea of others? **S3:** Do they support the learning of other children? **S4:** Do they collaborate effectively with other children? **S5:** Do they seek ideas, assistance and expertise from others? **S6:** Do they give feedback on the outputs of others (including when asked to do so)?	

FIGURE 9.1 Makerspace Learning Assessment Framework (MLAF)

can be mapped simultaneously across all five areas, but they have been separated below as a means of highlighting the key elements of each theme.

Playing and Exploring

In Nursery 1, a group of children created collages on an interactive whiteboard using an overhead projector and a collection of resources such as transparent coloured shapes and feathers. The following excerpt from field notes identifies the role of play and exploration in learning.

> Three boys are engaging with an interactive whiteboard and an overhead projector (OHP). Two of the boys place a range of shapes and other miscellaneous items on the glass plate of the overhead projector as it is projected onto the interactive whiteboard. This stimulates much talk and excitement. Mustafa takes a pen and begins to draw on the whiteboard, drawing at first to the right of the projected collage (see Figure 9.2).

> At one point, Mohammed takes a piece of orange cellophane and places it on the top of the glass plate of the OHP. It is then projected onto the whiteboard, alongside the collage and the marks made with pen. He runs over to the board, shouting excitedly, "Orange!" Mohammed then realises that his shadow can be seen on the board and runs backwards and forwards towards the screen with his arms outstretched and his fingers in a claw-like shape, saying, "A giant [unclear]!" Liz asks, "Can you see the shadow on there?" Mahmood says, "Yes, a shadow!" He then moves to the board, tracing his hand across some of the marks and colours. Mustafa continues to draw in a very focused way throughout this play. This episode reminds me of the collaborative drawing some children did earlier in the session, in which they drew on paper and then added LEDs and copper tape to their pictures in order to

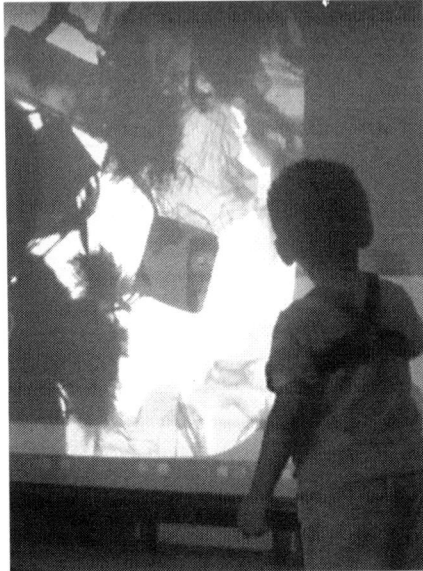

FIGURE 9.2 Mustafa drawing on the interactive whiteboard

illuminate areas of their drawing. This seems to me to be the digital equiva-
lent – joint playing and exploration with the way marks, light and colour can
interact.

(Jackie Marsh, Field notes, 8 December 2017)

This play and exploration engaged a range of senses, primarily sight, touch and
hearing, as the children experimented with the tools to hand and transformed the
resources to create their collaborative physical and digital collages.

Active Learning

In Nursery 2, the three and four year olds were busy creating lights for the model
houses they had made with their parents. James, the maker working on the project,
had laser cut bases for the children to work with, and they had to use copper tape,
a battery and a LED to construct their light.

Helen has spent most of the session this morning building her light. She has
carefully attached copper tape to the wooden post, then linked the tape to the
battery. However, when she places her LED light at the top of the post, it
does not light up. She takes a peg and clips it on to the middle of the stand,
then clips another to the top of the stand, as I encourage her and comment on
her actions. This action serves the purpose of ensuring the LED prongs attach
securely to the copper tape, and her bulb lights up.

(Jackie Marsh, Field notes, 7 November 2017)

In this activity, Helen's concentration was sustained, and she did not give up when
her LED did not light up initially. Persistence is important in learning (Claxton &
Carlzon, 2019), and Helen demonstrated an ability to keep going in the face of initial
failure. This was typical of the majority of children who participated in this activity; their
motivation to develop a light for their house was significant in driving their learning.

Critical Thinking

In School 1, children created theatres from shoe boxes, in which they placed their
laser-cut Moomin characters, attached to dowels. Children also created backdrops
to their theatres, which contained lighting:

James wants to place four LEDs on his backdrop. He has punctured the back
of the box with four holes. James pushes the first LED through the hole, and
realises that to keep it in place, he can extend the legs of the LED across the
back of the shoe box, so that it does not fall out of the hole. He then does that
with two other LEDs, and places the final LED to the right of the others.
James gets the copper tape and begins to measure it out, initially attempting to
measure across all four bulbs. Prompted by an adult, who says "Should we cut

two different pieces?" James then realises that he needs two sets of copper tape, as the LED to the right requires a different connection. Pointing to the LEDs, he says, "So there may be two different pieces that link across." He carefully places the copper tape to create the circuit for the lights. Once that is completed, he attempts to light the LEDs by connecting the battery pack to the copper tape using crocodile clips. When this does not work, he looks at the battery pack to see if it is switched on. The adult helper points out the black lead, and James realises that he has connected it to wrong end of the copper tape. He changes it over, and the LEDs light up.

(Video recording, 24 April 2018)

In this excerpt, James demonstrates a range of critical thinking and problem-solving skills. At times, it was the intervention of the adult helper that prompted James to think in a different way about the problem, which indicates the value of scaffolding learning in makerspaces as well as sometimes leaving children to find out the solutions to their problems.

Creativity and Design

In School 2, the children had created clay models to populate imaginary playspaces. Using the app *Qlone*, these physical models were represented as 3D digital images, which were imported into *Google Tilt Brush*. The children could then create a Virtual Reality (VR) imaginary playspace in which the models were placed. Donning VR they were given the hand controls of the HTC Vive and set off to create their 3D worlds. It was notable for all of the adults involved in the activity that the children were able to create imaginative designs very quickly, realising that they could reach up, around and behind them using the handsets to create 3D drawings. They experimented with the drawing tools, which allowed them to change colours, create rainbow lines, clusters of stars, and so on. The children produced a range of VR worlds, which featured their 2D models.

Through a trial and error approach, the children experimented and learned to use the design features of the software.

Social Learning

Across all of the makerspaces, social learning was key to the learning experiences. Jane, a teacher in Nursery 1, offered her reflections on social learning:

And then I think it also helped them sort of socially because there was a lot of co-operation, especially coming back to the Play Doh activity, where it wasn't working. They were quite keen to try to work together to think of ways to make the bulb light up, and why shouldn't it, "Hey, have you tried doing it this way, what if we do this?" and I think that was a lovely sort of knock-on really, how helpful they were. And there was a particular child at that time who started in the September and he was very much a follower of some of the others. And they were very kind with that little boy, really helping him to get up to speed.

(Judith, teacher in Nursery 1)

This was typical across the makerspaces in all of the settings, in that they fostered a range of collaboration, interaction, peer support and learning.

These vignettes illustrate how makerspaces develop characteristics of effective learning in a range of ways, and, therefore, highlight the value of the MLAF in capturing this learning. Nonetheless, there are other ways of assessing children's learning in makerspaces that may involve the children more actively in reflecting on their learning, which are explored in the following section.

Other approaches to assessing learning in makerspaces

Alongside practitioner-led approaches to observation, models that involve documentation of children's activities could also be adopted in order to develop a portfolio approach to assessment. The Mosaic approach is one such multi-method framework (Clark, 2005; Clark and Moss, 2011), historically designed to explore children's perspectives in a participatory way. A key feature of the Mosaic approach is the 'concept of competence', whereby children are not positioned as 'passive objects' but as 'social actors' with lived experiences and perceptions. This 'notion of the competent child' underpins the 'pedagogy of listening' and the 'pedagogy of relationships' that form the basis of the Mosaic approach (Clark, 2005, p.30). The 'pedagogy of listening' includes three elements:

- Internal listening or self-reflection
- Multiple listening or openness to other 'voices'
- Visible listening including documentation and interpretation *(Clark, 2005, p.16)*.

These three aspects of 'listening' that underpin the multi-method framework of the Mosaic approach could be used as a framework for assessment in makerspaces. Listening in this context becomes a reflective process for children as they 'consider meanings, make discoveries and new connections and express understandings' (Clark, 2005, p.35) of their makerspace activities. Samuelson and Carlsson (2008) state that 'the starting-point as well as the result of learning has to be traced in terms of the child's perspective' (p.631) and that the child should be listened to and respected (p.633). Enabling children to be 'active participants' is in keeping with makerspace as a constructivist pedagogy where 'problem-finding, problem-solving and the power of social learning through sharing and collaborative work' is fundamental (Marsh et al., 2017, p.39).

Internal listening is a strategy that enables 'children to make sense of their world', providing them with the opportunity to 'reflect on their lived experiences rather than an abstract concept', and giving them 'the freedom to express an idea for the first time or in a new way' (Clarke, 2005, p.35). Multiple listening is an opportunity for children, facilitators, researchers, teachers, parents and other collaborators to 'listen to each other and themselves' (p.38). Visible listening uses a process of documentation to record the learning process, 'bringing it into being' and 'making it visible' (p.42). It is proposed that all three aspects of listening can be utilised to assess processes within the makerspace and use these assessments to communicate children's learning to other interested parties, for example, the child's teacher or parent.

It is envisaged that this assessment strategy would be ongoing over the course of the child's time participating in the makerspace project as a way of building a picture of the journey of learning that has been undertaken. Observations, photographs, book making and children's drawings could be used as a continuous source of documentation, and these artefacts could be used as a stimulus for discussion with children about their learning. These artefacts and transcripts from discussions could then be collated into an assessment folder or 'learning journey' to communicate to others what children have done and achieved during their time participating in makerspaces.

Learning Stories may also be of value in makerspaces. These constitute the documentation of children's progress through a narrative approach. The focus is on formative assessment that offers 'feed-back and feed-forward to learners, other staff, and families in the interest of better teaching and learning' (Lee & Carr, 2006, p.2). Underpinned by socio-cultural and ecological perspectives, Learning Stories work to:

i   Enhance children's sense of themselves as capable people and competent learners.
ii Reflect the holistic way that children learn.
iii Reflect the reciprocal relationships between the child, people and the learning environment.
iv Involve parents/guardians and, where appropriate, extended family (ibid, p.3).

In a similar way to the Mosaic approach, Learning Stories include written narratives, photography and video footage, and examples of children's work (p.4). The documentation process utilises technology, aligning comfortably with the ethos of the makerspace, and this could enable assessment to be a co-construction between the child and facilitator. The use of technology also makes assessments much easier to share with parents, and the child's teacher, and allows the sharing of other perceptions within this process.

Current assessment practices in early years often utilise the use of online learning journals such as *Tapestry* and *Kinderly*, which are built upon the same concept as Learning Stories. Using these tools allows observations to be recorded digitally in real time, photographs and videos can be taken which can be annotated, and parents and other interested parties are also able to view and contribute to this evidencing of a child's achievements. The use of these tools to record observations through technological media, and the ease with which they can be shared with other parties make them an interesting proposal when considering assessment opportunities for makerspace activities.

Conclusion

Along with the new affordances provided by makerspaces for learning come new implications for pedagogy and assessment, both in terms of principle and practice. This chapter outlines in detail one approach to assessing learning in makerspaces, focusing on characteristics of effective learning. Whilst this approach aligns well to the Early Years Foundation Stage requirements in England, it is the case that because these characteristics are universal, they can inform approaches to assessment elsewhere. In addition, these characteristics are not only specific to nurseries and kindergartens; as some of the vignettes in this chapter demonstrated, they are also of value when considering children's learning in primary school.

The chapter has also considered other methods of assessment which can involve children more actively in the documentation of, and reflection on, learning. All of these approaches have value within the context of makerspaces. This is not to suggest that assessment needs to be undertaken in all makerspaces; in some contexts, this will not be appropriate. As early years settings and schools begin to incorporate makerspaces within their work, however, assessment will be important in order to ensure that children's learning is sufficiently well documented and can inform approaches to teaching and learning in other areas of the school's work, such as subject lessons. The principle of the transferability of skills and knowledge across contexts is an important one, and, thus, developing the tools to foster such transfer by acknowledging what has been learned in specific learning spaces is key. In the years ahead, this challenge will be one that is taken up in various ways by those settings that are forging ahead to create new and innovative approaches to learning in makerspaces.

References

Allina, B. (2018). The development of STEAM educational policy to promote student creativity and social empowerment. *Arts Education Policy Review*, 119(2), 77–87.

Bakhshi, H. & Mateos-Garcia, J. (2014). Fix the pipeline for STEAM talent in the creative economy. Retrieved from www.nesta.org.uk/blog/fix-pipeline-steam-talent-creative-economy, 21 May 2018.

Barniskis, S.C. (2014). Makerspaces and teaching artists. *Teaching Artist Journal*, 12(1), 6–14.

Beghetto, R.A. (2005). Does assessment kill student creativity? *The Educational Forum*, 69(3), 254–263.

Bevan, B., Ryoo, J.J., Shea, M., Kekelis, L., Pooler, P., Green, E., Bulalacao, N., McLeod, E., Sandoval, J., & Hernandez, M. (2016). *Making as a Strategy for Afterschool STEM Learning: Report from the Californian Tinkering Afterschool Network Research-Practice Partnership*. San Francisco, CA: USE: The Exploratorium.

Biggs, J. & Tang, C. (2007). *Teaching for Quality Learning at University*. Maidenhead, UK: SRHE and Open University Press.

Blackley, S., Rahmawati, Y., Fitriani, E., Sheffield, R. & Koul, R. (2018). Using a Makerspace approach to engage Indonesian primary students with STEM. *Issues in Educational Research*, 28(1), 18–42.

Blikstein, P., Kabayadondo, Z., Martin, A., & Fields, D. (2017). Assessment of technological literacies in makerspaces and FabLabs. *Journal of Engineering Education*, 106(1), 149–175.

Boud, D. (2009). How can practice reshape assessment? In G. Joughin (Ed.) *Assessment, Learning and Judgement in Higher Education*. Dordrecht: Springer.

Bristol Learning City (2017). *Bristol Early Years Characteristics of Effective Learning (CoEL)*. Retrieved from www.bristolearlyyears.org.uk/wp-content/uploads/2017/04/Bristol-EY-CoEL-Final-Document.pdf, 16 July 2018.

Care, E. & Luo, R. (2016). *Assessment of Transversal Competencies: Policy and Practice in the Asia-Pacific Region*. Paris, France: UNESCO Bangkok Office.

Chuter, A. (2016). What does assessment look like in makerspaces? Retrieved from https://ict4kids.ca/2016/04/04/what-does-assessment-look-like-in-makerspaces/, 7 June 2017.

Clark, A. (2005). Ways of seeing: Using the Mosaic approach to listen to young children's perspectives. In: A. Clark, P. Moss & A. Kjørholt (Eds.) *Beyond Listening: Children's Perspectives on Early Childhood Services* (pp. 29–49). Bristol, UK: The Policy Press.

Claxton, G. and Carlzon, B. (2019). *Powering Up Children: The Learning Power Approach to Primary Teaching*. Carmarthen, Wales: Crown House Publishing.

Davis, R., Kafai, Y., Vasudevan, V., & Lee, E. (2013). The education arcade: Crafting, remixing, and playing with controllers for Scratch games. *Proceedings of the 12th International Conference on Interaction Design and Children*, pp.439–442. New York: ACM.

Department for Education (DfE) (2017). *Statutory Framework for the Early Years Foundation Stage*. London: Crown Copyright.

European Skills/Competences, Qualifications and Occupations (ESCO) (2018). Skill reusability level. Retrieved from https://ec.europa.eu/esco/portal/escopedia/Skill_reusability_level, 4 June 2018.

Fleming, L. (2015). *Worlds of Making: Best Practices for Establishing a Makerspace for Your School*. London: Corwin.

Flores, C. (2014). The role of peer assessment in a maker classroom. Retrieved from http://fablearn.stanford.edu/fellows/blog/role-peer-assessment-maker-classroom, 4 June 2017.

Fontchiaro, K. (2015). *Design Thinking*. Ann Arbor, MI: Cherry Lake Publishers.

Gahagan, P.M. (2016) Evaluating Makerspaces: Exploring methods used to assess the outcomes of public library makerspaces. Retrieved from http://researcharchive.vuw.ac.nz/handle/10063/5193, 4 June 2017.

Gaskins, N. (2014). *Techno-vernacular Creativity, Innovation and Learning in Under-represented Ethnic Communities of Practice*. PhD thesis, Georgia Institute of Technology.

Hague, C. & Payton, S. (2010). *Digital Literacy across the Curriculum*. Bristol, UK: Futurelab.

Hughes, J. M. (2017). Digital making with "At-Risk" youth. *International Journal of Information and Learning Technology*, 34(2), 102–113. http://doi.org/10.1108/ijilt-08-2016-0037

Isabelle, A. & Valle, N. (2015) *Inspiring STEM Minds*. Rotterdam, the Netherlands: Sense Publishers.

Jenlink, P. (2015). STEM teacher education: Imagining a metadisciplinary future. *Teacher Education Practice*, 28(2/3), 197–207.

Julian, K. & Parrott, D. (2017). Makerspaces in the library: Science in a student's hands. *Journal of Learning Spaces*, 6(2), 13–21.

Kohn, A. (2000). *The Case Against Standardized Testing*. Portsmouth, NH: Heinemann.

Land, M. (2013). Full STEAM ahead: The benefits of integrating the arts into STEM. *Procedia Computer Science*, 20, 547–552

Lee, W. & Carr, M. (2006) *Documentation of Learning Stories: A Powerful Assessment Tool for Early Childhood*. Retrieved from http://newzealand.anniewhite.cikeys.com/wp-content/uploads/2016/04/Documentation-of-Learning-Stories-Wendy-Lee-Margaret-Carr.pdf, 10 July 2018.

Marsh, J., Kumpulainen, K., Nisha, B., Velicu, A., Blum-Ross, A., Hyatt, D., Jónsdóttir, S. R., Levy, R., Little, S., Marusteru, G., Ólafsdóttir, M.E., Sandvik, K., Scott, F., Thestrup, K., Arnseth, H.C., Dýrfjörð, K., Jornet, A., Kjartansdóttir, S.H., Pahl, K., Pétursdóttir, S.,

& Thorsteinsson, G. (2017). *Makerspaces in the Early Years: A Literature Review.* University of Sheffield: MakEY Project. Retrieved from http://makeyproject.eu/wp-content/uploa ds/2017/02/Makey_Literature_Review.pdf, 2 September 2019.

Marsh, J., Nordström, A., Sairanen, H., & Shkul, M. (in press). Making the Moomins: A Finnish/English adventure. In: K. Kumpulainen & J. Sefton-Green (Eds.) *Multiliteracies in Finland and Beyond: International Perspectives on an Early Years Innovation.* London: Routledge.

Martinez, S. & Stager, G. (2013). *Invent to Learn: Making, Tinkering, and Engineering in the Classroom.* Torrance, CA: Constructing Modern Knowledge Press.

Organisation for Economic and Co-operative Development (OECD) (2012). *PISA 2012 Results: Creative Problem Solving Students' Skills in Tackling Real-life Problems, Volume V.* Retrieved from www.oecd.org/pisa/keyfindings/PISA-2012-results-volume-V.pdf, 11 June 2018.

Papert, S. (1980). *Mindstorms: Children Computers, and Powerful Ideas.* New York: Basic Books.

Papert, S. (2001). Project-based learning. Accessed from www.edutopia.org/seymour-pap ert-project-based-learning, 5 June 2017.

Peppler, K., Halverson, E., & Kafai, Y. (Eds.) (2016). *Makeology: Makerspaces as Learning Environments* (Volume 1 and 2). New York: Routledge.

Race, P. (2001). *A Briefing on Self, Peer & Group Assessment.* York: Learning and Teaching Support Network Generic Centre. Retrieved from: https://phil-race.co.uk/wp-content/ uploads/Self,_peer_and_group_assessment.pdf, 2 September 2019.

Samuelson, I. & Carlsson, M. (2008) The playing learning child: Towards a pedagogy of early childhood. *Scandinavian Journal of Educational Research*, 52(6), 623–641.

Stewart, N. (2014). Active learning. In: H. Moylett (Ed.) *Characteristics of Effective Early Learning: Helping Young Children Become Learners for Life* (pp. 54–71). Maidenhead, UK: Open University Press.

10

CONNECTING LEARNING

Parents and young children in museum makerspaces[1]

Alicia Blum-Ross and Sonia Livingstone

Introduction

On a crowded Saturday at the Bay Area Discovery Museum (BADM), toddlers and ten-year-olds ran in and out of buildings, blowing bubbles and making gigantic constructions from foam building blocks or using unusual objects to make music. Within the former military barracks tucked into the fog below the northern end of the San Francisco Golden Gate Bridge, the facilitators have built on learning research to create spaces for "STEM-focused, inquiry-driven experiences that help children develop creativity and creative problem-solving skills".[2]

At the edge of the courtyard was what the facilitators called the "world's first early childhood FabLab".[3] Founded in conjunction with the Fab Foundation, it had equipment similar to that of adult makerspaces – 3D printers, a laser cutter and a CNC router, a table piled with tablets – along with bins of markers and child scissors, stacks of cardboard and multi-coloured tape, plasticine, hammers and nails.[4] Crowded around the low hexagonal tables were rotating crowds of children, sitting by themselves or on their parents' laps. Although the entry sign advertised that today's activity – designing and making an aerodynamic flying machine using the tablets and laser cutter – was for children aged five and above, the room also bustled with toddlers and older siblings.

Children's making activities in museums are generally facilitated by adult intermediaries – the accompanying parent or caregiver as well as by the facilitators.[5] Parents enable the making by identifying the opportunity and finding the resources (cost of entry, transportation). In some cases, they also get involved in helping children learn, though others are hopeful but unsure of their role. Indeed, their role may remain unclear, even as their child is welcomed into the makerspace and quickly occupied with tasks. Should a parent sit with their child or hang back? How 'helpful' should they be? What is expected of them by the facilitators, or indeed by other onlooking parents?[6]

Drawing on ethnographic research conducted in 2017–2018 in three museum makerspaces in the San Francisco Bay Area (California, USA), this chapter focuses on the role of families, usually parents but sometimes grandparents or other relatives or caregivers, in facilitating young children's activities in museum makerspaces. Our enquiry is situated in the 'connected learning' framework, which explores the benefits for young people of informal and non-formal learning across sites, especially in the context of new digital opportunities to "hang out, mess around and geek out" (Ito et al., 2010). Connected Learning proposes that digital media provide unique opportunities for children and young people to follow their passions and interests across the multiple (traditionally siloed) spaces of their lives – home, school, peers and interest-driven learning spaces (Ito et al., 2013; Livingstone and Sefton-Green, 2016).

When we joined the MakEY project we noted some of the same observations we had made in our previous project, *Parenting for a Digital Future* (P4DF, Livingstone and Blum-Ross, forthcoming), in which we had studied families and technology use including observations of children in digital media and learning sites. We saw how in initiatives to facilitate digital media learning, parents are often left hesitant on the sidelines – neither positively invited to join in nor really able to leave. Whether hanging around in corridors outside classrooms or at the edge of a busy room of child-focused activity, parents are often at a loss, not introduced to each other and so unable to chat, instead filling the time by staring at their phones. We wondered, like them, what the facilitators expect of them. We also wanted to know, what do the parents expect – of their child, the facilitators, themselves? What led them to bring their child here, and what might they do differently when they return home? As in the graphic design or music technology classes we had previously observed during P4DF, we noted some of the same hesitancy. However, in the case of making, here, with younger children involved and with a more direct invitation to parents from facilitators (as we discuss below), we noted the capacity for more active engagement. In this chapter we argue that parents can play a role in connecting or disconnecting learning across people and sites, especially when children are young. We explore how this role is conceived and how it can be intentionally designed.

There is very little research on parents and making (Marsh et al., 2017, although see Roque, 2016) and little more on families and museums (Ellenbogen, 2003; Nadelson, 2013). Parents value the promised 'educational' benefits, although families differ in their interests depending on multiple factors. Insofar as families arrive at the museum as a unit (however composed), they act as 'dispersed learning systems', and so are unlike individual visitors in the sense that they move through the museum together and apart, reinforcing one another's experiences (Brahms and Crowley, 2016, Benjamin, Haden and Wilkerson, 2010).

In this chapter, we first consider how the institutional and physical arrangements of museums and the relationships with museum facilitators 'invite' (or not) parents to participate alongside children in making activities. Second, we map the range of ways in which parents enact more or less supportive roles during children's making experiences. Our findings are based on observations made and interviews conducted with facilitators, parents and children during visits to three museums in or near Silicon Valley in 2017 and 2018 – the Bay Area Discovery Museum (BADM), The Tech Museum of Innovation ('The Tech') and the Lawrence Hall of Science (LHS), each described below. We visited each museum three to five times, for several hours per visit. We began with 'gatekeeper' interviews with senior museum staff, then scoping follow-up visits to capture the range of activities and participants (for instance, by arranging some visits on no-cost or outreach days). In each location, the museum facilitators placed a sign at the makerspace entrance notifying parents of our research and informing them of their option to decline participation – by telling us or the facilitators. We conducted interviews with families opportunistically, giving parents an information sheet, asking for permission to audio- or video-record activities, and for signed consent for interviews. Some parents were happy to speak with us but declined to be recorded. The interviews, photos and video recordings were hand-coded inductively according to emergent themes, framed by relevant research (as cited in this chapter).

Museum makerspaces

Museum makerspaces present opportunities and challenges within the aim of involving parents with young children in the process of making. All the museum makerspaces we visited prioritised easy-to-achieve activities that could be completed in a quick visit, although some families stayed for longer periods of time (Sheridan et al., 2014). But museums are often crowded and filled with other things to see and do. Parents may discourage children from staying too long in one place.

The three museums had different characteristics and aims. Although some of the activities were similar (this was unplanned, although the activities are also reminiscent of other projects described in this volume – there being an emerging canon of age-appropriate making activities for young children), these were adapted to their particular environment or emphasis. In each, we saw such mechanical engineering challenges as creating an aeroplane or designing a vehicle to carry a 'payload'. Differences among the museums are neatly illustrated by their gift shops: at The Tech the shop was filled with T-shirts and mugs emblazoned with the word 'Geek'; at LHS they sold science-oriented gifts (geodes, a periodic table); at BADM they sold fairy costumes and craft kits.

The Tech is located in San José, a mixed ethnicity city at the Southern end of Silicon Valley. Just a few miles from where Steve Jobs founded Apple computers, it was the most technology focused, with permanent exhibits on microprocessors, cybersecurity, robotics, VR and more, sponsored by such companies as Intel, Google and Lockheed Martin. Its makerspace – the **Design Lab** – occupied a substantial area on the lower floor cordoned off with barricades. This required parents to enter through a designated opening staffed by a greeter, a technique also employed by the other museums. The Tech's exhibits were fairly conceptual, perhaps explaining why the families we interviewed here had children at the older end of our age range (6+). Facilitators described their 'sweet spot' as eight-to-nine-year-olds, although in practice there were many older and younger children.

Unsurprisingly, given its location, many families we spoke with worked in technology or related industries.

The LHS is across the bay from San Francisco in Berkeley, California, and affiliated with the University of California, Berkeley, university home to the world-renowned physics laboratory where the 'cyclotron' (a particle accelerator) was invented; the museum is built in brutalist concrete to resemble the cyclotron. Many of the younger facilitators and volunteers at LHS are drawn from UC Berkeley. The target age for visitors was a bit younger – children aged four or five years, although again there was a range. LHS's dedicated makerspace – the **Ingenuity Lab** – was in a dedicated downstairs classroom. Some of the parents we spoke with 'worked in tech', but the range of experiences was wider, including university parents also.

The Bay Area Discovery Museum (BADM) is located in Marin, at the northern end of San Francisco Bay, at the end of a long winding road that leads onto historic parkland where the museum is housed in former army barracks. Of the three museums, BADM has the most visible emphasis on 'creativity', in addition to science. Rather than emphasising 'engineering', as at The Tech or LHS, BADM facilitators talked more of 'design' or 'imagination', describing it not as a "children's museum or a science museum but an early childhood centre with a science focus". However, its makerspace was by far the most digital of the three museums – with activities including designing prototypes on paper, then on tablets using the design software Tinkercad, then cutting out shapes and assembling before testing and iterating designs.[7] Visitors were a mix of local parents from a range of professions, including tech; being located near the Golden Gate Bridge and within a national park, BADM also attracted many tourists.

We were not able to collect demographic data on the museum visitors, instead inferring some socio-economic circumstances from our observations or from information gleaned in interviews. Many parents were high in economic and cultural capital, for instance working in software engineering or academia, and most were White or Asian. That said, the museums were sensitive to diversity, attempting to attract new visitors through targeted outreach.[8] At BADM a senior staff member told us:

> We do have an over-representation of… college-educated, wealthy, affluent, privileged families. Our school groups definitely are one way that diversify the audience of kids that we are bringing in, and we are spending a lot of time thinking about how, how to diversify further, given the immediate communities are very affluent.

BADM had created a mobile makerspace they called the Try it Truck, to bring making activities – including some specialist digital equipment – into surrounding low-income communities. The truck had taken considerable resources to build, although the staff told us that it was "very donation friendly; family and corporate donations have been pouring in and it's actually fully funded for the next 2–3 years which is awesome". The

Tech ran similar outreach with local schools and held a quarterly 'sensory day' for young visitors on the autism spectrum.

Are these inviting spaces for parents? In all three museums, the 'greeters' subtly telegraphed to parents their responsibilities – for example, giving them instructions to get their child started and, thereby, reinforcing the idea that the activity was not a 'drop-off' session where parents could leave children unattended. In each museum, although especially at BADM, the makerspace was scattered with table-top signs and posters giving prompts to parents about the activity – some were heavily text-based giving explicit 'tips to support your child' or explaining the activity. However, we rarely saw parents glance at these signs, preferring to turn to museum facilitators with questions instead.

In other respects, each makerspace was different in how it invited (or didn't invite) parents into the activities designed for their child. At BADM the tables and chairs were very low (similar to those that might be found in primary schools) or activities took place on cushioned mats on the floor. Parents had to physically crouch, lean over awkwardly or sit on the ground if they were to join their children. Although many did so willingly, or crowded in with children on their laps, the material arrangements were more comfortable for children than adults. At The Tech, tables were at waist height (on an adult) and there were no chairs at all. The facilitators explained this was designed to help parents get involved (since when they had chairs previously, parents tended to sit to one side). At LHS the makerspace resembled a classroom for older children, with tables at a more comfortable height for adults; here the parents spent the most time sitting next to their child(ren) – this space was most comfortable for those with limited mobility, and here we saw the most active grandparents. Far from casual, these material arrangements occupied a lot of facilitator effort. A senior staff member at The Tech described how they worked to

> support whole family groups... One of the points of friction can potentially be the fact that we have these longer dwell time activities [such as making] now. So, you know, if an older sibling who is eight or nine or ten really wants to do one of our activities, there's got to be something for the rest of the family like a nearby exhibit or naptime space. We are trying to think about the family experience holistically, not just focusing on the eight-year-old.

How facilitators view parents

Planning for whole families is demanding in terms of resources, and because facilitators generally know little of parents' skills, concerns or circumstances. In makerspaces for young children, relating to parents cannot be avoided. In our interviews with facilitators, although they strove to be positive we found them sometimes critical of parents, since their efforts were most needed in the face of problematic parental behaviour. Our questioning drew out how their observations of parents' interactions with children led them to alter their own practice or reconfigure the makerspace. For example, they worried about the 'problem' of parents who were either uninvolved in their children's activities or so involved that they 'took over' what their child was doing. A librarian in the space visited by the Try it Truck explained to us that she

> sees a lot of different parenting styles… sometimes there are parents who are very encouraging. Sometimes I do get some parents who are literally on their phone the entire time and not paying attention to what their child is doing. There's everything from being really engaged, sometimes actually doing the activities for them, to being more of a supportive role and encouraging them to do it on their own. It's a mixture of all of those things, sometimes with the same parent.

While parenting styles indeed vary, for any activity, makerspaces face the particular pedagogic challenge that their very ethos is one of open-ended tinkering, iterating and learning from mistakes. A young BADM facilitator suggested that parents were tempted to take an overly "hands-on approach" because

> I think that the protective parents don't want their kids to fail. But that's part of what this space is – a safe place to fail; the design process *is* failing, and testing and improving.

To persuade parents to leave behind their focus on outcomes and recognise the distinctive learning *process* of the makerspace, the BADM facilitators had created signs which read: 'Think, Make, Try'. Faced with sometimes 'pushy' parents who seemingly could not let their child do the activity by themselves, stepping in when failure was threatened, one facilitator described how parents often "underestimate what kids are capable of doing".

Recognising that parents have "so many different mindsets", a Tech facilitator explained how she tried to avoid a "one-size-fits-all" approach, trying

> to keep parents involved, whether it's having them play a supportive role like holding pieces together or having parents be a documentarian, taking photos and really celebrating the different parts of the process.

One BADM facilitator went so far as to suggest that parents are their 'true impact audience', the makerspace's aim being

> about changing the behaviour of adults. Because we have a kid here for 45 minutes, that doesn't change their life. But if in their parents coming here or their teachers coming here they see something differently, they think about how to, to set up learning experiences for their kids differently… [this makes] parents much more meta-aware of what kids can do.

Thus, facilitators talked of 'modelling' to parents the brokering and scaffolding activities needed to facilitate children's learning. For example, a BADM facilitator described how she would try to "spoon-feed more open-ended questioning" to parents, showing them how to elicit questions in turn from their child (rather than just asking the child the kinds of yes/no questions which turn the interaction into a test of knowledge). This dual goal – of educating parents through educating their children – remained unstated in a museum context where formal evaluation emphasised attendance figures and customer satisfaction as much as learning outcomes. Facilitators were uncomfortably aware that parents might not take kindly to being instructed, as a young undergraduate working as a facilitator at LHS explained,

> whenever I'm talking I make sure to make eye contact with the parent and the child. I make sure they're all included in the conversation of what we're doing, getting them both excited... for the most part it's not a problem. But when a parent is not really involved or just sitting with the kid, I always try to go and try to build with the kid and then find little ways for the parent to pay attention... like saying 'do you want to show your mom?'... I'm still navigating that, to be honest, because I don't want to be necessarily rude and be like, 'Hey, you should look at what your child's doing.'

The view of parents, by facilitators, was thus ambivalent – both acknowledging the strengths of some by aiming to shape the actions of others. How, then, did we see this play out in practice?

Parent roles in makerspaces

Building on research on how parents, of diverse backgrounds, support children's digital interests and the development of digital literacy (Barron, Martin, Takeuchi and Fithian, 2009; Barron and Levinson 2018; Brough, Cho and Mustain, forthcoming) and how parents act to support children's emergent interest in STEM-related subjects, even when they lack subject-area knowledge themselves (Brahms and Crowley, 2016; McClure et al., 2017), we developed a typology of different ways in which parents interacted with children within makerspaces. Before detailing this typology, we should note that these categories are not static, and many parents moved between and amongst different roles even within the same visit. Compared with the facilitators, our advantage as 'outsider researchers' was that we could interview these diverse parents about their perceptions and choices, asking parents about their expectations of the makerspace and how they conceived of its relation to their child's learning at home or school,[9] bringing a rarely heard parent perspective into research on children's digital media learning.[10] This typology is a set of composite actions, bringing together observations we made across different sites.

Babysitting

Although facilitators realised that parents may "need a break" when they come into the makerspace, accepting that they may not always take part, they were disparaging of parents they saw as disengaged. For some parents, basic supervision seemed sufficient for their role in makerspaces. But is there more to it? At BADM we observed an Asian-American mother enter with three sons aged six to ten to do the cardboard sculptures activity. As the boys gathered materials on the floor, she found a low chair to the side of the room and checked her phone while the boys began enthusiastically hacking at the thick cardboard with the available tools. Our fieldnotes recorded:

> She sits nearby, takes lots of pictures on her phone… periodically shouts out 'careful!' or 'watch your hands!' but doesn't really give any other guidance. Oldest kid in particular is enthusiastically singing, designing with pencil and then cutting with a saw.

In conversation with the mother, she described her careful attention to her children's diet and activities and her overall concern for their "health and safety". We learned, too, that she thought coming to the makerspace was the 'right' thing to do, but she lacked a language for what they were doing there. This was not necessarily a matter of social class, for museum entry and her phone were costly, and she told us not only of other museum visits but also that she only buys organic food. So perhaps puzzlement about making and makerspaces helps explain some parents' adoption of a 'babysitting' role across the economic spectrum.

In the Try it Truck in the low-income community (parked outside a public library), we saw another mother, a Filipina elder care worker, who had brought her daughters aged six and eight to the after-school activity because they were regulars at the library and found it 'relaxing'. On this occasion, after helping the girls get set up with one of the activities, she spent the session outside on the library computers, checking in periodically. The two girls helped each other through the different activity stations, requiring minimal supervision. Although the librarian we interviewed expressed some frustration at parents who simply dropped off their children and didn't engage in the activity, she was sensitive to the fact that within the low-income community, "a lot of parents are really overworked, they're working multiple jobs. A lot of times they are really dependent upon our resources".

At the end of the session we interviewed the family together. The older girl described her yearning for Minecraft, which her parents did not want to pay for, saying "my dad said he doesn't like to buy stuff on the app store. He said why would you pay for it when you can get a free one? But the free ones, but they're not even one bit like Minecraft". The mother had begrudgingly agreed to the purchase of Minecraft for the daughter's upcoming ninth birthday because, she said, "it's creativity and, you know, maths". At the makerspace, the girls were using tablets loaded with Tinkercad, which their mother considered good because it was "hands on", in contrast with their use of tablets at home, when she would lose track of time while "busy, cooking, so we forget what time it is already, like two hours of playing and then I feel disappointed when it's too long for them… it's going to break their eyes". Thus, while minimally 'babysitting' her children within the space, the mother had brought them because she believed in its benefits, in contrast to her worries about 'screen time' at home (Blum-Ross and Livingstone, 2018). Seemingly, in neither space did she conceive of an active or engaged role for herself in supporting or connecting her daughters' learning. As we know from wider public discourses, insofar as parents adopt a babysitting role, whether at home or in museums or elsewhere, they are tacitly judged.

Supervising

Some parents engaged in what initially seemed to be 'babysitting' but instead turned out to be a subtle form of supervision. Far from disengaged, we discovered in our conversations with their parents that they were practising a highly engaged but 'hands-off' form of encouragement. For example, at The Tech Museum, we met an African-American mother who was standing nearby but several feet back from the high table where her daughters (aged eight and ten) were taking part in the 'from here to there' activity, where they had to deliver a 'payload' across a model of the San Francisco Bay. Though not asking questions or offering advice, nor was she looking at her phone or doing anything else, saying when asked: "I just want to let them do it themselves." When the girls took their contraptions over to the map she moved with them, staying nearby, asking a couple of questions like "is it too heavy?" but not touching the materials herself. Her daughters stayed an unusually long time within the activity, testing out their designs over and over again, changing and tweaking their configurations to make the rubber bands more taut or change the angles on the beam. Their mother stood quietly but steadfastly nearby – only very occasionally asking or prompting by helping (especially the younger daughter) solve a problem.

Supervising independent learning in this way was not entirely unusual. At LHS we interviewed a White mother of a six-year-old boy, attending for his birthday, who similarly stood back from a child's activity. She too had an articulated philosophy as to her seeming disengagement:

> If I'm with him, he will want me to help him. So I often try and just leave him alone. I want him to feel challenged when his mind doesn't know how to do something, or when he thinks he might not be able to do something. If I'm not there, and he is forced to figure it out, then that's where the magic happens, and that's where growing happens.

Thus, what may look like disengaged parenting may in fact be a highly conscious effort to give children space to let their ideas evolve themselves.

Cheerleading

Both babysitting and supervising were often combined with *cheerleading* – in which parents praised and celebrated their child's accomplishments, often loudly, often too by taking photos or video. Indeed, it seemed to us that the advent of the smartphone exacerbated the normative expectation that parents would join in with cheerleading, the ritual of recording children's activities seemingly hard to resist, and with some children often watched most closely through the phone's camera lens. Cheerleading may also have been common because it did not require parents to have any specialist knowledge or understanding of the activity itself – and as we saw in the instances above, parents did not always grasp the nature or purpose of the activity, and they could be intimidated by the presence of 3D printers and laser cutters, as well as by the young and confident facilitators. It offered a familiar form of parental engagement for those inclined to sit out the session on their phone, or who were preoccupied with accompanying babies or toddlers, looking up when their child returned from an activity to regale them with their success.

As already discussed, cheerleading tends to transform what's meant to be learning-by-doing into learning-as-outcome – as when parents waited for the end of the activity to take a photo, hoping for a completed product (however rough and ready) to be held up proudly. Relatedly, cheerleading favours successful outcomes over learning by iterating through trial and error, for all that a facilitator may explain that learning by reflecting on why things went wrong can be far better than the lucky fluke of early success. For example, in our fieldnotes we recorded myriad times in which parents made supportive but relatively banal statements like "that looks great!" or "good job!" This is not to say that there is not a place for these enthusiastic responses, for children were often quite evidently pleased to have made their parents happy, but such statements were rarely tailored to the task at hand or helpful in helping a child understand the strengths or weaknesses of the approach they had taken.

Problematic from the connected learning perspective, cheerleading individualises the activity; a facilitator may have mobilised children to collaborate as a group, but over and again we saw parents take a photo of their own child at the end – possibly being nervous to photograph other people's children, possibly not recognising the collective nature of the activity. Indeed, the very moment of celebration easily dominates a 'teachable moment', often shared with a group, when at the end of an activity, had parents not gathered so excitedly with their congratulations and flashing phones, facilitators might have drawn out of the children some reflections on what worked, or not, why and what to try next.

Collaborating

Some parents took a more hands-on approach to scaffolding their child's learning in the makerspace, e.g. by physically assisting in the creation of a designed artefact or collaborating on envisioning what the child might complete. At BADM we met a mother who was attending with four children aged six to nine, two of her own and two of her neighbours'. The mother, an immigrant from Armenia, worked part-time in science policy with a husband who was a software engineer. Amidst a creative cardboard box activity, she sat on the floor to work with the two youngest children, while also cheerleading for the older ones.

Unlike many of the parents we observed during this activity, she started the children off by looking at the sample pictures provided by the facilitators to illustrate the different constructions they might make. First, they brainstormed together, and then she encouraged the children to create 'shelters' for their stuffed animals. The mother alternated between different postures – prepping materials for the children to add to their creations (e.g. ripping off pieces of tape for the child to stick on) and providing feedback and encouragement. She was clearly resisting 'taking over' the task, as our fieldnotes recorded:

> The son is trying to get a piece of cardboard onto the base of his pyramid shape – mum says 'It's not big enough, honey, get a pencil and measure it.' He goes and gets a pencil and a bigger piece of cardboard – she shows him how to hold the shape onto the base and draw around but hands the pencil back to him after making the first mark. Then he gets the small saw, starts cutting the cardboard while holding it in the air. She says, 'that's a dangerous way to do it, here let me help you' – braces the piece on the floor and scores a cut about an inch deep at the top to hold the knife in place and then hands it back so that he cuts it himself.

While the mother engaged in cheerleading (saying "awesome! It's perfect") her feedback was more concrete and specific – for example telling one child, "I really like the pattern you made with the tape." Not all parents managed to resist taking over the task, and not all recognised the value of specific feedback from which a child could learn. However, it was just such activities that the facilitators sought to encourage in parents, with some success.

This collaborative or scaffolding model of parental engagement was enacted differently depending on the age and abilities of the child(ren). Parents of younger children collaborated more physically and their artefacts reflected more of a co-design process in which the parent had been nearly as involved as the child. Often, we observed a parent–child pair crowding together over a task, or a child sitting on a parent's lap, or the parent physically holding a hand over a child's hand or helping open and close scissors. In such ways, parents acted as children's 'eyes' and 'hands', helping them see the potential in materials and physically realise their designs. Such physical intimacy supported collaboration in ways that professional facilitators cannot generally undertake (Sheridan et al., 2014).

Parallel play

In some cases, we found that parents and children engaged in making in close proximity to but in some ways separate from each other. We thought of this as 'parallel play' (drawing on the term from early childhood development research).[11] For example, at LHS, we met grandparents (White) visiting the Bay Area from Pennsylvania attended a 'jitterbots/artbots' session in the makerspace with their five-year-old granddaughter. The activity involved making circuits to animate a construction that would then draw patterns on a sheet of paper. The grandfather explained to us that he is a furniture maker, so while he was new to the concept of circuitry he understood how to make a stable construction. The girl worked mainly with her grandmother who acted as a collaborator, while her grandfather was sat next to her making his own construction. The three quietly concentrated on constructing their bots, with the girl occasionally glancing at her grandfather's progress, iterating ideas for her own bot – and sometimes they swapped objects to check out each other's creations.

Some facilitators reflected on these scenarios, describing how they would specifically give materials to a parent to encourage them to play and experiment alongside their children. For example, a facilitator from The Tech told us that if she saw a parent taking over too much she would

> introduce a new set of materials for them to both work on projects independent of each other or next to each other but they are both working on their own projects. And then you can play up the 'try them out against each other and try to learn from each other's'.

We saw similar scenarios multiple times, especially with older children engaging in friendly competition with parents to create effective designs. Sometimes this competitive edge backfired, with parents taking over by *directing* their children's designs and preventing them from pursuing their own ideas.

As noted, parents did not always stick within one of these categories but rather moved between and amongst them. For example, at The Tech Museum, we met a family of four – a father from India and an Indian-American mother with an eight-year-old boy and an eleven-year-old girl. The mother and daughter worked quietly side by side to each create their own version of a Mars Rover which could, powered by a fan, deliver a 3D printed cupcake up a ramp and over a gap. Each created their own design, walking back and forth from the trial table to the materials table to iterate and improve their design after testing it. The father, who described himself as an engineer, worked with the son directly, creating a shared idea that varied between the son's initiative but with the father increasingly directing the action by telling where the son to put the ballast on his small 'ship'. The father announced "it's a competition!", before egging on not only his wife but also his son and his daughter to see who could create the most aerodynamic design. At times the dad heavily directed the son, physically lifting the design out of his hands to make something more secure; still, after tinkering with the design for a few moments he generally handed it back to his son to continue iterating – changing the direction of the sail and ensuring a smooth journey.

Parents as connectors

Although one might be tempted to judge some of the parents – especially those 'babysitting' for being too hands-off or those 'directing' or taking over for being too controlling – we have instead sought to understand how they may be tailoring their actions (or inactions) in accordance with their own understandings, skills and values, as well as the needs of their children. Our initial views of the parents were frequently challenged by talking to them, at times leading us to turn a critical lens instead on the facilitators, especially in their assumptions about parents and parental understanding, and the design of the makerspace and the degree of welcome it offers.

One specific contribution of the parents – easily overlooked by the facilitators during the busy sessions – was the work they did in connecting their child's learning experiences across sites, helping them make sense of the makerspace activities in relation to other parts of their lives. For example, at LHS we observed a Native American mother building artbots with her two young daughters (three and five). She linked the activity to other things they had seen in the museum, and other lessons they had participated in as part of their small community of home-schooled families, for instance explaining how the artbots were "like R2D2" (a reference to the girls' love of Star Wars). At the same time, she looked to the professional facilitators to explain the scientific concepts to her daughters so she could build upon them. As one facilitator observed, parents can be helpful in the makerspace

> because they know that child so much better than a facilitator would know them and just having met them for the first time… a parent may know better how far they can challenge their kids.

Another facilitator commented that

> one powerful thing that the parents can do is help to bring that back to the connected learning throughout their life. So, you know, if they can call attention to something that they did that was similar in another place, or say, like: Oh do you remember when we were trying to do this thing, this is really similar to this. Like, how would you apply what you learned there, here?

This facilitator's use of the term 'connected learning' was independent from the learning theory of the same name, but it supports our argument that parents can play a key role within the learning ecosystem that surrounds a child. Although we expressed concerns earlier about the role of smartphones recording makerspace activities, we also recognise that one practical way in which many parents attempted to connect a child's learning is by taking photographs or video of the child's creations, thereby providing a vehicle for revisiting the experience later, although it is unclear whether in practice many in fact did this.

Ultimately, our observations of parents have led us to advocate for an asset-based approach to understanding the role of parents in makerspaces. By an asset-based approach, we mean that typically perceived deficits can instead be considered assets, bringing something unique to a particular encounter (Alper, Katz and Clark, 2016). Here this means that while in some cases parents felt themselves to be, or were considered by facilitators, lacking in knowledge when they entered makerspaces – they nonetheless present a powerful and highly unique asset by supporting children's making by connecting their learning between and across spaces.

While professional facilitators were informed by institutional theories of learning, and viewed parents sometimes as too 'hands-off' or, alternatively, too 'hands-on', they also acknowledged (as we observed) that parents were drawing on unique "repertoires of practice" (Gutiérrez and Rogoff, 2003) or "funds of knowledge" (González, Moll and Amanti, 2005). These repertoires were informed not only by the parents' own sets of knowledge and experiences – including their sense of self-efficacy – but also their understanding of the interests and strengths of their own child(ren). Some parents saw themselves as learning resources by helping directly steer their children within activities, while acquiring new skills (Martin, Erete, Pinkard and Sandherr, 2017; Roque, Lin, & Liuzzi, 2016). Others consciously disengaged from children in order to give them space. Even those parents who did not take part in activities at all often had their own 'theory of learning' that had led them to bring their child to the makerspace in the first place (Sefton-Green, 2013).

Conclusion

In this chapter we have considered the design of the physical and social space, the perspectives of facilitators and the roles for parents in three museum makerspaces in order to understand the different ways in which intergenerational learning occurs through 'making'. What we have also noted is the very different ways in which parents support children through making, as opposed to professional facilitators.

Parents presented a different form of support to children from the professional facilitators. Parents' intimate knowledge of their children, knowing when to push and what might motivate, was also complemented (especially for parents of younger children) by their physical intimacy and ability to help children when needed. However, in some cases, that intimate relationship could also occlude parents' ability to see when they needed to step back, an outside perspective that professional facilitators were sometimes more able to assess. Facilitators also had greater subject knowledge of making itself, professional knowledge that in ideal cases worked in tandem with parents' more intimate but hard-won expertise.

Reading through the typology above one might be tempted to produce normative analyses of parents based on their behaviour – the hands-off parents too uninvolved, the hands-on parents too 'helicopter-y'. Yet in our observations we saw that parents often made reasoned choices (based on their knowledge of their children) as to why they chose one role over another, or their own experiences or pressures framed these choices in more or less beneficial ways. We suggest that creating this typology of parent actions (rather than of individual parents, for some moved between and amongst these categories) is helpful in elucidating these differences and, hopefully, in providing some reflections that can be shared with the facilitators to help develop new initiatives and support for parents, either separately or together with their children, in the future. Our observations of parents lead us to argue that parents play a unique role in connecting children's learning in makerspaces with their learning elsewhere. They are experts not in 'making' but in their *own children* – and this makes them able to foster helpful interactions grounded in the intimacy of their relationships. Facilitators and parents, when operating in tandem, can together help develop new forms of shared knowledge creation by building on children's enthusiasm for and engagement with making – and bring this knowledge and experience to bear after the making experience has been completed.

Notes

1 Research for this chapter was made possible by the Horizon 2020 programme grant no. 734720 for the MakEY project and by a grant from the John D. and Catherine T. MacArthur Foundation as part of the Connected Learning Research Network. Our thanks also to Paige Mustain for editorial assistance and to the staff from The Tech, Bay Area Discovery Museum and the Lawrence Hall of Science for their generous help in facilitating this research.
2 From the BADM website, accessed 8 December 2018, "Bay Area Discovery Museum" (n.d.)
3 The Fab Foundation was created at MIT and encompasses a network of about 1,000 fabrication labs meant to provide access to digital fabrication. The Fab Foundation and maker culture stem from MIT Professor Seymour Papert's theory of constructionism which posits that learners construct their own knowledge by making and tinkering with objects and having agency over the learning process (Papert, 1980).
4 3D printers create three-dimensional solid objects from a digital file by printing layers of material until the object is complete. A laser-cutter is a machine that uses lasers to precisely cut through a wide range of materials. A CNC (computer numerical control) router is also used to cut various materials, such as wood, plastic and steel.
5 By which we mean an adult with caring responsibility for a child – in practice in our fieldwork this was usually parents, occasionally grandparents or another family member (an aunt or uncle, an older sibling) or a paid caregiver like a nanny. Because the focus of our research was on families we spent less time with paid caregivers and do not include observations of professional teachers in this chapter. For ease we will refer to 'parents' and specify cases where we observed a caregiver of a different type.
6 We use the term 'facilitator' in keeping with our previous work on digital media and learning (Blum-Ross and Livingstone, 2016), which draws from Paulo Friere's (1970) conception of 'critical pedagogy' in order to distinguish between 'facilitators' who enable participatory learning versus 'teachers' who may be more traditional in their approach as givers of information.
7 Tinkercad is a free browser-based app that allows users to create 3D designs ("Tinkercad", n.d.).
8 Their schools programme welcomed anyone who signed up, but they – like the other museums – had also created special outreach for 'Title 1' schools (schools with a high percentage of students receiving free or reduced-cost lunch, a national poverty marker in the US) (Dawson, 2014).
9 Our research for Parenting for a Digital Future (Livingstone and Blum-Ross, forthcoming) revealed the multitude of ways in which everyday family activities already resemble maker experiences – think of crafting, gaming, cooking, DIY or various forms of play, many of which now involve YouTube tutorials or other kinds of 'joint media engagement' (Takeuchi and Stevens, 2011; see also Gauntlett, 2011; Barron and Levinson, 2018).
10 See Roque (2016) as an example of studying parental involvement.
11 See Parten (1933).

References

Alper, M., Katz, V. & Clark, L. S. (2016) Researching children, intersectionality, and diversity in the digital age. *Journal of Children and Media*, 10(1), 107–114.
Barron, B., Martin, C., Takeuchi, L. & Fithian, R. (2009). Parents as learning partners in the development of technological fluency. *International Journal of Learning and Media*, 1(2), 55–77.

Barron, B. & Levinson, A. (2018). Media as a catalyst for children's engagement in learning at home and across settings. In E. Gee, L. Takeuchi, & E. Wartella (Eds.), *Children and families in the digital age: Learning together in a media saturated culture* (17–36). New York: Routledge.

Bay Area Discovery Museum. (n.d.). Retrieved 12 August 2018 from: https://bayareadiscoverymuseum.org/

Benjamin, N., Haden, C. & Wilkerson, E. (2010). Enhancing building, conversation, and learning through caregiver–child interactions in a children's museum. *Developmental Psychology*, 46(2), 502–515.

Blum-Ross, A. & Livingstone, S. (2016). From youth voice to young entrepreneurs: The individualization of digital media and learning. *Journal of Digital and Media Literacy*, 4(1–2), 1–22.

Blum-Ross, A. & Livingstone, S. (2018). The trouble with "screen time" rules. In G. Mascheroni, C. Ponte & A. Jorge (Eds.), *Digital parenting: The challenges for families in the digital age*. (179–187). Göteborg: Nordicom.

Brahms, L. & Crowley, K. (2016). Learning to make in the museum: The role of maker education. In K. Peppler, E. R. Halverson, & Y. Kafai (Eds.), *Makeology: Makerspaces as learning environments* (Vol. 1, 15–29). New York: Routledge.

Brough, M., Cho, A. & Mustain, P. (forthcoming). Making connections: Encouraging touchpoints, sharing digital authority, and sandboxing among low-income families. In M. Ito et al. (Eds.), *Connected learning: New directions for design, research, and practice*. New York: NYU Press.

Dawson, E. (2014). "Not designed for us": How science museums and science centers socially exclude low-income, minority ethnic groups. *Science Education*, 98(6), 981–1008.

Ellenbogen, K. (2003) Museums in family life: An ethnographic case study. In G. Leinhardt, K. Crowley & K. Knutson (Eds.), *Learning conversations in museums* (81–102). New York: Routledge.

Friere, P. (1970). *Pedagogy of the oppressed*. New York: Herder and Herder.

Gauntlett, D. (2011). *Making is connecting: The social meaning of creativity, from DIY and knitting to YouTube and Web 2.0*. Cambridge: Polity Press.

González, N., Moll, L. & Amanti, C. (2005). *Funds of knowledge: Theorizing practices in households, communities, and classrooms*. Mahwah, NJ: Lawrence Erlbaum Associates.

Gutiérrez, K. D. & Rogoff, B. (2003). Cultural ways of learning: Individual traits or repertoires of practice. *Educational Researcher*, 32(5), 19–25.

Ito, M., Baumer, S., Bittanti, M., boyd, d., Cody, R., Herr-Stephenson, B….Tripp, L. (2010). *Hanging out, messing around, geeking out: Kids living and learning with new media*. Cambridge, MA.: MIT Press.

Ito, M., Gutiérrez, K., Livingstone, S., Penuel, B., Rhodes, J., Salen, K., Schor, J….Watkins, C. (2013). *Connected learning: An agenda for research and design*. Irvine, CA: Digital Media and Learning Research Hub.

Livingstone, S. & Sefton-Green, J. (2016). *The class: Living and learning in the digital age*. New York: NYU Press.

Livingstone, S. & Blum-Ross, A. (forthcoming). *Parenting for a digital future: How hopes and fears about technology shape our children's lives*. Oxford: Oxford University Press.

Marsh, J., Kumpulainen, K., Nisha, B., Velicu, A., Blum-Ross, A., Hyatt, D., Jónsdóttir, S. R., Levy, R., Little, S., Marusteru, G., Ólafsdóttir, M. E., Sandvik, K., Scott, F., Thestrup, K., Arnseth, H. C., Dýrfjörð, K., Jornet, A., Kjartansdóttir, S. H., Pahl, K., Pétursdóttir, S. and Thorsteinsson, G. (2017). *Makerspaces in the early years: A literature review*. Sheffield: University of Sheffield, MakEY Project.

Martin, C., Erete, S., Pinkard, N. & Sandherr, J. (2017). Connections at the family level: Supporting parents and caring adults to engage youth in learning about computers and technology. In Y. Rankin & J. Thomas (Eds.), *Moving students of color from consumers to producers of technology* (220–244). Hershey, PA: IGI Global.

McClure, E. R., Guernsey, L., Clements, D. H., Nall Bales, S., Nichols, J., Kendal-Taylor, N. & Levine, M. (2017). *STEM starts early: Grounding science, technology, engineering and math education in early childhood*. New York: The Joan Ganz Cooney Center at Sesame Workshop.

Nadelson, L. (2013). Who is watching and who is playing: Parental engagement with children at a hands-on science center. *Journal of Education Research*, 106(6), 478–484.

Papert, S. (1980). *Mindstorms: Children, computers and powerful ideas*. New York: Basic Books.

Parten, M. B. (1933). Social play among preschool children. *The Journal of Abnormal and Social Psychology*, 28(2), 136–147.

Roque, R. (2016). Family creative learning. In K. Peppler, E. Rosenfeld Halverso & Y. Kafa (Eds.), *Makeology: Makerspaces as learning environments* (47–63). New York: Routledge.

Roque, R., Lin, K. & Liuzzi, R. (2016). "I'm not just a mom": Parents developing multiple roles in creative computing. In C. K. Looi, J. L. Polman, U. Cress & P. Reimann (Eds.), *Transforming Learning, Empowering Learners: The International Conference of the Learning Sciences (ICLS) 2016*. Vol. 1. Singapore: International Society of the Learning Sciences.

Sefton-Green, J. (2013). What (and where) is the 'learning' when we talk about learning in the home? *Occasional Paper Series*, 2013(30). Retrieved from https://educate.bankstreet.edu/occasional-paper-series/vol2013/iss30/2

Sheridan, K., Halverson, E. R., Litts, B., Brahms, L., Jacobs-Priebe, L. & Owens, T. (2014). Learning in the making: A comparative case study of three makerspaces. *Harvard Educational Review*, 84(4), 505–531.

Takeuchi, L. & Stevens, R. (2011). *The new coviewing: Designing for learning through joint media engagement*. New York: The Joan Ganz Cooney Center.

Tinkercad. (n.d.). Retrieved from www.tinkercad.com/

11

TEACHING FOR SOCIAL IMAGINATION

Creativity in an early-learning makerspace

Anne Burke and Abigail Crocker

Introduction

This chapter integrates recent scholarship surrounding creativity, social imagination and makerspaces, sharing a case study focused on a pre-service teaching programme, where students shared their experiences teaching environmental sustainability and stewardship to early-learning classrooms. The project data suggest that interactions within a maker-space foster play, exploration and participatory learning, and instil a culture of creation rather than consumption. This 'mindset concept' sets the standard for growing teaching pedagogies that sustain exploration in low-risk but high-reward environments, where students are agents of their own creativity and problem-solving. This chapter will challenge the belief that 'creativity' is goal oriented, individualistic and leads to original outcomes. Instead, it is through collaboration and tinkering that the children observed within this case study developed creativity as 'recycled' knowledge and utilised maker-space as a process-driven learning experience, and not a product-driven one.

Overview of makerspaces in Canada

Any adult who has spent time among young children has observed how much they enjoy playing with construction and craft toys of all sorts, be they blocks, modelling clay, sticks or cardboard and glue. Given time and space they are inherently creative, though all too often, as they grow older, this creativity is pushed aside in favour of more assessment-based learning models.

A 'maker', as defined by Kylie Peppler, Erica Halverson and Yasmin B. Kafai in their text *Makeology Volume 1*, is "anyone who builds or adapts objects by hand, often with the simple pleasure of figuring out how things work, creating an aesthetic object, or seeking to solve an everyday problem" (Peppler, Halverson & Kafai, 2016, p.25). Using this definition, many people may be viewed as having been 'makers' all their lives and taking pride in the things they make. In our own province, on the island of Newfoundland situated on the east coast of Canada, historically, people were 'makers' as a means of survival – even now many people manufacture their own fishing nets, wooden boats, furniture and sealskin clothing. In classrooms, 'makers' draw upon their own interests and unique skills to create art or artefacts, or solve problems and meet challenges. Regardless of one's goal, makerspaces empower learners by providing them with agency over their learning process. Makerspaces also teach critical thinking skills and encourage the collaborative investigation of complex learning themes by building a context of experimentation and trial-and-error. In combination, these skill traits work together to create a positive relationship with learning for young children.

The maker movement in Canada, however, has a complex history – the impetus for which was popularised by *Make Magazine* in 2005. In 2013 *Make Magazine* popularised Maker Fairs as a way for 'makers' to showcase their creations, which further contributed to building dedicated space for makerspaces in classrooms, libraries, museums and community centres. In 2014, the Canadian Library Association (CLA, 2014) established a *Standards of Practice for School Library Learning Commons in Canada* with the aim of rebranding libraries as "learning commons" – accessible spaces that use digital media for all learners of differing backgrounds and at different stages in their educative careers. Makerspaces in school libraries align with three of the CLA's five core standards of practice: "Facilitating collaborative engagement to cultivate and empower a community of learners"; "Fostering literacies to empower life-long learners"; "Designing learning environments to support participatory learning" (CLA, 2014, p.10).

Programmes like Brilliant Labs and Canada 2067 Makerkids further encouraged a maker culture in children by capitalising upon the entrepreneurial spirit fostered through makerspaces. Programmes like these bring mobile makerspaces in Canada to schools and community centres (Brilliant Labs), or develop after-school programmes, camps and weekend events that focus on components of STEM learning (Makerkids), such as robotics and coding. Fourteen professional makerspaces participate in the Canadian Maker Passport begun by ThingTankLab, inspiring collaborative designing between individuals working creatively at the intersections of art and technology. This programme also encourages travel between provinces from Alberta to Ontario, expands artistic and personal global views, and treats these spaces as destinations and those who visit them as creative tourists (ThingTankLab, 2019).

However, professional makerspaces like these often are not apt spaces to encourage young children's learning. And while programmes like Brilliant Labs and Makerkids meet success where they visit, not all school districts can fit these programmes into their schedules, have funds available to spare, or have access to professional spaces like those found in a community library, community centre or museum. In addition, there has been much research conducted in middle and high schools regarding student engagement with makerspaces, but not much conducted with early-learning students.

The maker movement has gained traction in Canada, but there is still much room for further exploration and expansion. Outside of classrooms, professional makerspaces usually require a subscription fee, and they are not accessible spaces to the very young. Programmes that bring makerspaces into schools are generally organised by for-profit enterprises, and finding access to these programmes is difficult, if not impossible, and more so for schools in geographic and economically disadvantaged areas. Furthermore, there is no network of schools across Canada that can showcase the work educators are doing with makerspaces in their classrooms. Giving notice of such events is left to newspapers, almost all of which have a dwindling clientele. While government and library association educational mandates do not yet stress the full importance of hands-on learning in Canada, they are gradually working towards the academic and philosophical goal that learning is immersive and experiential, and that makerspaces are the ideal setting to enhance these learning opportunities.

Creativity in making

In theory, Canadian teaching philosophies encourage creativity, but unfortunately, due to the written and unwritten rules of schools, they often unknowingly emphasise conformity (Meng, 2016; Robinson, 2006). And the creativity that schools hope to teach can differ significantly from the more inventive do-it-yourself creativity that the professional world wants to deliver (Perry & Collier, 2018). This contrast has caused a paradox as to what should be considered creativity, especially if we accept Stein's (1953) definition that creativity equates to originality and innovation (Marsh et al., 2017).

Perry and Collier argue that processes of 'recycling', 'upcycling', 'repeating', 'remixing' or 'relocating', while not traditionally original, still constitute a valuable creative process (Perry & Collier, 2018). Pahl (2007) agrees and, by considering Perry and Collier's view that creativity is contextual, contends that children draw from past events and integrate them into their classrooms (Pahl, 2007). Craft calls this reformation 'little-c creativity' (Craft, 2005) and suggests that this can be seen as "everyday creativity, or 'democratic creativity'. It could be said that an idea or action could be deemed novel or original within the terms of reference of the individual" (Craft, 2005, 52). Applying 'little-c creativity' within classrooms "could be seen as a way of expanding what one knows, understands and can do – in which case it could be said to be an aspect of learning" (Craft, 2005, p.52).

Meanwhile 'Big-C' Creativity refers to the common belief that true creativity is new and innovative – something triggering an earth-shattering and unique discovery. Perry and Collier (2018) argue that this belief is harmful to students, as very few of them are equipped to meet this standard. When students see themselves falling short of 'Big-C' Creativity's high expectations, a natural response is to quit being 'creative'. In our own experience, we have observed that some students might conclude that they are not creative at all because they have never, and will never, see themselves achieving the 'Big-C' Creativity level that society values. In classrooms, therefore, 'little-c' creativity is much more helpful and inclusive. 'Little-c' creativity encourages students to imitate images, actions and ideas that they have already experienced. By doing so, children can nurture their creative expression and grow to incrementally understand how their individuality sparks creative ideas and can be revealed in their work. 'Little-c' creativity creates an achievable standard that all students can reach. It validates the learning process, but it also validates the self-worth of students who can now see themselves as creative beings.

By incorporating digital media through makerspaces into lessons and curricula, educators can help young children navigate communicative practices that are used in social, political, economic, technological and activist forums worldwide. Such lessons also encourage young children to begin to develop the necessary skills for participating in these forums by cultivating mindsets of positivity, creativity, possibility and citizenship, as producers and disseminators of information (Carrington & Dowdall, 2015).

Marsh, Arnseth and Kumpulainen (2018) argue that citizenship and creativity are undeniably linked through makerspace activities, and can result in contributions to citizenship even on a small scale. Children learn about collaboration, entrepreneurship and positive ways to impact on society through makerspace activities that expand learning beyond the boundaries of the classroom and into the community. Ratto and Boler (2014) in their work identify this process of engagement as DIY Citizenship and Critical Making.

Research conducted by Ratto and Boler (2014) shows that social activism is a crucial component of the Maker Movement and key to helping participants understand and contribute positively to the world around them. Ratto and Boler call the practice of uniting makerspaces with social activism 'Critical Making', because it focuses on the creation of products to advance more philanthropic and ideological goals through 'connective action' and 'collective or networked individualism' (Ratto & Boler, 2014, p.1). In our study, critical making was an outlined goal for the project, to be achieved with pre-service teachers' use of environmental books in combination with maker technologies and young children. This was achieved through critical activities that acted as 'an activity that provides the possibility to intervene substantively in systems of authority and power and that offers an important site for reflecting on how such power is constituted by infrastructures, institutions, communities and practices' (Ratto & Boler, 2014, p.1). Such was the case in this project when the children met with the city mayor to convey their concerns about the harbour clean-up, and to share the Sea Sweeper prototype they made during their critical making session, as will be outlined.

Further to this point, Ratto's earlier work argues that critical making connects critical thinking with creative expression, inviting 'makers' to engage with the community that surrounds them (Ratto, 2011). The young learners in this study drew from what they had studied, but also gathered information and perspectives from personal knowledge and experiences in order to share and inform their peers and teachers about the ocean. By, 'sharing [results] and an ongoing critical analysis of materials, designs, constraints, and outcomes, participants in critical making exercises together perform a practice-based engagement' (Ratto & Boler, 2014, p.253).

Ratto, Boler and Deibert also argue that reflexive Maker Cultures (cultures created through participation in makerspace communities rather than as a result of them) promote systems of lived or DIY citizenship that emphasises 'individual engagement with the processes of personal and cultural construction' (Ratto & Boler, 2014, p.137), which further situates the learning of participants within the context of the community.

Participants in DIY citizenship culture use making in ways to improve the lives of their peers, community and world by focusing on collaboration and empowerment. Pre-service teachers in the study observed this type of empowerment as children shared in collaborative efforts to address environmental factors that were a result of ocean pollution and global warming. In addition, much like 'little-c' creativity as described by Perry and Collier (2018), 'little-c' citizenship as it is manifested in the children of the project site expressed the foundational skills and habits of mind needed to cultivate 'Big-C' Citizenship: a person or movement that impacts on the world in an 'earth-shattering', 'society-shaking' way.

While makerspaces can reinvigorate young children's 'little-c' creativity, they also reflect Schulte and Thompson's (2018) research that finds that young children's engagement with critical thinking and creativity grows *with* materials at hand. Schulte and Thompson describe how the process of drawing liberated their students' ability to think creatively. They argue that the use of materials spurs children to think, express and create within early childhood settings, because it allows children to engage their views of the world. The researchers found that children were able to see beyond the materials placed in front of them, changing them into something new and creative through imitation, recycling or mimicry. Schulte evokes the perception that each person is only part of the larger picture (Schulte & Thompson., 2018). Holly Carrell Moore and Jennifer Keys Adair (2015) also assert that using digital tools, such as the computerised drawings of Logo from 25 years ago, or the 3D printing CAD programs and Makey Makey of today, can promote early-learning student creativity because it orients students towards a process-driven enquiry into meaning-making (Moore & Adair, 2015). Moore and Adair argue that for the best results, student learning and digital technology should be applied in ways that are open-ended and promote active student learning. Students should be engaged both intellectually and kinaesthetically for the most invested learning processes to occur (Moore & Adair, 2015, p.26). In the present study, students used themed environmental picture books, paper crafts and inventive drawings to capture their ideas, and to create 3D designs and prototypes using a computer program called Tinkercad. Pre-service teachers encouraged young children to be creative in remaking craft materials, with the goal of developing a sustainable solution to an environmental problem.

Materiality inspired creativity within the makerspace and encouraged children to be playful with their learning in ways that Angela Eckhoff says are 'important to the development of personal and social identity' (Eckhoff, 2017, p.116), a developmental process that 'cannot be separated from its social context' (Eckhoff & Urbach, 2008, p.180). This was evident in the present study, where pre-service teachers observed children's social identity as an emerging social self that materialised in the form of 'stewardship', through their voiced understandings of the plight of the polar bears in Canadian arctic waters and their vows to clean up the polluted St. John's harbour. All decisions made by the children were about changes that could be made within their communities for the greater good. Eckhoff's observation of the vital role of context was made true in this study as the research site encouraged creative exploration, and the institutional structure in the child-care space played a role in advocating the ideals of social justice as important components of their curriculum (Eckhoff, 2017, p.116). In this case, a social justice advocacy focus placed in a local learning context, such as the children's community, enhances the environmental understanding underlining the makerspace, with digital literacy and creativity being utilised together to inform a common goal.

Context

This project took place at Memorial University and was created through an interdisciplinary research initiative to introduce Faculty to the pedagogies around makerspaces. The technological tools associated with maker technologies used in educational makerspaces are very costly, and can require both training and background knowledge to operate (Resta & Laferriere, 2015). Due to this, the university chose to have the Engineering and Education faculties work together on developing joint technology-based projects, including this one designed especially for the university's childcare facility. The project drew on this collective expertise, and this expertise was also shared with the pre-service teachers in the project, through the creation of maker activities designed for children aged 4–7 years at the early childcare centre located on campus.

This case study design combined environmental books focused on ocean pollution and makerspaces. A case study, as defined by Merriam, is 'an examination of a specific phenomenon' (Merriam, 1998, p.9). The phenomenon in question may be an individual, a group, an event or a programme in which the researcher is interested in gaining more insights (Merriam, 1998). Yin explains that a 'case study method allows investigators to retain the holistic and meaningful characteristics of real-life events' (Yin, 2009, p.4). We were interested in how pre-service teachers could observe play and creativity in the context of early learning, with young children harnessing an environmental subject with digital tools in the context of a makerspace.

Connecting young learners to the oceans

Makerspaces provide the context for early learners to physically engage with their learning process in encouraging, creative and low-risk ways. The pre-service teachers considered the following research questions:

1. How do children's environmental picture books introduce knowledgeable information which may be used to enhance their makerspace activities?
2. When exploring sustainability themes, how does a maker mindset encourage creative idea-sharing among children?
3. How are materials important to inspire literacy in the makerspace?

With the goal to teach about environmental sustainability and stewardship, pre-service teacher researchers guided early-learning students through a creative exploration of issues around ocean conservation. Environmental children's books chosen included *Why Should I Recycle?* (Green & Gordon, 2002), *Polar Bear, Why is Your World Melting?* (Wells, 2008) and *Over the Ocean* (Gomi, 2016). These texts were shared in read-aloud sessions with the young children. Pre-service teachers shared the picture books with children, and facilitated a wide range of activities. *Polar Bear, Why is Your World Melting?* (Wells, 2008) was used to inform early-learning students about the greenhouse effect, global warming and how these two events negatively impact on the world. *Over the Ocean* (Gomi, 2016) prompted students to consider the organisms that live in the sea that could be harmed through global warming. *Why Should I Recycle?* (Green & Gordon, 2002) encouraged students to think about the reasons why recycling is important.

Early-learning practitioners modelled a number of open-ended questions for the pre-service teachers, including, 'What are some ways we can help improve our oceans?', 'Why do you think the ocean is important?' and 'How can we stop pollution from getting in the water?' The nature of the open-ended questions challenged the children's prior knowledge, illustrating to pre-service teachers that children's prior knowledge can be joined with classroom literacy materials. Once a common understanding of the environmental themes had been established, pre-service teachers were able to use the children's picture books to scaffold the learning of new concepts related to sustainability.

The pre-service teachers encouraged the children to draw upon their prior knowledge and creative self to engage in exploratory talk. The reutilisation of this knowledge in a new way exemplifies Craft's and Pahl's theories that 'low creativity' engages 'possibility thinking' (Craft, 2005; Pahl, 2007). For example, we observed that when Marla, one of the pre-service teachers, asked children, "Do you think the water is cold? Have you ever been to the ocean before?", while pointing to an illustration in *Over the Ocean*, 5-year-old Daniel moved closer to the picture book, excitedly pointed to a puffer fish in the illustration and shared "I see spike balls." "Spike balls ARE puffer fish," another student loudly chimed in. Children also challenged each other on the word 'starfish' and the origins of the 'star' in starfish. Four-year-old Tia shared, "That's not true, starfish come from the sea." In adding to the discussion, Thomas shared with authority, "You're not allowed to pick up seahorses," drawing from his recent experiences of a glass-bottom boat trip his family experienced while on vacation in Mexico, "You have to go underwater to see them because if you pick them up they'll be dead."

Pre-service teachers built on these discussions to funnel the early-learning students' creative energies into the process, which led to the design of a prototype to address ocean conservation. Two groups created 3D printed prototypes based on drawn student designs: Sea Sweeper and Polar Bear Pants.

Discussion: Learning from young creative minds

A significant part of this project considered ways in which early years practitioners could mentor pre-service teachers in observing and documenting early literacy engagement. Many of the data were collected by the research team, along with the pre-service and early childhood practitioners, who recorded field notes of literacy engagements, took photos of the children's playmaking sessions, and monitored the children's early prototypes using the 3D program Tinkercad. Read-aloud and creative technology sessions were videotaped by the early childhood practitioners, and followed childcare, university research and ethics protocols. Pre-service teachers reflected upon their experiences in journal entries, and shared in mentoring group discussions with the early childhood practitioners.

Little-c creativity

Many of the youngest children demonstrated 'little-c' creativity by re-localising, reapplying and reshaping prior knowledge and experiences to create their makerspace project. This was a pleasant surprise for the pre-service teachers. Discussions during their classes shared a common thread of concern that 4- and 5-year-old children would not be able to grasp complex ideas such as environmental stewardship and sustainability. Further to this, the pre-service teachers also wondered if the creativity exhibited by the children would not match up to established expectations of discipline-altering 'Big-C' Creativity. Instead, the children's application of Craft's 'possibility thinking' (Craft, 2005) instinctually caused the pre-service teachers during the project to re-evaluate their previous learning, where the pedagogical approach was to emphasise 'Big-C' Creativity as the sole possible creative outlet. Pre-service teachers considered their own experience with creativity as only being 'new and remarkable' and that their observations of children applying creativity in the form of recycling, integration and collaboration indicated a change in a viewpoint of creativity as solely that of an individual as opposed to a collective creativity – where children exchange ideas and guiding questions in low-risk contexts unbounded by practicalities so as to invite collective creative knowledge between teachers and children. A student teacher, Hayden, shared in class:

> For example, one child knew that a polar bear is not really white, but in fact has black skin and hollow fur that gives off a white colour… I started to realise that we were not there to just teach children about polar bears, global warming or ocean protection, we were also there to learn from them.
>
> *(Hayden, 2018)*

The pre-service teachers engaged the children in playful games around how climate change affects polar bears that they had read about together in other picture books, such as *Ice Bear* by Nicola Davies. Beginning the lesson, a student–teacher named Britta asked the children what ice pans are. Ella, age 4, said, "Ice pans are like cookie pans, they are square and made of ice." Daniel interjected "But ice melts! And it's hard for polar bears; they can't fish when the ice melts!" Hayden and Britta invited the children to play an ice-pan game by laying squares of white cardboard on the floor with fact questions printed on the back. Each time a fact was read to the children from one of the chosen picture books, the children had to decide whether it was true or false. This exchange of knowledge shows Craft's (2005) possibility thinking in action in relation to how these young children understood the harmful actions of society to polar bears. On a poster entitled 'How to Save Polar Bears', children included lines like "humans put garbage in the ocean and it makes ice melt", "fish gets trapped in the garbage and polar bears eat it", "when an ice pan goes away it's hard for the polar bears because they have to swim so far". The children brainstormed ideas on how to save the bears, showing their creativity when Portia suggested, "We can make a boat for them" and Aidan added, "Make a machine to feed polar bears", while Kierin suggested a "Propeller that the bear could wear and a remote to control it" like "floating shorts". The children drew pictures of prototypes for the pre-service teachers (see Figures 11.1–11.4).

Fostering play-based creativity through digital materials

Another project created by the children was a machine called the Sea Sweeper, a robot that could clean the ocean floor. One of the pre-service teachers named Sharon recounted that her lesson "involved showing students new technologies for reducing ocean pollution and then letting them play with the idea in their own way, creating their own blueprint". Early childhood practitioners said that the children were so inspired by a reading from the book *Why Should I Recycle?* (Green & Gordon, 2002) that they engaged in discussions while leaving with their parents at the end of the day on how they were going to construct their new Sea Sweeper prototype. Even in the following weeks, children returned to the day-care centre with drawn prototypes for the Sea Sweeper, and were, according to a teacher, "eager to begin the process of construction" (Figure 11.5).

The children's reaction suggests that when students are provided with a low-stakes space to explore, make mistakes, collaborate, create, tinker and invent, they are connected more viscerally to their learning and are more likely to continue their learning outside the classroom. This understanding of how learning can be expansive was shared by a student-teacher named Maureen in a written diary reflection after working with the group: "I have realised that a makerspace is not only a space, but 'a concept'. It is more than a space for exploring, it is really a mindset for creativity" (Maureen, 2018). In this case, makerspaces establish low-risk, high-reward environments where students are unbounded by unpracticalities, encouraged to explore and learn through play. Wohl-wend suggests that "Creativity is the result of imagining otherwise, that is, expanding the embodied cultural practices of here-and-now worlds, by improvising to 'make do' with the available resources, by negotiating to reimagine constraints into possibilities, and by remaking to transform immediate contexts into alternatives" (Wohlwend, 2015, p.549). The concept of the makerspace as a 'mindset for creativity' encourages teachers and students alike to forego mentally bound and place-bound limitations, such as practicalities or culture. This is best exemplified by the children observed in the project, as they were observed utilising the makerspace as a process-driven learning experience, not solely focusing their energies on a product outcome. Guided by open-ended questions inspired by environmental picture books, the children engaged with a complicated dialogue to devise imaginative solutions. Even though no one child owned the entirety of the result, all the children had a stake in the product, thus all of them had a stake in the learning process. Overall, it was a collective learning experience that demonstrated how creativity can build utilising a spiral effect.

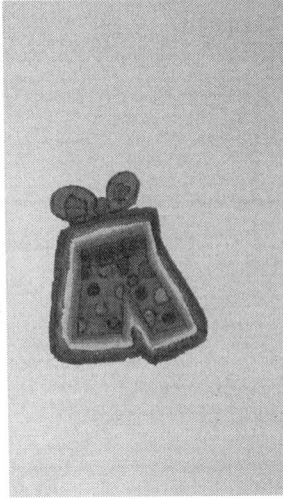

FIGURES 11.1 –11.4 Children's prototypes of inventions to save polar bears

Creative, collective designing

Throughout this project, students developed a communal and personal connection to environmental sustainability. The context of cleaning St. John's city harbour, a body of water well known to both children and teachers, helped provide a sense of obligation that further invested the children in their lessons about environmental stewardship and sustainability. With the goal of cleaning up the harbour in mind, the pre-service teachers worked with the children, learning together about the harm from pollution, the importance of keeping our oceans clean, and how to design prototypes, work with partners and develop ideas in a positive way. This is reflective of the early childhood practitioners' modelling of learning as a process of engagement and conversation, shared through collaborative ideas, without judgements being made.

Environmental sustainability is not a new concept, nor is cleaning St. John's harbour. However, makerspaces provided the context for the children to have novel ideas that were valuable in their remixing, re-localisation and recycling of ideas, included digital and non-digital materials, and involved the discovery of surprise. Their solutions to these problems were at once their own, and both socially and collectively developed. The children embraced open, playful problem-solving in their risk-taking, imagination and play.

STEPHEN: We could dive into the ocean, have a little bag, and put the cans and garbage in it. Then we can get bigger bags and put the little bags in it.
ANNA: Well, BE CAREFUL if you do that because a SHARK could EAT YOU!
ALESSA: You'd have to wear a snorkel.

The children were excited and engaged with the premise of cleaning St. John's harbour. We noted the excited chatter of small voices as they bounced ideas off one another. When one child shared a creative idea, other children suggested critical solutions or made other suggestions. This critical making (Ratto & Boler, 2014) and community problem-solving is a systemic process with makerspaces, one that encourages students to create tangible objects from new and existing knowledge in order to facilitate their learning. The final product – a 3D printed prototype – is the

FIGURE 11.5 Sea Sweeper prototypes

result of collective process knowledge showing the power of social imagination. No one student developed the prototype alone. Each student had a stake in its development, whether through conversation or by contributing elements from their drawings.

Exploring stewardship-role-taking through makerspaces

During a subsequent group reflection, early childhood practitioners discussed how the pre-service teachers had reacted to the activities. The practitioners' field notes documented that while the pre-service teachers saw validating the children's role-taking as important, they, and we too, were accepting of the children's desire to be seen as scientists while playmaking. Importantly, this was also key to the children understanding the next steps towards stewardship and civic engagement. One of the practitioners, Dalia, shared that working with crafts, digital prototypes, experts from the field and creating prototypes on a 3D printer was a way in which young children can express themselves, learn that their ideas have value in bringing change, and that their suggestions have worth. She also realised that through social and collaborative imagination generated from play, children's ideas may be used to solve complex problems by visualising a concept in a new way. This was even more evident in discussions the children had with experts on oceans at the local science centre, where the children eagerly shared their ideas and designs for ocean clean-up. The pre-service teachers witnessed how collaborative knowledge-sharing and critical discussions on the part of the children had begun to resemble Ratto and Boler's (2014) notion of DIY citizenship, with a pronounced desire to improve their community and world through addressing issues of pollution and global warming. Empowered by their experiences, the children invited the city's mayor to a round-table discussion, during which children shared their drawings and committed to being responsible citizens of their city, protecting the harbour by supporting recycling programmes in their homes and at the childcare centre.

Discussion

This type of field experience introduced pre-service teachers to a tangible window into children's unbounded creativity, social imagination and play, sharing a collective learning process through critical making possibilities. More often than not, early years

FIGURE 11.6 Mayor Danny Bree's tweet thanking children for explaining their project called the Sea Sweeper

practitioners found that pre-service teachers misinterpreted the children's day-to-day 'little-c' creativity (Craft, 2005), often because they themselves had felt so removed from childhood and their own playmaking experiences, and social imagination was not easily recalled from childhood. As one pre-service teacher shared, "How many times has someone suggested 'think outside the box' or 'approach this from a different angle'?" He, like others in the group, admitted that they were unsure as to what this creative process meant when working with young children. This resonates with Craft's ideas around possibility thinking. The pre-service teachers learned that, in maker-spaces, the usual rules of creativity did not apply. Despite the pre-service teachers' predisposition to focus their practice on the assessment of skills, they saw children taking agency of their own creativity, and positively engaging with surprise without concern for feasibility or practicalities. The playmaking experience through maker-spaces exemplified the children's empowerment through trial-and-error. However, we must admit that the childcare makerspace differs significantly from a traditional classroom, where students are not always encouraged to take control of their learning, nor to experiment and play with ideas, nor to craft solutions to open-ended problems. Overall, we saw that the learning within makerspaces was a basis for children's creative enquiry, and helped develop social imagination, showing qualities such as inquisitive-ness, cleverness and thoughtfulness. Eventually, such projects could play a role in influencing children who are engaged citizens and open to environmental action, through the critical making championed by Ratto and other scholars.

Furthermore, this case study typifies an acceptance that young children are agentive citizens within their communities as opposed to passive onlookers. Marchant and Kirby (2004) argue that the recognition of children as citizens is important to initiating support for the fulfilment of the principles of democratic life, and thereby improving society. Stephen and Gadda (2017) observe that young children are often not given full rights of citizenship based on their perceived level of maturity or immaturity. As a result, children are taught how citizenship might be enacted as adults in the hope that these skills will shape their behaviour as children (Stephen and Gadda, 2017). However, what is missing from this argument is how children can be active and positive forces for citizenship if viewed as agents of positive societal change. The message that society sends to young children is that in order to be citizens, one must be an adult – further positing that like the dichotomy between 'big and little-c' creativity, there also exists a dichotomy between 'big and little-c' citizenship.

This case study exemplifies a type of creativity that is not new – both children and adults recycle, integrate and re-localise knowledge in collaborative ways to solve critical and complex real-world problems – but one that has not been ubi-quitously recognised or encouraged as a type of creativity within classrooms. For example, Marsh, Arnseth and Kumpulainen's (2018) findings show that each of the maker projects they studied 'fostered collective agency by empowering the chil-dren to make their multimodal works and voices public via a joint exhibition in a local city or library [which is likely to] contribute to the ways in which the chil-dren think, view, and situate themselves in the world' (Marsh, Arnseth and Kum-pulainen, 2018, p.11). Similar to Marsh et al.'s study, our project with young children on building citizenship focused on environmental and ocean sustainability, and fostered a new critical consciousness among the children, in order to make changes through the creation of new prototypes with innovative possibilities that can make a significant change within their local communities.

Kate Orton-Johnson (2014) asserts that the inclusion of digital technology within makerspaces helps to promote citizenship, collaboration and creativity on a global scale by expanding the possible communities involved. The children gained experience with maker technologies such as Makey Makey and 3D printing though working closely with engineering students at the university maker lab. In addition, their community was enlarged through the engagement with pre-service teachers' introduction to environmental books focusing on ocean pollution and global warming. Connecting makerspace learning to a community helps learners feel their creativity and critical thinking is valued in the adult world, it validates their sense of inclusion within a given community, and develops both individual and collective identities through shared experiences (Orton-Johnson in Ratto & Boler, 2014, p.143). One of the key findings here was the development of collective identities, where pre-service teachers saw their learning coincide with that of young children. The data showed that pre-service teachers saw how the opportunities afforded in makerspaces are high-reward and low-risk, and also open-ended collective learning environments that help learners develop a 'maker' identity in relation to their identity of being a citizen. This type of learning challenged the pre-service teachers to re-examine their own perspectives on the capabilities of young children and to consider Bal, Nolan and Seko's (2017) argument that the view of children as 'vulnerable' and 'underdeveloped beings' actively hinders children's learning process. It also acknowledges that young children are capable of being citizens both within and outside the classroom, despite their perceived vulnerability or stage of development. In this way, using makerspaces to enact 'little-c' citizenship – a process of allowing children to practise being a citizen while acknowledging that children are citizens whose opinions and values are affirmed by the communities in which they participate – is a valuable process working towards connecting children and their learning, but also encouraging children to act upon and use what they learn to improve their homes, communities and the world.

This case study used a makerspace to provide opportunities for young children to engage with three communities: their community within the centre, which was a familiar space to practise the skills needed to become agentive within a collaborative community and critical making practices (Ratto & Boler, 2014); the community of pre-service teachers shared experiences with the young children and encouraged them to see themselves as capable citizens; and creative playmaking with materiality in which students created personal and social identities as experts of the ocean and citizens who care about how the ocean impacts on their island home. The application of Orton-Johnson's 'sense of self' not only coincides with feelings of value, validation and capability that the children outwardly shared and experienced, but also encouraged pre-service students to think more deeply about creativity and how children can be provided opportunities to engage with civic engagement within communities, which for young children might not be easily accessible.

Perhaps through makerspaces both teachers and students can work to solve the paradox that Perry and Collier (2018) suggest exists between schools and the professional world, by creating learning experiences validated by the wider community, integrating digital literacy into their play, and guiding life-long learners, advocates and community members through encouragement, play, social imagination and creativity.

Conclusions

This study opens up several avenues for future research. First, there is a need to explore how pre-service teachers are introduced to applied digital literacy topics within early-learning classrooms. Studies like this one offer valuable insights into how the pre-conceived ideas of pre-service teachers might be addressed and altered when working with early-learning students. Second, further research should focus on how early-learning students can engage with complex global topics through makerspaces, multimodal communities and digital literacy.

In policy and practice, research regarding how creativity is viewed at a social and institutional level, and best practices for 'recycling' creativity, would be a valuable avenue of study. It would speak to the need to reconsider the ways in which society values 'creative' minds – 'big-C' vs 'little-c' creativity – and the possible detrimental effects this can have on children's creativity if not validated and encouraged. Makerspaces provide equity for learners. While each child can construct and deconstruct their personal identity, the collaborative and positive atmosphere encourages children to work together to develop interpersonal connective skills.

Makerspaces can also be a positive force for social and institutional change at a grassroots level. This study shows how young children can civically engage with complex topics in collaborative, experiential, positive and creative ways. For pre-service teachers, makerspaces are a way of conceptualising a new mindset, one in which children are encouraged to recycle their creativity, build on their prior knowledge, and share in collective ideas in the pursuit of a common goal.

References

Bal, A., Nolan, J. & Seko, Y. (2017). Melange of Making: Bringing Children's Informal Learning Cultures to the Classroom. In: M. Ratto & M. Boler (eds.), *DIY Citizenship – Critical Making and Social Media*. Cambridge, MA; London: MIT Press, pp. 157–169.

Brilliant Labs. (2017). www.brilliantlabs.ca/

Canada 2067. (2017). Inspiring Students Through Maker Culture. Retrieved from: https://canada2067.ca/en/articles/inspiring-students-through-maker-culture/

Canadian Library Association (CLA). (2014). *Leading Learning: Standards of Practice for School Library Learning Commons in Canada 2014*. Retrieved from: http://clatoolbox.ca/casl/slic/llsop.pdf

Carrington, V. and Dowdall, C. (2015). Vernacular Creativity in Urban Textual Landscapes. In: R. H. Jones (ed.), *The Routledge Handbook of Language and Creativity*, ed.. Abingdon: Routledge, pp. 415–430.

Craft, A. (2005). *Creativity in Schools: Tensions and Dilemmas*. London; New York: Routledge Falmer.

Eckhoff, A. (2017). Images of Play Experiences Through a Child's Lens: An Exploration of Play and Digital Media with Young Children. *International Journal of Early Childhood*, 49 (1): 113–129.

Eckhoff, A. & Urbach, J. (2008). Understanding Imaginative Thinking During Childhood: Sociocultural Conceptions of Creativity and Imaginative Thought. *Early Childhood Education Journal*, 36(2): 179–185. doi:2a-proxy.mun.ca/10.1007/s10643-008-0261-4

Gomi, T. (2016). *Over the Ocean*. San Francisco, CA: Chronicle Books LLC.

Green, J. & Gordon, M. (2002). *Why Should I Recycle?*London: Hachette Children's Group.

Makerkids (2019). https://makerkids.com/

Marchant, R. & Kirby, P. (2004). The Participation of Young Children: Communication, Consultation and Involvement. In: B. Neale (ed.), *Young Children's Citizenship*. York: Joseph Rowntree Foundation, pp. 92–158.

Marsh, J., Kumpulainen, K., Nisha, B., Velicu, A., Blum-Ross, A., Hyatt, D., Jónsdóttir, S. R., Levy, R., Little, S., Marusteru, G., Ólafsdóttir, M. E., Sandvik, K., Scott, F., Thestrup, K., Arnseth, H. C., Dýrfjörð, K., Jornet, A., Kjartansdóttir, S. H., Pahl, K., Pétursdóttir, S. and Thorsteinsson, G. (2017). *Makerspaces in the Early Years: A Literature Review*. Sheffield: University of Sheffield, MakEY Project.

Marsh, J., Arnseth, H. C. & Kumpulainen, K. (2018). Maker Literacies and Maker Citizenship in the MakEY (Makerspaces in the Early Years) Project. *Multimodal Technologies and Interaction*, 2(3), 50.

Meng, T. K. (2016, May 18). Everyone is Born Creative, but It Is Educated Out of Us at School. *The Guardian*. Retrieved from: www.theguardian.com/media–network/2016/may/18/born-creative-educated-out-of-us-school-business

Merriam, S. B. (1998). *Qualitative Research and Case Study Applications in Education*. San Fransisco: Jossey-Bass Publishers.

Moore, H. C. & Adair, J. K. (2015). "I'm just playing iPad": Comparing Prekindergartners' and Preservice Teachers' Social Interactions While Using Tablets for Learning. *Journal of Early Childhood Teacher Education*, 36(4): 364–378.

Orton-Johnson, K. (2014). DIY Citizenship, Critical Making, and Community. In M. Ratto & M. Boler (eds.), *DIY Citizenship – Critical Making and Social Media*. Cambridge, MA; London: MIT Press, pp. 141–157.

Pahl, K. (2007). Creativity in Events and Practices: A Lens for Understanding Children's Multimodal Texts. *Literacy*, 41(2): 86–92.

Peppler, K., Halverson, E. & Kafai, Y. B. (eds). 2016. *Makeology: Makerspaces as Learning Environments* (Vol. 1).

Perry, M. & Collier, D. (2018). What Counts as Creativity in Education? An Inquiry into the Intersections of Public, Political, and Policy Discourses. *Canadian Journal of Education*, 41(1): 24–43.

Ratto, M. (2011). Critical Making: Conceptual and Material Studies in Technology and Social Life. *Information Society an International Journal*, 27, 252–260.

Ratto, M. & Boler, M. (2014). *DIY Citizenship – Critical Making and Social Media*. Cambridge, MA; London: MIT Press.

Resta, P. & Laferriere, T. (2015). Digital equity and intercultural education. *Education and Information Technologies*, 20(4): 743–756.

Robinson, K. (2006). Do Schools Kill Creativity? TED Talks. Retrieved from: www.ted.com/talks/ken_robinson_says_schools_kill_creativity?language=en

Schulte, C. M. & Thompson, M. (2018). *Communities of Practice: Art, Play, and Aesthetics in Early Childhood*. Cham, Switzerland: Springer International Publishing.

Stein, M. I. (1953). Creativity and Culture. *Journal of Psychology*, 36: 311–322. doi:10.1080/00223980.1953.9712897

Stephen, C. & Gadda, A. (2017). *Nurturing Citizenship in the Early Years*. Stirling: University of Stirling.

ThingTankLab. (2019). www.thingtanklab.com/makerpassport/canadian-maker-spaces/

Wells, R. E. (2008). *Polar Bear, Why is Your World Melting?* Chicago, IL: Albert Whitman & Company.

Wohlwend, K. (2015). Making, Remaking, and Reimagining the Everyday: Play, Creativity, and Popular Media. In J. Rowsell & K. Pahl (eds), *Routledge Handbook of Literacy Studies*. Hoboken, NJ: Routledge, pp. 548–560.

Yin, R. (2009). *Case Study Research: Design and Methods. Fourth Edition*. Applied Social Research Methods Series, Volume 5. Thousand Oaks, CA: SAGE Inc.

12

CONCLUSION

Jackie Marsh, Alicia Blum-Ross and Kristiina Kumpulainen

As the chapters in this book indicate, the MakEY project has been successful in meeting its original aims, which were to identify the role and value of makerspaces for young children in both formal and non-formal settings. In this concluding chapter, we draw together the project's findings across the three levels of analysis outlined in the introduction: personal, relational and institutional. This is not to suggest that these three areas can be separated in a simple manner, given that they are interrelated. Nonetheless, this approach to analysis enables a close look at the micro-, meso- and macro-level factors at play in the provision of makerspaces for children aged under eight years.

Impact of makerspaces at the personal level

Identity plays a significant role in the ways in which children take up, or not, as the case may be, the opportunities offered by makerspaces. Given the links between makerspaces and STEM learning, it is worth considering some of the barriers to engagement. Whilst patterns of participation across post-compulsory STEM education, training and careers differ across the disciplines, some key trends are clear. Engagement by certain groups (girls, some Black, Asian and Minority Ethnic (BAME) groups and individuals from working-class families) in STEM is problematic, and research has identified that these patterns are evident in the choices made in subjects available to pupils in compulsory schooling in some countries (Archer et al., 2017), as well as in future educational and career choices (DeWitt et al., 2011). There are a number of reasons that have been identified for this situation, such as the stereotypes of scientists in society, who are often portrayed as White males, feelings of a lack of identification with the subject matter of STEM curricula, and a lack of family engagement in science subjects or pursuits, such as visits to science museums (Archer et al., 2012, 2013; Dabney, Tai and Scott, 2016). Given these challenges, makerspaces could offer a valuable means of providing more positive experiences for girls and for children from low socio-economic BAME communities. In many of the case studies outlined in this book, this was found to be the case. It was felt by many of the country project leaders that the development of a STEAM approach was more conducive to inclusive practice, as it enabled children to draw on their interests in non-STEM subjects. This has been identified in other projects (Kang et al., 2012), although these studies have focused on older children. In addition, a STEAM approach aligns with established practice in early childhood education, in which topic-based approaches to the construction of the curriculum are common.

The MakEY project was also found to have an impact in terms of 'projective identities' (Gee, 2003), in which individuals can imagine themselves otherwise. There were numerous cases across the studies in which children self-identified as makers, though they had not necessarily done so previously. Given the timescale of this project, it was not possible to determine whether or not this impact is long-standing in nature. If the practices established in makerspaces are not embedded in everyday curricula, then children will have limited opportunities to rehearse the maker identities developed within makerspaces. This is also the case in relation to the impact of the study on children with special educational needs. Whilst many of the practitioners involved discussed the way in which the project had benefited children who had cognitive, linguistic, and/or physical special needs, it remains to be seen if this impact continues beyond engagement with the MakEY project.

In line with other analyses of makerspaces (Peppler, Halverson and Kafai, 2016), children across the case studies followed interest-driven pursuits. This was not always possible in those makerspaces that focused on specific outcomes, but even within those contexts, children spent longer on those activities that were of specific interest to them. It was not always the case, however, that makerspaces fostered engagement of all the children in the case studies. In those pre- and after-school settings in which the opportunity to choose whether or not to participate was available to children, some children did not want to engage, either partly or fully, as, for example, the Romanian case study indicates. Marsh, Wood, Chesworth, Nisha, Nutbrown and Olney (2019) point to the way in which 'maker capital' and 'maker funds of knowledge' (drawing on Moll et al.'s (1992) concept) impact on children's engagement in makerspaces. Children's previous experiences as makers impact on their levels of confidence and interest.

Finally, in a consideration of the impact of the study at a personal level, a focus on children's acquisition of digital skills and knowledge indicates that engagement in makerspaces can enhance children's learning in numerous ways. Across the projects, children learned to operate and use a range of hardware and software, and they observed the use of equipment that was too complex for them to operate themselves, such as 3D printers and laser cutters. The makerspaces enabled children to learn how to code, how to create animations and films, and how to operate virtual reality (VR) tools, amongst other things. What was of value in this process was the way in which the acquisition of skills and knowledge was embedded in meaningful activities; children were not acquiring skills in isolation. In addition, makerspaces enabled the children to encounter playful approaches to the use of digital technologies, which is of value given the well-established relationship between play and learning (Vygotsky, 1938/67). It is important to note, however, that children did not simply acquire operational skills in the makerspaces; their cultural and critical skills and knowledge were also developed (Marsh, Arnseth and Kumpulainen, 2018). Further, it soon became clear that the project's original focus on digital literacy and creativity was too narrow; across the makerspaces, a rich range of skills and knowledge were developed across STEM and arts and humanities subjects.

It is important to note that when studying young children's creativity in makerspaces, there needs to be an acknowledgement that digital and non-digital practices are intimately related, and that practices will be fluid across domains. MakEY was interested in digital making, but the team recognised that much of children's making takes non-digital forms, and they were interested in the creativity embedded in those practices, too. Rather than pose a false dichotomy between digital and non-digital making, the project explored young children's making in a range of forms and across physical and virtual domains, identifying the ways in which these domains were sometimes quite separate, and at other times merged, as in the Danish, German and UK case studies.

Impact of makerspaces at the relational level

Early childhood educational provision places great emphasis on the importance of providing space and time for children's social development. Given the significance of the early years in terms of, as the US National Scientific Council on the Developing Child terms it, 'Establishing a level foundation for life' (2012), and the evidence on the relation between social development and academic success (Denham and Brown, 2010), it is of little surprise that almost all early childhood curricula across the globe place emphasis on this aspect of development (Bertram and Pascal, 2002). Therefore, early-years practitioners foster values such as interacting with, and caring for, others. As Hatch's (2013) emphasis on 'sharing' indicates, makerspaces offer such opportunities. Petrich, Wilkinson and Bevan (2013: 53–54) argue that makerspaces foster solidarity with others, and David Gauntlett, in his book *Making is Connecting*, makes the point that 'acts of creativity usually involve, at some point, a social dimension and connect us with other people' (2011 2). Thus, makerspaces offer children the potential to develop their social capacities.

Across the case studies, it was clear that social interactions were key to makerspace activities, with rich exchanges taking place not just between children, but between children and practitioners, older siblings, parents, grandparents and volunteer helpers, as was evident in the US case study, for example. Children provided support and scaffolding for other children's learning in the spaces, and listened to each other's ideas and reflections. It is important to note, however, that the nature of social interaction in the makerspaces was not always positive. Difference and conflict are embedded in daily social practices (Kumpulainen and Renshaw, 2007; Rajala and Sannino, 2015). Children did not always share the same thoughts about their work, and some found it difficult to share resources at times. Whilst not documented within the case studies outlined in this book, there were, occasionally, differences of opinion between some of the various professionals engaged in the study with regard to how to plan and conduct the makerspaces. This is, perhaps, unsurprising when one considers the different backgrounds and experience of the various professionals involved in the study. Rather than viewing this as problematic however, the team felt that this process enhanced the project, as it forced members to articulate the underlying principles and philosophies that shaped their practice, and it changed beliefs and practices in productive ways.

As outlined in the introductory chapter, the project team was also interested in understanding the ways in which the social and material resources of the makerspaces supported diverse children's joint engagement, digital learning and creativity. There were particular technical resources that supported collaborative work, such as tablets, given the affordances they have for this (such as touchscreen interfaces that enable more than one child to use them at the same time) (Burnett et al., 2017). However, even when resources appeared to preclude collaborative work, children still found opportunities to collaborate. For example, in the case studies in Germany and the UK, the use of VR equipment meant that only one child could wear a headset and experience the 3D environment at any time, but in fact in many of the activities, other children stood near the child wearing the headset, commenting on the VR drawing on the computer screen and talking with the VR artist about what they were doing.

The extent to which some of the makerspace activities fostered social relations was dependent on how they were organised by the practitioners. As the examples from Iceland, Norway and Romania indicate, for example, where a more open pedagogical approach was adopted, interaction and collaboration were encouraged, but even when a more closed pedagogical approach was adopted, joint activities were planned. Only in those maker activities which focused on individual tasks related to a specific skill were opportunities for collaboration fewer. In addition, how far an activity became a collaborative one was frequently shaped by the children themselves. At times, children engaged in activities that were set up to foster collaboration, but they worked in such a way that they deliberately excluded engagement with others. A key point to reflect on when considering this issue is that each makerspace is unique in the way in which it fosters, or closes down, social interaction, and much of that is shaped by the makerspace provider in addition to the types and tools of resources offered, but it is also the case that individual children's agentic actions can open up, or close down, opportunities for social interaction. Timely interventions by the pedagogue can ensure that these situations are managed effectively when necessary.

Impact of makerspaces at the institutional level

The project explored makerspaces across both formal and non-formal settings, and examined both temporary and permanent spaces. Given this level of heterogeneity, it is not possible to identify a singular institutional impact across these contexts.

However, it was clear that there were some key principles that enabled makerspaces to flourish across this range of settings.

Firstly, having knowledgeable and committed individuals in institutions was key to ensuring that the legacy of MakEY makerspaces was sustained beyond the project. In order to ensure this sustainability, a range of professional development opportunities were offered to participants in the study. Practitioners in some of the countries were able to participate in makerspaces prior to engaging in them with children, which developed their confidence and subject knowledge. The project as a whole developed a range of resources to support professional engagement in makerspaces.[1] Makers from independent Fab Labs and open-access makerspaces for the general public were brought into the project in some countries in order to share their expertise. Secondly, key to the sustainable nature of makerspaces is the ability to resource them, in terms of space, tools and resources. For some of the museums and libraries involved in the project, it was possible to set up permanent makerspaces, which enabled ongoing access to a range of tools and resources. Obviously, this was much more problematic for the early-years settings and schools, which in the main tended to set up pop-up makerspaces. In some cases, the nature of the makerspace shifted over the course of the project, from a pop-up one, in which practitioners could try out activities and approaches, to a more permanent space once the warrant for such provision was established.

The project also considered how far the makerspaces created equitable opportunities for children's learning and identity development and how this process operated at an institutional level. Whilst a number of claims have been made about how makerspaces can promote democratic participation in society (Anderson, 2012), the reality is rather different. The majority of makerspaces are located in urban spaces, which immediately excludes many people living in rural communities from participating. Further, Alper (2013: 1) reported a US survey that found that '8 in 10 makers are male, their median household income is $106,000, and 80% have a post-graduate education'. This, indeed, was a major driver for setting up the MakEY project in the first instance. If makerspaces are going to be offered to young children in both formal and non-formal settings, then issues of equity are significant. In the preschool settings and schools involved in the project, equity of access to such provision is well-established in practice, and this was no different in relation to the makerspaces. Practitioners were attentive to the need to ensure inclusive practice and utilised a range of strategies to ensure such inclusivity, such as ensuring that topics were diverse and relevant to children's cultural backgrounds, that children in the early stages of acquiring the national language as a second language were given support in understanding key terms, and that the engagement of children who might not otherwise have participated was facilitated through mentoring arrangements.

In some of the libraries and museums involved in the study, inclusive practice was also possible because of public funding, as was the case in the US-based project. However, for some of the independent organisations and SMEs involved in the study, makerspaces could only be provided for children by requiring parents to pay for them, and this then restricted the opportunity for all children to participate.

This situation could be addressed by the inclusion of such spaces in public-funded programmes that promote makerspaces in non-formal learning settings, a point that will be returned to later in the chapter.

At the institutional level, the MakEY project also considered the kinds of pedagogical and assessment practices that supported children's engagement in makerspaces. In general, it was found that more open pedagogical practices in which children could take an agentive role in planning and conducting their activities were productive in terms of children's engagement and learning, as discussed in the chapters written by the Danish, Icelandic and Norwegian teams. This is not to suggest that the makerspaces in which children had fewer choices about what to make were not successful, as the Finnish and UK case studies indicate. In those instances, even though the teachers wanted the children to meet specific learning objectives, which reduced the children's possibilities for agency in terms of the types of making, the children were fully engaged in the activities and gained a lot from them, as they were able to be creative and innovative. Therefore, it is clear that children gain different things from different kinds of makerspaces, and it is valuable for them to experience variety in terms of the set-up of makerspaces and the educational possibilities they offer.

Finally, the project examined the value of the partnership between academic and non-academic participants in creating makerspaces for young children. The project was highly successful in this regard, in that it enabled rich knowledge exchanges to take place. Early-years teachers acquired a range of technical skills and specialist maker knowledge from makerspace staff, who in turn became knowledgeable about the developmental needs of young children. Academics learned about exploratory approaches to creative production from artists, who themselves enjoyed extending their understanding to include approaches to undertaking research with young children and families. Library staff and museum educators taught others about the value of interest-driven learning, and they gained valuable knowledge about how to identify and capture the learning taking place in makerspaces. The project moved beyond simple knowledge exchange, however, to embody the key principles of co-constructed research, in which all parties contributed to knowledge creation, ensuring that, between them, new understandings were developed regarding the provision of makerspaces for children aged under eight. This project has also enabled learning across national boundaries, and it has fostered a conversation between different disciplines (education, media and communication, sociology, urban studies and planning) and across different sectors (SMEs, public services, third sector). Despite the challenges in this process, the value of such exchanges is inestimable. It is only through interdisciplinary and inter-sector work that some of the key challenges that face society in the years ahead can be addressed.

Implications of the project for research, policy and practice

The project has a number of implications for future research, policy and practice. In relation to research, whilst the project has identified the role and value of makerspaces in the early years, there is much more to explore with regard to this provision. Firstly, the longitudinal impact of children's engagement in makerspaces needs to be traced. It is to be hoped that, through positive engagement in innovative and creative approaches to STEM subjects in makerspaces in early childhood, children will maintain their interest in these subjects throughout primary and secondary school, but this needs to be the subject of sustained study. Secondly, the relationship between the knowledge and skills gained in makerspaces, and the subject knowledge required when studying single disciplines, deserves further exploration. The interdisciplinary nature of learning within makerspaces means that, inevitably, the development of subject-level knowledge will be uneven in nature, and experiences may not map easily onto disciplinary expectations. This may not matter, if the main value of engaging children in making spaces is to excite them about subjects that they might not otherwise be attracted to. However, further sustained links between experiences in makerspaces and the curriculum would offer a more integrated educational experience for children. Finally, this project demonstrated that there is much synergy between the principles that underlie makerspaces and early childhood philosophy and practices, yet there are still some misunderstandings about the relation between them. As suggested in Chapter 1, this means that some observers may query the need for makerspaces to be set up in early-years settings, arguing that this is everyday practice. This stance, we would argue, overlooks the fact that making in many preschool settings has traditionally focused on a relatively narrow set of tools and resources, and there is a need to broaden the sets of tools and resources made available if children are to become competent makers in the fourth industrial age. In addition, real-world applications of making, which are frequently seen in makerspaces, are not prevalent in early childhood education. Further research should be undertaken that examines the value of fostering authentic maker activities in preschool settings and primary schools, activities that can be linked to issues of citizenship and community action (Marsh, Arnseth and Kumpulainen, 2018).

The project also has a number of implications for policy. Given the rich range of learning that was observed across the case studies in this project, education ministries should carefully consider the need to fund the resourcing of makerspaces in early childhood and primary education, and in non-formal settings such as museums and libraries. It is clear that makerspaces can boost the kinds of skills and knowledge required to enable nation-states to compete globally in future employment markets, and so this investment will offer growth opportunities in later years. There is a particular need to support the provision of makerspaces in areas of high unemployment and deprivation, given that these are the areas most likely to be digitally excluded (Helsper, 2012). This is not to suggest that makerspaces are a panacea for poverty and a lack of equal opportunities; it would be foolish to suggest that through attendance at makerspaces, individuals will automatically develop the kinds of skills and knowledge that would provide entry to the job market. Nevertheless, such experiences can spark interest in the pursuit of further education and training in relevant areas. In addition, it may make employment in the creative and technical industries, or related future pathways, more accessible to a wider group of people, thus tackling the lack of diversity which is prevalent in these areas (O'Brien et al., 2017).

Finally, there are numerous implications for practice from this study. The project team has developed a wide range of resources for practitioners in early-years settings, schools, libraries and museums, and therefore we point readers to the project website, as detailed previously. In addition to these resources, which provide guidance on setting up and running makerspaces, the project has also identified implications for practice in open-access spaces and Fab Labs. In many communities, there is an appetite for attending makerspace activities aimed at young children, with some parents willing and able to pay for out-of-school makerspace workshops. We would encourage not-for-profit makerspaces and SMEs to consider this market, and to identify ways in which they may be more inclusive of this age group. This may lead to collaborations with early-years settings in primary schools in their vicinity.

Conclusions

This book has outlined the main findings from the MakEY project, and it has considered the implications of these findings for research, policy and practice. The collaboration across different countries has been crucial to the success of the programme, as it has led to a more informed understanding of the way in which specific cultural contexts shape policy and practice with regard to the provision of makerspaces for young children. As the literature reviewed throughout this book identifies, there is a worldwide concern that our educational systems are outdated and failing to promote the necessary digital literacies that will adequately prepare our children for the future. One of the major concerns of educators is to ensure that every young person is equipped early on with adequate digital literacy skills and knowledge that will support their academic and civic engagement and lifelong, and lifewide, learning opportunities. In many countries the availability of technology is adequate, but the primary challenge to overcome is the lack of readiness for the pedagogically meaningful use of digital technologies and media to enhance young people's digital literacies in connection with other disciplinary and 21st-century skill sets. The MakEY project, with its interest in understanding the potential of makerspaces for enhancing young children's digital literacy and creativity across various settings, has made an important contribution to furthering understanding in this area.

Note

1   See: http://makeyproject.eu/resources/

References

Alper, M. (2013). Making space in the makerspace: building a mixed-ability maker culture. IDC'13, 24–27 June 2013, New York, NY, USA. Retrieved from https://pdfs.semantic scholar.org/8d8a/ef7ff1f842a65e4fcbec9fb7d10deb46711a.pdf

Anderson, C. (2012). *Makers: The New Industrial Revolution*. New York: Crown Business.

Archer, L., DeWitt, J., Osborne, J., Dillon, J., Willis, B. & Wong, B. (2012). Science aspirations, capital, and family habitus: How families shape children's engagement and identification with science. *American Educational Research Journal*, 49(5), 881–908.

Archer, L., DeWitt, J., Osborne, J., Dillon, J., Willis, B. & Wong, B. (2013). Not girly, not sexy, not glamorous: Primary school girls' and parents' constructions of science aspirations. *Pedagogy, Culture and Society*, 21(1), 171–194

Archer, L., Moote, J., Francis, B., DeWitt, J. & Yeomans, L. (2017). Stratifying science: A Bourdieusian analysis of student views and experiences of school selective practices in relation to 'Triple Science' at KS4 in England. *Research Papers in Education*, 32(3), 296–315.

Bertram, T. & Pascal, C. (2002). *Early Years Education: An International Perspective*. International Review of Curriculum and Assessments Framework Internet Archive (INCA). Retrieved from www.nfer.ac.uk/early-years-education-an-international-perspective/

Burnett, C., Merchant, G., Simpson, A. & Walsh, M. (Eds.) (2017). *The Case of the iPad: Mobile Literacies in Education*. Singapore: Springer.

Dabney, K.P., Tai, R.H. & Scott, M.R. (2016). Informal science: Family education, experiences, and initial interest in science. *International Journal of Science Education, Part B*, 6(3), 263–282.

Denham, S.A. & Brown, C. (2010). "Plays nice with others": Social-emotional learning and academic success. *Early Education and Development*, 21(5), 652–680. doi:10.1080/10409289.2010.497450

DeWitt, J., Archer, L., Osborne, J., Dillon, J., Willis, B. & Wong, B. (2011). High aspirations but low progression: The science aspirations–careers paradox amongst minority ethnic students. *International Journal of Science and Mathematics Education*, 9(2): 243–271.

Gauntlett, D. (2011). *Making is Connecting: The Social Meaning of Creativity, from DIY and Knitting to YouTube and Web 2.0*. Cambridge: Polity Press.

Gee, J.P. (2003). *What Video Games Have to Teach Us about Learning and Literacy*. New York; Basingstoke: Palgrave Macmillan.

Hatch, M. (2013). *The Maker Movement Manifesto*. New York: McGraw-Hill.

Helsper, E. (2012). A corresponding fields model for the links between social and digital exclusion. *Communication Theory*, 22(4), 403–426.

Kang, M., Park, Y., Kim, J. & Kim, Y. (2012). Learning outcomes of the teacher training program for STEAM education. International Conference for Media in Education, Beijing.

Kumpulainen, K., & Renshaw, P. (2007). Cultures of learning. *International Journal of Educational Research*, 46(3), 109–115.

Marsh, J., Arnseth, H.C., & Kumpulainen, K. (2018). Maker literacies and maker citizenship in the MakEY (Makerspaces in the Early Years) project. *Multimodal Technologies and Interaction*, 2, 50. doi:10.3390/Mti2030050

Marsh, J., Wood, E.A., Chesworth, L., Nisha, B., Nutbrown, B. & Olney, B. (2019). Makerspaces in early childhood education: Principles of pedagogy and practice. *Mind, Culture, and Activity*, 26(3), 221–233.

Moll, L.C., Amanti, C., Neff, D. & Gonzalez, N. (1992). Funds of knowledge for teaching using a qualitative approach to connect homes and classrooms. *Theory Into Practice*, 31(2), 132–141.

National Scientific Council on the Developing Child. (2012). *Establishing a Level Foundation for Life: Mental Health Begins in Early Childhood*. (Working paper 6). Retrieved from Center on the Developing Child website, Harvard: Harvard University, www.developingchild.harvard.edu

O'Brien, D., Allen, K., Friedman, S. & Saha, A. (2017). Producing and consuming inequality: a cultural sociology of the cultural industries. *Cultural Sociology*, 11(3), 271–282. doi:10.1177/1749975517712465

Peppler, K., Halverson, E. & Kafai, Y. (Eds.) (2016). *Makeology: Makerspaces as Learning Environments* (Volume 1 and 2). New York: Routledge.

Petrich, M., Wilkinson, K. & Bevan, B. (2013). It looks like fun, but are they learning. In M. Honey & D. Kanter (Eds.), *Design, Make, Play: Growing the Next Generation of STEM Innovators* (pp. 50–70). New York: Routledge.

Rajala, A., & Sannino, A. (2015). Students' deviations from a learning task: An activity-theoretical analysis. *International Journal of Educational Research*, 70, 31–46.

Vygotsky, L. (1938/67). Play and its role in the mental development of the child. *Soviet Psychology*, 5(3), 6–18.WES (2016). Statistics on women in engineering. Retrieved from www.wes.org. uk/sites/default/files/Women%20in%20Engineering%20Statistics%20March2016.pdf

AFTERWORD

Reflecting on process

Kylie Peppler

UNIVERSITY OF CALIFORNIA, IRVINE

This volume encourages us to shift our focus from the products reached through the making experience to the process in which makers learn and create. While an increasing number of young children are making and creating digital media, so often in early childhood education we resist technology use and even creative uses of technologies, preferring paper, pencil, and paints over iPads and augmented reality. Equally challenging is the constraints on time for exploration and activity that leave us trying to accomplish ambitious learning goals in very short periods of time, saving very little time for open-ended making. This unintentionally stresses product over process in the time that remains. In an era of high-stakes accountability, there can be a pressure to have something to be handed to the parent, or displayed on the bulletin board, instead of recognizing that the time spent in making should be designed to foster deeper communication between the individual and their materials, regardless of the end product.

Not only is the appreciation for process over product a helpful frame for viewing the diverse forms of making across ages, cultures, and topics, but it is also a poignant reminder of how scholars and practitioners can unlock new understandings by changing the methods of the ways in which they work. This edited volume is the result of many minds working together across national boundaries and professional fields not just to share the work they've done within their respective quadrants but to earnestly synergize their understandings in order to create a new field of research. In this case, the understudied focus—the untapped potential of bringing making and digital literacies to young children—is tremendously important, though just as impactful is the unique model for field-building that Jackie Marsh and colleagues envisioned in order for this work to occur.

This project was designed very differently than most cross-institution research efforts by placing an emphasis on network-building at the center. It brought together cultural epicenters of making activity across eight countries. Across each node of the network, the project afforded ample opportunity for researchers and practitioners to communicate and share insights, artifacts, processes, and challenges through shared writings, guest speakers, poster presentations, and the creation of this edited volume. The project also connected these individual labs of exploration within a broader international network involving people that are researching and studying in this area. This was done both by bringing a large advisory group together to view and provide feedback during research meetings, but also to place scholars within the network within residencies among other laboratories and makerspaces internationally over the span of weeks and months. This, in and of itself, is rare, providing a level of cultural exchange not commonly afforded through typical research activities. It also allowed the participants within the network to dive more deeply into the work that each other was doing, to offer an opportunity to see the unique contributions that each view makes toward a much larger understanding.

I was incredibly fortunate to have Dr. Sara Sintonen and Jasmiina Korhonen from the University of Helsinki, Dr. Anca Velicu from the Romanian Academy, and Dr. Fiona Scott from the University of Sheffield in residence with the Creativity Labs at Indiana University, where we shared our work, offered workshops, visited local early childhood programs, and developed new prototypes around making music through tracking whole-body movement through space over time. Ours was but one of several such residencies between collaborators on this volume, where professional relationships were forged between people, institutions, and projects. The accumulation of residencies like this not only lays a firm foundation for the clarity of understanding articulated in this volume, but also catapults the field forward in ways that are bound to reap the benefits of this research project in many years to come.

This focus on deepening connections within this network helped new understandings emerge. The authors of this volume undertake a radical and important re-thinking of the impact of bringing making and digital literacies to young children. By placing an emphasis on young children, this volume gives us several paths forward for viewing the role of the personal, relational, and ultimately institutional, in countering prevalent discourses on media and technology usage among children in a way that is expansive and agentic. While making is universal in nature, this is one of the first projects to understand the cross-cultural nature of making that moves beyond a set of kits and materials to how deeper pedagogies, philosophies, and educational infrastructures offer a new vision for education in the 21st century that is connected to the histories and cultures of the lives of young children.

What does this mean for the larger field of making? The process of getting people together within the network allowed the foundation built through our various collaborations to grow, not only through the project but beyond. This network of authentic relationships and engaged scholarship, forged through the process of doing this work, continues to help fuel new ideas around making across cultural contexts. Especially in an age of telecommuting and remote work, scholars across a range of disciplines should view the activity in this broader collaboration as a way to build strong foundations and alliances toward future effort. It's through this kind of activity that change can be enacted.

In closing, this volume provides researchers, policy makers, educators, parents, philanthropists, and makers with high-quality research, methods, and theoretical understandings to shape the future of making. As we face the fourth industrial revolution, it becomes apparent that young children need to be ready to become creative problem solvers around their use of technology. While this book pushes our theoretical understandings forward to help us better understand this increasingly tech-immersive world and the experience of young children within it, the roots in Vygotsky and Activity Theory across many of the chapters remind us of what should be perennially preserved in high-quality learning experiences through making, both in- and out-of-school. My hope is that this volume will arm you with the means to defend what is already working in your makerspaces or, alternatively, to inspire something new; to bring the world of making and digital literacies to your school or your household.

INDEX

Page numbers in *italics* denote figures, those in **bold** denote tables.

Printed in Great Britain
by Amazon